Did God Do It?

Figurative or Literal

Our Good, Just, and Merciful God

Judy E. Coad

Did God Do It? Figurative or Literal: Our Good, Just, and Merciful God

Copyright © 2019 by Judy E. Coad

Published by God is Light (visit http://GodIsLight.com)

All rights reserved. No part of this publication may be reproduced, stored in a retrieval system, or transmitted in any form by any means (electronic, mechanical, photocopy, recording, or otherwise) without prior permission of the publisher, except as provided for by USA copyright law.

This study quotes Scripture from the *The Holy Bible, English Standard Version* (ESV). Copyright © 2011 by Crossway Bibles, a publishing ministry of Good News Publishers. Used by permission. All rights reserved.

It quotes Scripture from other versions with a mark indicating the source:

AMP: *Amplified Bible*. Copyright © 1954, 1958, 1962, 1964, 1965, 1987 by The Lockman Foundation. Used by permission.

BBE: *Bible in Basic English* (1949/1964). Public domain.

DBY: *Darby Translation* (1890). Public domain.

HCSB: *Holman Christian Standard Bible*. Copyright © 1999, 2000, 2002, 2003, 2009 by Holman Bible Publishers. Used by permission.

KJV: *Authorized King James Version* (1611). Public domain.

NASB: *New American Standard Bible*. Copyright © 1960, 1962, 1963, 1968, 1971, 1972, 1973, 1975, 1977, 1995 by The Lockman Foundation. Used by permission. All rights reserved.

NIV: *Holy Bible, New International Version, NIV*. Copyright © 1973, 1978, 1984, 2011 by Biblica, Inc. Used by permission of Zondervan. All rights reserved worldwide.

Phillips: *The New Testament in Modern English by J.B Phillips*. Copyright © 1960, 1972 J. B. Phillips. Administered by The Archbishops' Council of the Church of England. Used by Permission.

RV: *Revised Version of the Bible* (1881/1885). Public domain.

WTJ: "Working Translation" from *A Journey through the Acts and Epistles, Volumes 1 and 2*. Copyright © 2006 and 2013 by Walter J. Cummins. All rights reserved.

YLT: *Young's Literal Translation* (1898). Public domain.

Paperback ISBN 9780975978610

10 9 8 7 6 5 4 3 2 1

Contents

Preface	1
How this Study Came About	1
A Firm Foundation	2
Organization of Study	3
Scope of Study	5
Versions Quoted	6
Acknowledgments	7
1 The Problem and Essential Background	9
Statement of the Problem	10
This Study's Approach	13
Essential Background: God Is Light	17
Essential Background: One of a Different Nature	20
Essential Background: Opposing Natures	21
Essential Background: Choices and Sources of Information	25
Essential Background: God Is Just	31
Essential Background: Recognizing What Is Just	37
Summary	39
2 Moses and an Unusual Expression	41
An Unusual Expression	42
Wider Context	42
Closer Context	45
Related Scriptures	50
Ways to Understand the Scriptures	51
Figures of Speech	51
Idioms	52
Idioms and Context	55

	Biblical Idioms and the Western Mind	56
	Three Important Cultural Influences	58
	Cultural Influence: Name Not Mentioned	59
	Cultural Influence: Not Yet Fully Known	61
	Cultural Influence: Do Mention the Lord God	66
	Recap: Idioms, Context, and Culture	69
	Summary	70
3	**Pharaoh and the Heart**	**73**
	Who Hardened Pharaoh's Heart?	74
	The Context of these Expressions	75
	God's Covenant with His People	76
	Continuing in the Context	77
	Related Scriptures: Other Hard Hearts	86
	Who Is Responsible for the Heart?	87
	Idiomatic Espressions with the Word "Heart"	92
	Summary	95
4	**Pharaoh and the Passover**	**97**
	Unusual and Seemingly Difficult Wording	98
	Background	99
	Context	100
	The Destroyer and Related Scriptures	106
	A Consideration for Another Time	114
	Justice and Mercy	115
	Summary	117
5	**More Essential Background: Covenants and Justice**	**121**
	Time Periods	122
	Adam	122
	Abraham	126
	The Mosaic Law and the Nation of Israel	133
	God's People	138
	The Whole Congregation of Israel	142
	Kings of the Nation of Israel	146

The Promise of a New Covenant	148
Justified Freely by His Grace	150
God's Purpose In Christ	153
God's Eternal Perspective	154
Summary	155

6 Abraham — 157

Two Unusual Expressions	158
Review	159
Background	160
More Background: Related Scripture	162
Genesis 12:17 Context	164
Genesis 20:18 Context	169
Promises Fulfilled	174
Comparing Pharaoh and Abimelech	174
Summary	175
God's Eternal Purpose in Christ	176

7 Saul — 179

An Unusual Expression	179
Background	180
Context: Complementary Accounts	184
Related Scripture	187
Summary	196
Review: A Particular Biblical Idiom	197
A Closing Note	199

8 David — 201

Two Sets of Unusual Expressions	202
Background: To Number Israel	204
Unusual Expressions in the Opening Verses	205
Digression: The Anger of the Lord	207
Context: I Chronicles 21:14	208
Review: Angels and Cost to God	212
Continuing in the Context	213

	More Review: Just Standards	217
	God's Plan for Life	219
	Summary	220
	A New Standard of Justice in Christ	221

9   II Thessalonians 2 and God's Enduring Mercy   225

	Review: Acts 16:14	227
	An Unusual Expression	229
	Wider Context	229
	Essential Background: Three Terms	231
	The Context	240
	Review	244
	Summary	245
	God's Enduring Mercy	247

10   Nehemiah 9 and God's Great Mercy   249

	Nehemiah 9	249
	Three Unusual Expressions	257
	Related Scriptures	257
	Summary: Figurative, Literal, or We Do Not Know	259
	Our Faithful and Merciful God	261

11   No Wrongdoing and What It Is not   263

	Background	264
	Naomi and Ruth	264
	The "But Not Always" Provision	270
	Job, The Lord, and Satan	273
	The "But Not Always" Provision	278
	Elijah and the Widow Woman	280
	The "But Not Always" Provision	285
	Hannah, the Mother of Samuel	287
	Summary—No Wrongdoing	293
	What It Is Not and Closing Notes	294

12 Considerations and Summary — 297
Working Considerations — 298
Summary — 301

Appendix A Justice and Judgment — 307
Two Hebrew Words for Justice — 307
Things Associated With God's Justice — 308
What God Calls Good and Desirable — 311
Administering Justice — 313
Jesus Christ Spoke Regarding Judgment — 316
Summary — 317

Appendix B Working List–Literal — 319
In the Time of Noah — Genesis 6:13 and 17 — 320
Abraham — Genesis 20:18 — 321
Abraham — Genesis 12:17 — 321
Sodom and Gomorrah — Genesis 19:24-25 and 29 — 321
Pharaoh and the Passover — Exodus 12:12 — 322
Aaron and the Golden Calf — Exodus 32:35 — 323
Nadab and Abihu — Leviticus 10:2 — 324
Korah's Rebellion — Numbers 16:35 — 326
Baal Worship at Peor — Numbers 25:11 — 327
The Sin of Achan at Ai — Joshua 7:25 — 331
Joshua against Amorite Enemies — Joshua 10:8 and 11 — 336
Joshua against Enemy Kings — Joshua 11:6 and 8 — 340
The Ark of God and the Philistines — I Samuel 5:6-7 and 9 — 341
The Ark of God and Men of Beth-shemesh — I Samuel 6:19 — 343
The Ark of God and Uzzah — II Samuel 6:7 — 343
David — II Samuel 24:15 and I Chronicles 21:14 — 345
Uzziah, King of Judah – II Chronicles 26:20 — 346
Herod — Acts 12:23 — 348
Observations — 349

Appendix C Working List–Figurative — 351
Review from Chapter Two of this Study — 352

How this Appendix Is Organized	**353**
Idiom (Basic)	**353**
Moses — Exodus 5:22	353
Joshua and the City of Ai — Joshua 7:7	354
Elders of Israel — I Samuel 4:3	359
Saul and the Harmful Spirit — I Samuel 16:14-16 and 23	361
The End of Saul's Life — I Chronicles 10:14	363
Idiomatic Expressions with the Word "Heart"	**364**
Pharaoh — Exodus 4:21; 7:3; 9:12; 10:1, 20, 27; 11:10	364
King Sihon — Deuteronomy 2:30	366
Israel against the Amorite Enemies — Joshua 10:10	366
Joshua against Enemy Kings — Joshua 11:20	367
David — II Samuel 24:1	368
Darius, King of Assyria — Ezra 6:22 and 7:27	369
Zerubbabel, Governor of Judah — Haggai 1:14	372
Lydia — Acts 16:14	374
Unjust People — Romans 1:24, 26, and 28	374
Titus – II Corinthians 8:16	376
Some in Future Times — II Thessalonians 2:11	378
Idiom without Wrongdoing	**378**
Sarah — Genesis 16:2	379
Joseph's Brothers — Genesis 42:28	380
Moses — Numbers 11:11	382
Ruth — Ruth 1:13 and 20-21	385
Hannah — I Samuel 1:5-6	387
Elijah and the Son of the Widow Woman — I Kings 17:20	388
Job — Job 2:3	389
To Close	390

Scripture Index   393

Preface

People have struggled for centuries with making sense of certain Bible passages, particularly in the Old Testament, that seem to connect God with negative actions. Lack of understanding about these actions has eroded some people's regard for the God of the Scriptures. This should not be so.

How this Study Came About

My journey to make sense of such passages began one evening after a Bible study in the spring of 2007. After the study, three of us talked about certain statements from an article, "A Consideration of Job." The article stated that the expression in Job 2:3, "although you [Satan] incited me [God] against him [Job], to destroy him without reason" is a Hebrew idiom, in which God was said to do something that He did not do. What the article said next caught our attention:

> A further study of the Scriptures would reveal that there are…also records in the Scriptures of calamities that occurred to people (such as the children of Israel) when they broke a covenant agreement with God. There are

also records of calamities that happened to people (such as the Egyptians) who fought against God's people.[1]

The three of us were saying to one another that someone should do a further study. As we talked back and forth among ourselves, it was as if we were tossing a hot potato around to see who would no longer toss it back. I decided to hold onto the hot potato. I decided to take a look at the considerations raised by these two sentences.

You may ask: why did this grab such attention? Up to then, when encountering any unclear wording that appeared to indicate that God did anything one might think of today as wrong or evil, we, and many other God-loving people, automatically thought of it as figurative. That approach was appropriate for some records, yet not for others. Thus we recognized the need to first consider the Scriptures themselves—and after doing so, to see if we could respectfully articulate an approach that, to our best understanding, would work for all such records.

A Firm Foundation

Some time after beginning this study, it became clear that a firm foundation in the very good nature of our God would be an essential consideration in this study.

---

1. See Walter J. Cummins, *Scripture Consulting Select Studies* (Franklin, Ohio: Scripture Consulting, 2010), Chapter 7 "A Consideration of Job," p. 236. This content was first published in *Scripture Consulting: A Journal for the Consideration of What the Scriptures Say*. October/November/December 2000.

> I John 1:5
> This is the message we have heard from him and proclaim to you, that God is light, and in him is no darkness at all.

God is light and in Him there is no darkness—none at all. We will see that God's light is associated with many good things. The intent of this study is to provide a context and scope to better appreciate certain actions credited to the God of the Scriptures that He may or may not have done. To that end we are considering certain expressions (often found in the Old Testament) that might seem to say God did something contrary to His nature. When not understood, these expressions may be puzzling or unsettling. Therefore, as we endeavor to understand these unusual expressions, we will hold firmly in mind what the Scriptures say regarding God's nature: that He is light and in Him is no darkness at all.

Organization of Study

This study is organized as one connected topic intended to be read in order, as each chapter of this study builds upon the previous one.

Chapter one introduces the statement of the problem and this study's approach to the Scriptures. Also included are six subsections of essential background that are foundational to this study.

Chapter two starts in Exodus 5 with an unusual expression that seems to say God did evil to His people. To help consider if the unusual expression is figurative or literal, figures of speech in the Scriptures are introduced. Also included are three important cultural influences applicable to a particular figure of speech used in the Bible.

Chapters three and four of this study, continue in Exodus and address several unusual expressions found in Exodus chapters 6-12. The unusual expressions in chapter three have to do with the hardening of Pharaoh's heart. Therefore, a scriptural consideration of who is responsible for the heart is included in chapter three. Chapter four goes on to consider the deliverance of God's people from bondage in Egypt. This section includes an unusual expression regarding the killing of all the firstborn of Egypt. Chapter four also considers what the Scriptures say about the destroyer of Exodus 12.

Chapter five, "More Essential Background: Covenants and Justice" provides essential background for the chapters that follow it. This chapter does not consider a specific unusual expression. Instead, this chapter looks at essential background regarding covenants, time periods, and standards of justice in the Scriptures. The goal of this chapter is to provide some breadth and scope of the Scriptures necessary to understand the following chapters.

Chapter six covers two unusual expressions about Abraham, one in Genesis 12 and one in Genesis 20. To make a determination if they are figurative or literal, or if we do not know, a review of promises God made to Abraham is included. The chapter ends with God's eternal purpose in Christ.

Chapter seven considers an unusual expression regarding the end of Saul's life from two complementary accounts.

Chapter eight explores who provoked David to number Israel and the regrettable outcomes that followed. This chapter also includes sections on what the Scriptures say about the anger of the Lord, angels, God's just standards in David's time, and God's plan for life.

Chapter nine considers a New Testament record in II Thessalonians and God's enduring mercy.

Chapter ten presents Nehemiah 9 and God's great mercies to the children of Israel.

Chapter eleven looks at expressions that are similar in pattern but different; it is entitled "No Wrongdoing and What It Is Not."

Chapter twelve sums up this study and offers some overall observations and considerations.

Appendix A is a brief consideration of what God associates with justice and judgment in the Scriptures.

Appendices B and C are working lists of other expressions that follow the pattern of words this study is considering. These working lists are not exhaustive, comprehensive, nor are they intended to be the final word on the topic. They are *working lists* of other literal and figurative expressions offered for further study and consideration.

Scope of Study

This study is about our good and just God, and what He may or may not have done; it is not intended to be comprehensive or exhaustive. There are many other related topics that could be considered but that are not the focus of this study. There are also topics touched on here, such as God's justice or good and evil that could be studied in much greater depth. Every study must limit its focus in some manner. This study will only consider our good and just God in records where wording such as "the Lord [did] evil to this people" or "the Lord put him [Saul] to death" occurs. That is to say, we will only consider records where certain expressions occur that at first glance might *seem* to say God did something contrary to His nature or a person's free will. Our main objective in this study will be to determine, from the Scriptures, if these expressions are literal or figurative, or if we do not know. It is hoped that this study will provide a scriptural pattern for making sence of these kinds of unusual expressions found in the Scriptures.

Versions Quoted

This study quotes Scripture primarily from the *English Standard Version*. Reading multiple Bible versions is often helpful when seeking to better understand a passage. Parallel Plus by TheBible.org provides tools that have been helpful to me in the preparation of this study. This app's customized parallel Bible mode provided simple access to reading the context and related passages in multiple versions. Sometimes how a certain word or phrase is rendered in another version is helpful to our study and appears in brackets. When other versions are quoted this study marks them with the following abbreviations (presented here in alphabetical order):

· AMP	*Amplified Bible, copyright 1965*
· BBE	*Bible in Basic English*
· DBY	*Darby Translation*
· HCSB	*Holman Christian Standard Bible*
· KJV	*Authorized King James Version*
· NASB	*New American Standard Bible*
· NIV	*Holy Bible, New International Version*
· RV	*Revised Version of the Bible*
· WEB	*World English Bible*

- WTJ   "Working Translation" from *A Journey through the Acts and Epistles*
- YLT   *Young's Literal Translation*

This study includes a Scripture index, presented in alphabetical order. In addition, the index identifies the version quoted.

Acknowledgments

The greatest acknowledgment is to my heavenly Father for His grace and provision as this book has come into fruition. I give thanks to God with my whole heart.

> Romans 16:27
>
> To the only wise God be glory forevermore through Jesus Christ! Amen.

To all who have prayed for this project in its various stages, I acknowledge your contribution of prayer and am thankful. I could not have done it without your prayers!

For those who have taught me the Scriptures and especially those who have contributed to my overall understanding of how the Scriptures interpret themselves, I am deeply thankful. I am indebted to many biblical resources and their authors that have provided a foundation and springboard for my growth in the Scriptures. Without these teachers and resources I would not have been equipped to handle God's precious Word.

I am especially thankful to Rev. Walter J. Cummins and the *Greek Scripture Conferences* for much valuable mentorship. As part of the *Greek Scripture Conference,* I led a small research group called "God Is Light." This group provided a rich forum for collaboration on some of the records that eventually ended up in this book. For the past three years I am humbled to have had opportunities to present my book in various fellowships and seminars. These presentations provided valuable feedback and in particular sparked the idea to add chapter eleven, "No Wrongdoing and What It Is Not."

I am most grateful for all the help I've received from others; however, I take full responsibility for the content of this study, including any mistakes. It certainly is not my intent to mishandle God's Word. Yet I am aware of my limitations. I have endeavored to handle God's Word honestly, accurately, and with integrity to the best of my ability and knowledge at the time of this publication.

I pray that this work, *Did God Do It: Figurative or Literal*, will help the reader better understand and appreciate how good, just, and merciful our God truly is as declared throughout the Scriptures.

You may reach the author at jcoad@Godislight.com.

1

The Problem and Essential Background

Those who love God, His Word, and His wonderful Son Jesus Christ often rejoice in God's light, love, and goodness. They have reason to do so, because the Scriptures continually speak of God's love and goodness toward all people. I John 1:5 declares, "God is light, and in him is no darkness at all." Psalm 5:4 says, "For you are not a God who delights in wickedness; evil may not dwell with you." God is light and there is no darkness or evil in Him—none at all.[1]

I John 4:7 adds, "Love is from God," and I John 4:8 says, "God is love." Exodus 34:6 tells us that God is "merciful and gracious, slow to anger, and abounding in steadfast love and faithfulness." Furthermore, Psalm 145:7 and 9 state, "They shall pour forth the fame of your abundant goodness," and "The Lord is good to all, and his mercy is over all that he has made."

---

1. Throughout this study scriptures are quoted from the English Standard Version, except where otherwise noted.

Numbers 23:19 proclaims that "God is not man, that he should lie...or has he spoken, and will he not fulfill it?" People may lie but God does not lie. People may not keep their word but God is faithful to His Word. II Thessalonians 3:3 states that "the Lord is faithful. He will establish you and guard you against the evil one." Lastly, Deuteronomy 32:4 affirms that He is "a God of faithfulness and without iniquity, just and upright is he."

These are just a few verses that tell us of God's abundant goodness. The God of the Scriptures is described as being a God of light, love, mercy, grace, faithfulness, and justness. The Scriptures say that God has no evil or iniquity dwelling in Him. No part of God is evil; there is no darkness in God—none at all. God's desire is always for what is best for His people. God is faithful to Who He is and He always fulfills His Word. With these scriptures in mind, we will consider the statement of the problem (in our understanding) addressed in this study.

Statement of the Problem

Having begun this chapter by briefly considering verses that credit many good characteristics to the God of the Scriptures, it is perplexing when we read passages that may seem to say otherwise. For example, the following verse seems to associate God with wrongdoing.

1. The Problem and Essential Background

> I Chronicles 10:14
>
> He did not seek guidance from the L<small>ORD</small>. Therefore <u>the L<small>ORD</small> put him [Saul] to death</u> and turned the kingdom over to David the son of Jesse.[2]

This verse says "the Lord put him [Saul] to death." These words are an unusual expression that seems to associate God with evil. The part of the verse that says, the Lord put Saul to death does not appear to agree with what we considered regarding the good nature of the God of the Scriptures. Such wording is often found in the Old Testament and may cause even those who love God to pause and ponder. Since Psalm 5:4 says that no evil dwells in God, it is understandable that these words might give us pause. Therefore, in an upcoming chapter of this study, we will take the time to consider this potentially difficult verse.

In Exodus we find other records with potentially troubling statements.

> Exodus 5:22
>
> Then Moses turned to the L<small>ORD</small> and said, "O <u>Lord, why have you done evil to this people</u>? Why did you ever send me?

> Exodus 9:12
>
> But <u>the L<small>ORD</small> hardened the heart of Pharaoh</u>, and he did not listen to them, as the L<small>ORD</small> had spoken to Moses.

---

[2]. The underlining added in this study is to mark out the expression or pattern of words being considered in this study.

> Exodus 12:12
>
> For I will pass through the land of Egypt that night, and <u>I will strike all the firstborn</u> in the land of Egypt, both man and beast; <u>and on all the gods of Egypt I will execute judgments</u>: I am the Lord.

Reading that the Lord did evil to His people or that He hardened Pharaoh's heart may be puzzling. Reading that the Lord smote all the firstborn in the land of Egypt may be unsettling. Upon initial consideration, such actions may appear to be in sharp contrast with God Who is light, merciful, and without iniquity. Therefore, we may have difficulty reconciling what the Scriptures say about God's nature, with records that associate such actions with our wonderful God. Upcoming chapters in this study will dig deeper into these unusual expressions. We will do so by considering the context and other related scriptures.

I Chronicles 21 presents another verse with unusual and potentially troublesome wording.

> I Chronicles 21:14
>
> So <u>the Lord sent a pestilence on Israel</u>, and 70,000 men of Israel fell.

This verse says that the Lord sent a pestilence so that seventy thousand Israelites died. Again, these words do not appear to agree with the many clear records about God's nature—He is light, He is love, and He is just. In an upcoming chapter of this study, we will spend the necessary time to consider this unusual wording.

Let us consider Psalm 12.

1. The Problem and Essential Background

Psalm 12:6

The words of the LORD are pure words, like silver refined in a furnace on the ground, purified seven times.

The words of the Lord God are as pure as perfectly refined silver. Therefore, in this statement of the problem, we recognize that any difficulty with the unusual wording in the above examples is in our understanding and not with God's Word. Although the words of the Lord are pure, we may not always understand what is written. So, how do we understand wording in the Scriptures that seems to associate God with evil?

One way that many God-loving Bible readers have dealt with such wording is to regard *all* such unusual expressions as figurative. So what is figurative? It is the *opposite of* what is true to fact or actually so. Figurative language is nonliteral and makes use of figures of speech. However, if we automatically label all unusual expressions, as in the above examples, as figurative then we would be trying to supply an answer before examining the Scriptures. To regard *all* such wording as figurative before examining the Scriptures would not be rightly handling the Word of the Lord.

Therefore, let us next consider what the Scriptures say about how to approach the Scriptures.

This Study's Approach

The following verses effectively state the approach to the Scriptures that this study is applying.

> Proverbs 1:7
>
> The fear [reverence] of the Lord is the beginning of knowledge; fools despise wisdom and instruction.

Here, the word "fear" is better rendered "reverence." Reverence for the Lord is the starting point of knowledge. To grow in our understanding of wording in the Scriptures, that seems to associate God with evil, we must begin with reverence for the Lord God. The basis of our consideration of the Scriptures ought to be an attitude of reverence for God and His Word.

> II Timothy 3:16
>
> All Scripture is breathed out by God and profitable for teaching, for reproof, for correction, and for training in righteousness [justness].

God's breath is associated with His voice and indicates the source of all Scripture. All scriptures are authored by God and are profitable to teach, to reprove, and to correct. God's Word instructs us in His righteousness (justness).

> II Peter 1:20-21[3]
>
> [20] Knowing this first of all, that no prophecy of Scripture comes from someone's own interpretation.
>
> [21] For no prophecy [of the Scripture] was ever produced by the will of man, but men spoke from God as they were carried along by the Holy Spirit.

---

3. See also Galatians 1:11-12: "For I would have you know, brothers, that the gospel that was preached by me is not man's gospel. For I did not receive it from any man, nor was I taught it, but I receive it through a revelation of Jesus Christ."

1. The Problem and Essential Background

What we read in the Scriptures are God's words. As these holy men of God wrote information from God, they used the language and vocabulary of the culture, place, and time in which they lived. While the writers used the manner of communication of their times, what they wrote originated with God. What God authored ought not to be subjected to any person's private interpretation. Therefore, in seeking to make sense of some of the records that *seem* to associate God with evil, we must first look at what the Scriptures say, rather than consider our private understanding or misunderstanding. We will consider certain seemingly difficult passages that include an unclear expression about God's actions. As we do so, we must set aside preconceived ideas and traditions and allow the internal integrity of the Scriptures to speak for itself.

> II Timothy 2:15[NASB]
> Be diligent to present yourself approved to God as a workman who does not need to be ashamed, accurately handling the word of truth.

To accurately or rightly handle the Word of truth we will allow the intrinsic evidence of the Scriptures to speak for itself. Our approach is to let the Scriptures interpret themselves. To understand what is written, we read the Scriptures themselves and not things written about them. We begin by reading the verse and the context. When the verse alone is not clear we want to consider a wider section of Scripture. Understanding certain difficult expressions may require a broad scope of the Scriptures from Genesis to Revelation. Therefore, we consider the unusual wording in the verse, in the context, and in a wider view of the Scriptures. By looking at related passages where the same word, event, or subject occurs, we will put together complimentary scriptures to give a more complete understanding. When these efforts do not yield the source of our misunderstanding, we need to consider if there are any applicable figures of speech, customs, or manners of speaking of the lands and times of the Bible. We may also need to consider additional keys that allow the Scriptures to interpret themselves.[4] These are some foundational considerations in this study's approach to the Scriptures.

To recap, it is *not* this study's approach to label unusual wording about God's actions as figurative without first examining the Scriptures. Instead we apply a pattern of allowing the Scriptures to interpret themselves. This allows the intrinsic evidence of the Scriptures to determine if certain unusual expressions about God's actions are literal or figurative. Let us also acknowledge that, at times, we may not know, and that's okay. This study will consider records with unusual wording that seems to say God did something contrary to His nature. We will consider the context and related passages and any additional scriptures necessary to determine if such unusual expressions are literal or figurative, or if we do not know. Along the way, we will see how good, just, and merciful the Lord God is—both in the Old Testament as well as the New Testament.

In the upcoming chapters of this study, we will look further at the unusual and potentially troublesome words introduced above in the

---

4. To read more about how the Scriptures interpret themselves, see Walter J. Cummins, *Scripture Consulting Select Studies* (Franklin, Ohio: Scripture Consulting, 2010), Chapter 1, "Considerations for Consulting the Scriptures."

1. The Problem and Essential Background

"Statement of the Problem." As we do so, we want to hold in mind the many good characteristics of our God, in Whom no evil dwells.

The remainder of this chapter will look at six areas of essential background that will lay a foundation for this study. We will consider in order: God Is Light, One of a Different Nature, Opposing Natures, Choices and Sources of Information, God Is Just, and Recognizing What Is Just.

Essential Background: God Is Light

In the opening paragraphs, we briefly considered passages that credit many good things to the God of the Scriptures. Let us now look at some of these records in more detail.

> I John 1:5
> This is the message we have heard from him and proclaim to you, that God is light, and in him is no darkness at all.

The Scriptures assure us that God is light and that there is absolutely no darkness at all in Him. Darkness is the absence of light, and it is not associated with God. Let us look at another record involving light and darkness.

> Genesis 1:2-4 and 31
> ² The earth was without form and void, and darkness was over the face of the deep. And the Spirit of God was hovering over the face of the waters.
> ³ And God said, "Let there be light," and there was light.

> ⁴ And God saw that the light was good. And God separated the light from the darkness.
>
> ³¹ And God saw everything that he had made, and behold, it was very good. And there was evening and there was morning, the sixth day.

God spoke light into being and called the light good. When there was darkness on the face of the deep, God introduced light to benefit the situation. God separated the light from the darkness and declared that the light was very good. Light was one of the very good things God made.

> James 1:17
> Every good gift and every perfect gift is from above, coming down from the Father of lights with whom there is no variation or shadow due to change.

In Genesis 1, God introduced light into a dark situation. In James 1, God is declared to be the Father of lights, Who gives good and perfect gifts. The expression "shadow due to change" refers to the variations of light and dark caused by the changing shadows of the moon and planets as they move about the night sky. The movements of the moon and planets in the night sky cause shifting shadows so that sometimes there is more light and sometimes there is less light. Sometime they appear bright and sometimes they are barely visible. This is never the case with God. God's light is not brighter one day and shadowy the next. God's light is always strong enough and big enough for any situation. What God gives is not light one day and dark the next. Instead, what God gives is always light.

1. The Problem and Essential Background

Psalm 86:5 and 15

⁵ For you, O Lord, are good and forgiving, abounding in steadfast love to all who call upon you.

¹⁵ But you, O Lord, are a God merciful and gracious, slow to anger [long-suffering] and abounding in steadfast love and faithfulness.

Psalm 145:7 and 9

⁷ They shall pour forth the fame of your abundant goodness and shall sing aloud of your righteousness.

⁹ The Lord is good to all, and his mercy is over all that he has made.

Exodus 34:6

The Lord passed before him and proclaimed, "The Lord, the Lord, a God merciful and gracious, slow to anger [long-suffering], and abounding in steadfast love and faithfulness.

In these scriptures, we see that God is abounding in steadfast love, faithfulness, and goodness. He is good to all who call upon Him. God demonstrates His goodness to all in His mercy over all that He has made. The God of the Scriptures is merciful, gracious, and long-suffering. These scriptures and many more assure us that the God of the Scriptures is constant light that never has any dark shadows. God is light and in Him is absolutely no darkness—none at all. What God gives is faithfully and reliably good.

Essential Background: One of a Different Nature

However, the Scriptures reveal another being who has different characteristics than God Who is light, love, and good.

> Revelation 12:9
>
> And the great dragon was thrown down, that ancient serpent, who is called the devil and Satan, the deceiver of the whole world—he was thrown down to the earth, and his angels were thrown down with him.
>
> I Peter 5:8-9
>
> [8] Be sober-minded; be watchful. Your adversary the devil prowls around like a roaring lion, seeking someone to devour.
>
> [9] Resist him, firm in your faith [believing]…

Satan, the devil, and the adversary are different names for the same being. Even though he has many different names, his nature is the same. This study uses the name that occurs in the relevant context; otherwise, the name used is "the devil."

From this brief look at the devil we can see that he seeks to deceive and devour people. Therefore, God's people are encouraged to be sober-minded, watchful, and firm or steadfast in believing God's Word. We can resist the devil by being firm in believing God's Word. By these verses, we begin to see that the devil's nature is quite different from God's nature.

1. The Problem and Essential Background

Essential Background: Opposing Natures

We have seen that God is associated with light, and not with darkness. This section will look at records, which speak of light and darkness to get a clearer idea of what the Scriptures associate with each.

In the next record, Jesus Christ is speaking to the apostle Paul.

> Acts 26:16-18
>
> ¹⁶ But rise and stand upon your feet, for I [Jesus Christ] have appeared to you [Paul] for this purpose, to appoint you as a servant and witness to the things in which you have seen me and to those in which I will appear to you,
> ¹⁷ delivering you from your people and from the Gentiles—to whom I am sending you
> ¹⁸ to open their eyes, so that they may turn from darkness to light and from the power of Satan to God, that they may receive forgiveness of sins and a place among those who are sanctified by faith [believing] in me.

The Lord Jesus Christ appointed Paul to minister the gospel of God to the Gentiles. Romans 1 defines the gospel of God as the good news concerning God's Son Jesus Christ.[5]

In Acts 26, darkness is associated with Satan and light is associated with God. Psalm 119:130 says, God's Word gives light.[6] The people of Acts 26 were in a dark situation; they needed deliverance from Satan's darkness. So God sent Paul to minister the gospel of God to them. The light of the gospel of God equipped them to turn

---

5. See Romans 1:1-4. See also Romans 15:16:[KJV] "That I [Paul] should be the minister of Jesus Christ to the Gentiles, ministering the gospel of God..."
6. Psalm 119:130: "The unfolding of your words gives light..."

from darkness to light so that they could receive forgiveness of sins and sanctification. They were to be sanctified by believing concerning Jesus Christ.

> Colossians 1:12-13
> [12] Giving thanks to the Father, who has qualified you to share in the inheritance of the saints [sanctified ones] in light.
> [13] He [the Father] has delivered us from the domain of darkness and transferred us to the kingdom of his beloved Son.

Putting this together with Acts 26, we see that all who believed the gospel of God concerning Jesus Christ are absolutely delivered out of Satan's domain of darkness. When we believed, we were transferred into the kingdom of God and of His Son and Satan has no legal authority over us.[7]

Regarding the kingdom of God, Jesus Christ told Nicodemus in John 3, that the way to see and enter the kingdom of God was to be born of God. Everyone who is born of God's spirit has been delivered and transferred into God and His Son's kingdom of light.

We are considering the opposing power and nature of God and the devil. Next we go to II Corinthians.

---

7. The Greek word rendered "transferred" in this context does not mean a physical transfer, but rather it means a transfer of position or status from one domain or kingdom to another. For more information, see footnote on "transferred" in *A Journey through the Acts and Epistles* translated and edited by Walter J. Cummins (Scripture Consulting, Franklin, Ohio 45005, First edition 2006) p. 453-454.

1. The Problem and Essential Background

II Corinthians 4:3-6

³ And even if our gospel is veiled, it is veiled to those who are perishing.

⁴ In their case the god of this world has blinded the minds of the unbelievers, to keep them from seeing the light of the gospel of the glory of Christ, who is the image of God.

⁵ For what we proclaim is not ourselves, but Jesus Christ as Lord, with ourselves as your servants for Jesus' sake.

⁶ For God, who said, "Let light shine out of darkness," has shone in our hearts to give the light of the knowledge of the glory of God in the face of Jesus Christ.

In Acts, we saw that the light of God's Word delivers people from the darkness of the power of Satan. The god of this world is another name for the devil or Satan, as we can see by the fact that he is engaged with similar activities as Satan. The god of this world blinds the minds of those who do not believe. He does so to keep them from seeing the light of the gospel of the glory of Christ and the deliverance it brings.

II Corinthians 4:6 quotes Genesis 1:3 and offers an interesting comparison. Just as God introduced light to deal with darkness in Genesis 1, so He has shone the light of the gospel of Christ to confront Satan's darkness. In this record, some believed concerning Jesus Christ and some did not. Those who believed were delivered from the power of darkness. Once again, God's light and the devil's darkness are set in opposition.

> John 10:10
>
> The thief comes only to steal and kill and destroy. I came that they may have life and have it abundantly.

Although the devil is represented here as a thief, we know that he is the same being because he is engaged in the same activities. John 10:10 contrast the activities of Jesus Christ with those of the devil. Jesus Christ came so that people might have life in abundance. On the other hand, Jesus Christ exposed the devil as a thief who steals, kills, and destroys.

> Hebrews 2:14[WTJ]
>
> Therefore, since the children share of flesh and blood, he [Jesus Christ] likewise partook of the same so that through death he [Jesus Christ] might render inactive [ineffective] him who holds the strength of death, that is, the devil.

Part of the purpose of the death, resurrection, and ascension of Jesus Christ was to render the devil ineffective. We again see the stark contrast between God and His Son Jesus Christ, and the devil. God is the originator and source of life while the devil is associated with death.[8]

From these records that contrast God and the devil, we are building a clearer picture (from the Scriptures) of their opposing natures and associated characteristics. We have seen that the devil is

---

8. Death entered the world when the devil deceived Eve and Adam sinned. See Genesis 3. See also Romans 5:12: "Therefore, just as sin came into the world through one man, and death through sin…"

Since eternal life spirit cannot die, one way the devil's hold on death is rendered inactive is by receiving eternal life spirit.

characterized by darkness, death, bondage, and destruction. On the other hand, the God of the Scriptures is characterized by life, light, and deliverance.

Essential Background: Choices and Sources of Information

In Genesis 1, God saw all that He had made and called it good. God created Adam in His image and put him into a very good environment. John 4:24 tells us that God is spirit, so in Genesis, when God created man in His image, that image was spirit.[9] Spirit gave them the means of communication and a close relationship with God. So we see that Adam was in an ideal situation. He had unrestricted access to fellowship with God by way of spirit. Adam was equipped for success and was surrounded by only good things. What would Adam do with all that God had provided?

> Genesis 2:15-17
>
> [15] The LORD God took the man and put him in the garden of Eden to work it and keep it.
>
> [16] And the LORD God commanded the man, saying, "You may surely eat of every tree of the garden,
>
> [17] but of the tree of the knowledge of good and evil you shall not eat, for in the day that you eat of it you shall surely die."

Because God had Adam's best interest in mind and wanted only good for mankind, God instructed Adam regarding the tree of the

---

9. For more information regarding man's two life forms and God's intention that man have spirit, see Walter J. Cummins, *The Acceptable Year of the Lord* (Franklin, Ohio: Scripture Consulting, 1998-1999, 2005), Chapter 1, "The World's Need for a Savior," pp. 2-8.

knowledge of good and evil. These instructions provided the possibility for two very different responses. Adam was free to decide if he would obey or disobey. Adam's choice is summarized in Romans 5.

> Romans 5:19
>
> For as by one man's disobedience the many were made sinners, so by the one man's obedience the many will be made righteous.

Adam disobeyed. If Adam was not free to choose then why would God give him a choice? Had God controlled Adam's responses then why go to the trouble of giving him instructions that contained a choice? Why not just say, "Here is the best decision, no choice."? However, God did give Adam a choice and regrettably Adam chose to disobey. Throughout the Scriptures we see that God always allows people to choose between the available sources of information. God does so because He is just. Thus, in order to rightly understand the Scriptures, we need to recognize that people have freedom of will.[10]

In Deuteronomy, God offered a choice to the people of Israel.

> Deuteronomy 30:10-16 and 19
>
> [10] When you obey the voice of the LORD your God, to keep his commandments and his statutes that are written in this Book of the Law, when you turn to the LORD your God with all your heart and with all your soul.
>
> [11] "For this commandment that I command you today is not too hard for you, neither is it far off.

---

10. See also Joshua 24:15; Psalm119:173; Proverbs 1:29, 3:31; and Jonah 1:1-3, 3:1-3.

1. The Problem and Essential Background

> [12] It is not in heaven, that you should say, 'Who will ascend to heaven for us and bring it to us, that we may hear it and do it?'
>
> [13] Neither is it beyond the sea, that you should say, 'Who will go over the sea for us and bring it to us, that we may hear it and do it?'
>
> [14] But the word is very near you. It is in your mouth and in your heart, so that you can do it.
>
> [15] "See, I have set before you today life and good, death and evil.
>
> [16] If you obey the commandments of the LORD your God that I command you today, by loving the LORD your God, by walking in his ways, and by keeping his commandments and his statutes and his rules, then you shall live and multiply, and the LORD your God will bless you in the land that you are entering to take possession of it.
>
> [19] I call heaven and earth to witness against you today, that I have set before you life and death, blessing and curse. Therefore choose life, that you and your offspring may live.

In this record, we see that God presented the people of Israel with three opposing choices: life or death; good or evil; and blessing or cursing. If they obeyed His voice to keep His commandments and turned unto God with all their heart and soul, they would be choosing life, good, and blessing. If they chose not to obey God's voice, they would be choosing death, evil, and cursing. As far as God was concerned, they were free to make up their own minds and make a choice. Yet, God set them up for success in that His Word was near and not far; it was accessible and doable. God gives His Word to benefit people and He allows people to choose to believe or not; He does not overstep anyone's freedom of will. As we can see from this record, God wanted His people to enjoy the blessings of living in His goodness; He exhorted them to choose life by choosing to believe His Word. God always allows people to make up their own minds. This will be important to remember as we go forward.

In order to have a choice there must be more than one source of information from which to choose. In this study, we are not considering the many choices people make daily in relationship to the physical world; instead we are considering sources of information about spiritual realities.

In the next record, Jesus Christ was having a discussion with some Pharisees about certain spiritual realities and their source.

> John 8:12-14
> [12] Again Jesus spoke to them, saying, "I am the light of the world. Whoever follows me will not walk in darkness, but will have the light of life."
> [13] So the Pharisees said to him, "You are bearing witness about yourself; your testimony is not true."
> [14] Jesus answered, "Even if I do bear witness about myself, my testimony is true, for I know where I came from and where I am going, but you do not know where I come from or where I am going.

1. The Problem and Essential Background

Jesus Christ is called the light of the world and those that followed him did not walk in darkness, but rather had the light of life. Moreover, Jesus Christ knew that he came from God and that the record concerning him was true. On the other hand these Pharisees did not follow Jesus Christ; they did not believe concerning him. Therefore, they walked in darkness. We will pick up another part of this discussion in verse 42.

> John 8:42-47
>
> [42] Jesus said to them, "If God were your Father, you would love me, for I came from God and I am here. I came not of my own accord, but he sent me.
>
> [43] Why do you not understand what I say? It is because you cannot bear to hear my word.
>
> [44] You are of your father the devil, and your will is to do your father's desires. He was a murderer from the beginning, and does not stand in the truth, because there is no truth in him. When he lies, he speaks out of his own character, for he is a liar and the father of lies.
>
> [45] But because I tell the truth, you do not believe me.
>
> [46] Which one of you convicts me of sin? If I tell the truth, why do you not believe me?
>
> [47] Whoever is of God hears the words of God. The reason why you do not hear them is that you are not of God."

It seems that those Pharisees were not only confused about Jesus Christ's parentage, but they were also confused about their own parentage. Jesus Christ told them that he came from God but that they were not of God but were of their father, the devil. The Pharisees claimed that they were associated with truth and light; however, Jesus Christ declared they were children of the devil associated with his lies and darkness. From this we see that during the earthly life and ministry of Jesus Christ, he revealed the devil and his nature of lies and darkness.

In this subsection, we are considering choices and sources of information. Let us again consider verse 44.

> John 8:44^{NASB}
>
> You are of *your* father the devil, and you want to do the desires of your father. He was a murderer from the beginning, and does not stand in the truth because there is no truth in him. Whenever he speaks a lie, he speaks from his own *nature,* for he is a liar and the father of lies.

Jesus Christ declared that the devil had no truth in him; whereas what Jesus Christ spoke was truth from the God of truth. The devil's nature is that of a liar in whom there is no truth. Revelation 12:9 adds that Satan is "the deceiver of the whole world." To deceive is to mislead by deception or delusion. That is quite a helpful description of what we can expect from the devil: untruth, lies, and deception. The devil is a source of information, but the information he provides cannot be trusted. What the devil gives is intended to deceive, delude, and blind people with his darkness. In contrast to the devil who is the father of lies, Numbers 23:19 says, "God is not man, that he should lie," and Titus 1:2 says, "God, who never lies." God is the source of information that is true and trustworthy.

In this section, we saw that the Father of lights and the father of lies are two opposing sources of information. Since God does not overstep anyone's freedom of will, people are free to choose between these opposing sources. Along with the choice, God lovingly exhorts His people to choose life, truth, and blessings.

Essential Background: God Is Just

We saw that God and the devil are opposing powers and opposing sources of information. God is abundant in goodness and truth. He is merciful, gracious, long-suffering, and just. As God's justness is essential to this study, let us consider more about our just God.

> Deuteronomy 32:4[NASB]
>
> "The Rock! His work is perfect, For all His ways are just; A God of faithfulness and without injustice, Righteous [just] and upright is He.

There is no injustice or iniquity in the God of the Scriptures. All His ways are just. Regarding the word "righteous," both the Hebrew and Greek[11] word families rendered as "right, righteous, righteousness" may also be accurately rendered as "just, justice, justness." This study uses: just, justice, and justness. Here, Deuteronomy 32:4 says all of God's ways are just. There is no injustice in God—none at all. God's faithfulness is linked with His justice; He is reliably just.

---

11. In this study Hebrew and Greek refer to biblical languages, not modern ones.

> Proverbs 2:7-9
>
> ⁷ He stores up sound wisdom for the upright; he is a shield to those who walk in integrity,
>
> ⁸ guarding the paths of justice and watching over the way of his saints.
>
> ⁹ Then you will understand righteousness [justness] and justice and equity, every good path.

In this context, the saints are those who walk uprightly in integrity. By guarding the paths of justice God watches over the way of the upright. Every good path includes God's justness, justice, and equity.[12]

> Psalm 19:9-10
>
> ⁹ The fear [reverence] of the LORD is clean, enduring forever; the rules of the LORD are true, and righteous [just] altogether.
>
> ¹⁰ More to be desired are they than gold, even much fine gold; sweeter also than honey and drippings of the honeycomb.

"Rules" may also be rendered "just decrees" or "judgments." The context of Psalm 19 refers to the covenant of the law, that is the Mosaic law given to Israel. The commandments and judgments of the covenant of the law set forth God's established standard for justice at that time. According to Psalm 19, God's established standard of

---

12. The Hebrew word rendered "justice" in Proverbs 2:8-9 may be understood as a decision based upon an established standard. See Walter J. Cummins, *Scripture Consulting Select Studies* (Franklin, Ohio: Scripture Consulting, 2010), Chapter 10, "Justification" p. 334.

1. The Problem and Essential Background

justice was more desirable than gold and sweeter than honey. That is quite a description of the desirable nature of God's just decrees.

Once Jesus Christ, the Son of God, came and fulfilled God's plan of redemption and salvation, there was another standard of justice that was not based on the covenant of the law.

> Romans 3:21-22
>
> [21] But now the righteousness [justice] of God has been manifested apart from the law, although the Law and the Prophets bear witness to it—
>
> [22] the righteousness [justice] of God through faith [believing] in Jesus Christ for all who believe. For there is no distinction.

This standard of justice is based on believing concerning Jesus Christ.[13] It is a standard God planned and brought to pass to redeem and deliver mankind from Adam's sin. We will consider more about this righteousness or justice in a later chapter. For now, we noted that Proverbs 2 associated equity with justice and here in Romans 3 we see that God's standard of justice in Christ is to all who believe with no distinction. God's just decrees are based on His established standards and are never fickle, erratic, or whimsical. God's standard of justice in all times is true, just, and equitable. His very nature is just and He demonstrates His justice in that all, without any distinction who believe concerning Jesus Christ, are made just.

---

13. The Greek word rendered "faith" may be rendered "believing." In the Scriptures, faith or believing does not refer to a church or denomination's doctrine or membership, nor does it refer to blind faith. Biblically believing starts with having information from God from the Scriptures or by way of His spirit. See Hebrews 11.

> Psalm 33:4-6
>
> ⁴ For the word of the LORD is upright, and all his work is done in faithfulness.
>
> ⁵ He loves righteousness [justness] and justice; the earth is full of the steadfast love of the LORD.
>
> ⁶ By the word of the LORD the heavens were made, and by the breath of his mouth all their host.

Psalm 33 is a psalm of praise to God. God is to be praised for His upright and powerful Word and for His love for justness. In verse 5, the psalmist links God's justness and justice with His steadfast love that fills the earth. God demonstrates His justice by His love that fills the earth.

> Jeremiah 9:24
>
> But let him who boasts boast in this, that he understands and knows me, that I am the LORD who practices steadfast love, justice, and righteousness [justness] in the earth. For in these things I delight, declares the LORD."

Psalm 33 says God loves justness and justice; Jeremiah 9 says God delights in justness and justice. In both, God's love is associated with His justness and justice. The Hebrew word rendered "steadfast love" in the English Standard Version is translated "mercy" in the Authorized King James Version because an underlying aspect of God's love is His mercy.

These verses begin to introduce the biblical truth that God's love, mercy, and justice are connected in a positive way in the Scriptures. However, in the societies and cultures of present times, some people call God's actions unjust or unloving. We ought to be cautious to not allow present-day culture to define how we think about God's justice.

> Isaiah 5:19-21
>
> ¹⁹ ...Let the counsel of the Holy One of Israel draw near, and let it come, that we may know it!"
> ²⁰ Woe to those who call evil good and good evil, who put darkness for light and light for darkness, who put bitter for sweet and sweet for bitter!
> ²¹ Woe to those who are wise in their own eyes, and shrewd in their own sight![14]

While this section of Isaiah is a list of woes addressed to the wicked, the exhortation is generally applicable. The people to whom the woes were addressed substituted darkness for light and called dark things the opposite of what God called them. They were wise in their own eyes. In contrast, we want to call things as God calls them. We ought to allow God's Word to determine what is good or evil and not present-day societal values. Our goal is to grow in our understanding of God's perspective of what is good, light, sweet, and just—and then to align our thoughts with God's Word, the Scriptures. What God calls good is good.

> Psalm 119:39
>
> Turn away the reproach that I dread, for your rules [just decrees] are good.

---

14. Isaiah 5:19-21 and its context are considered further in appendix A.

God's just decrees are described as good. God's justice is not based on arbitrary whims or on the currently fashionable ideologies of our times. God's justness and justice are established, reliable, and good.

> Psalm 98:8-9
> ⁸ Let the rivers clap their hands; let the hills sing for joy together
> ⁹ before the LORD, for he comes to judge the earth. He will judge the world with righteousness [justness], and the peoples with equity.

Rivers clapping their hands and hills joyfully singing represent a celebration of joy in that the Lord will come to judge. When God judges, He judges with justness and equity.

> Revelation 16:7
> And I heard the altar saying, "Yes, Lord God the Almighty, true and just are your judgments!"

Whenever the Lord God Almighty judges, His judgments are true and just. Throughout all times, God's justice is equitable, true, good, and just. For what the God of the Scriptures says is good or evil defines what is good or evil. We saw that guarding the paths of justice preserves and protects the way of the upright who walk in integrity. In the Scriptures, God's justness and justice are linked with God's steadfast love and goodness. There is great joy associated with God judging people and the world.

1. The Problem and Essential Background

Essential Background: Recognizing What Is Just

In the previous section, we considered God's justness and justice. This section will consider more about the devil's injustice. Our aim is to recognize when actions (that may appear similar) are according to God's justice versus the devil's injustice.

In John 8, Jesus Christ told certain Pharisees that they were of their father, the devil. In the following, Paul addressed another person whose father was the devil.

> Acts 13:9-10
> ⁹ But Saul, who was also called Paul, filled with the Holy Spirit, looked intently at him
> ¹⁰ and said, "You son of the devil, you enemy of all righteousness [justice], full of all deceit and villainy, will you not stop making crooked the straight paths of the Lord?

The apostle Paul had information from God by way of spirit. Here, Paul exposed the nature of the devil just as Jesus Christ had in John 8. Paul spoke to the son of the devil calling him an enemy of all that is just. Moreover, the devil's ways are full of deceit, villainy, and attempts to make God's straight paths seem crooked.

We have considered the contrast between the nature, characteristics, power, and information that comes from God as opposed to the nature, characteristics, power, and information from the devil. God's standard of justice is based on His nature and reflects Who He is. God is light and love. His ways are good, just, and merciful. God introduces light into dark situations to bring life and deliverance. On the other hand, the devil's acts reflect his nature. The devil's nature is to deceive and devour people; by his deception of Eve that led to Adam's transgression, death entered the world. The devil's ways bring death and bondage. Moreover, the devil is an enemy of all that is just and right.

In Romans 1:29-31,[15] the Scriptures link a long list of deeds and ways of thinking with injustice. These associated characteristics agree with what we have already seen regarding the devil's unjust ways. The list in Romans concludes with linking injustice with being unmerciful. The devil's injustice has no mercy at all.

When the devil steals, kills, and destroys it is rooted in his nature of lies, hatred, envy, strife, and lack of mercy. However, when God executes justice it is based on His established standards of justice. God's justice includes freedom of will—God always allows people to choose between available sources of information. On the other hand, the devil does not respect a person's freedom of will but seeks to control people for his unjust purposes. God's just standards include abundant mercy to all. His mercy provides a way to soften consequences. In contrast the devil shows no mercy. The fruit of God's justice is deliverance for those who turn to Him. We recognize the devil's injustice by its evil and arrogant characteristics. On the other hand, we recognize God's justice by its good, just, and merciful characteristics.

We must also recognize that God would never work against His established standards of justice. Since the fall of man, God's justice

---

15. Romans 1:29-31: "They were filled with all manner of unrighteousness, evil, covetousness, malice. They are full of envy, murder, strife, deceit, maliciousness. They are gossips, slanderers, haters of God, insolent, haughty, boastful, inventors of evil, disobedient to parents, foolish, faithless, heartless, ruthless [unmerciful, no mercy]."

across the ages was founded on and demonstrated in Christ Jesus our lord. Thus we would expect God's just acts to protect and provide for those who believe concerning Christ.

God's established standards of justice are a good path and are linked with His mercy and steadfast love. We recognize what is just by its characteristics according to God's established standards.

Summary

In this chapter we have set forth the aim and approach of this study. We briefly looked at a few introductory passages that, to some, may *seem* to associate God with evil. Since the Scriptures declare that God is light, love, and reliably good, the unusual words in these passages may be understandably unsettling. To proceed, we asked, "How do we go about understanding such unusual wording in the Scriptures?" We noted that to automatically view *all* such wording as figurative is not the best approach. Instead, this study's approach is to allow the intrinsic evidence of the Scriptures to determine if such unusual expressions are literal or figurative, or if we simply do not know. We will do so by examining the context and related passages of such expressions to see what God is communicating in His Word.

The Scriptures reveal a stark contrast between the justice of God and the injustice of the devil. They are opposing powers and opposing sources of information. The following chart summarizes our findings.

God	The devil
Light	darkness
Light of gospel	spiritual blindness
Deliverance	bondage
Good	evil
Life	death
Truth	lies and deceit
Just	unjust
Equitable	unfair
Mercy to all	no mercy
Justice	injustice
Father of Light	father of lies

As we consider certain potentially unclear or possibly unsettling records in God's Word, we must hold in mind God's nature as evidenced throughout the Scriptures. God's nature is good, true, just, faithful, merciful, gracious, and long-suffering. God's justness and justice are consistently linked with His steadfast love, mercy, and goodness throughout the Scriptures. When God executes justice, His actions reflect His nature. Since God is faithful to His nature from Genesis to revelation, we should expect to see His good nature in all that He does throughout the Scriptures. Thus, we must set aside preconceived ideas and read what is written. We must search the Scriptures so that we might call what God calls good, good; what God calls light, light; and what God calls sweet, sweet. There is absolutely no darkness at all in the God of the Scriptures—none at all.

2

Moses and an Unusual Expression

In chapter one, we established that the approach of this study is to consider what God's Word, the Scriptures, say and not what society or philosophers say. We saw that God is light, love, merciful, good, and just. God introduces the light of His Word to bring life and deliverance to people. Yet there is another who is unjust, unmerciful, dark, and who opposes God. God and the devil are opposing powers and opposing sources of information. The Scriptures show that each person has freedom of will to choose which source of information to believe. While God is just and faithful to His Word, the devil is an enemy of justice; he is unjust, a liar, deceitful, and seeks to steal the light of God's Word from people so that they do not believe and benefit from God's goodness. What God gives and does is based on His just nature, while what the devil gives and does is based on his unjust nature. In the Scriptures, God's judgments and justice are described as good.

More background and scope of the Scriptures is important to the overall subject of this book; however, we will delay further essential background until chapter five.

Did God Do It?

In this chapter, we will get right into an example of some potentially unclear or possibly unsettling wording. We will also handle a little bit about figures of speech, idioms, and biblical culture to help us understand an unusual expression that may seem difficult or unclear.

An Unusual Expression

Exodus 5 occurs at a time when the people of Israel were in bondage in Egypt.

> Exodus 5:22
>
> Then Moses turned to the LORD and said, "O Lord, why have you done evil to this people? Why did you ever send me?

Moses' manner of speech is puzzling. Moreover, saying God did evil to His people does not fit with so many clear scriptures about God's nature. Since we do not understand what is meant by this one verse alone, let us next consider the wider context of Exodus in the chapters leading up to this troublesome verse. Then we will consider the closer context of Exodus chapter five.

Wider Context

The book of Exodus begins with the people of Israel multiplying in the land of Egypt. Their situation in Egypt had started off good, but over time deteriorated.

> Exodus 1:11-14
>
> ¹¹ Therefore they set taskmasters over them to afflict them with heavy burdens. They built for Pharaoh store cities, Pithom and Raamses.

2. Moses and an Unusual Expression

> ¹² But the more they were oppressed, the more they multiplied and the more they spread abroad. And the Egyptians were in dread of the people of Israel.
> ¹³ So they ruthlessly made the people of Israel work as slaves
> ¹⁴ and made their lives bitter with hard service, in mortar and brick, and in all kinds of work in the field. In all their work they ruthlessly made them work as slaves.

The Egyptians made the people of Israel to serve with hard labor to build cities to store Pharaoh's treasures. History tells us that Pharaoh's building projects required large numbers of laborers. Thus the people of Israel's lives were bitter; they needed deliverance.

> Exodus 2:24-25
> ²⁴ And God heard their groaning, and God remembered his covenant with Abraham, with Isaac, and with Jacob.
> ²⁵ God saw the people of Israel—and God knew.

God heard, remembered, and had concern for the children of Israel. Next we will read from Exodus 3 concerning what God told Moses when He spoke to him by the burning bush.

> Exodus 3:6-11
> ⁶ And he said, "I am the God of your father, the God of Abraham, the God of Isaac, and the God of Jacob." And Moses hid his face, for he was afraid to look at God.
> ⁷ And the LORD said, I have surely seen the affliction of my people who are in Egypt and have heard their cry because of their taskmasters. I know their sufferings,

> ⁸ and I have come down to deliver them out of the hand of the Egyptians and to bring them up out of that land to a good and broad land, a land flowing with milk and honey, to the place of the Canaanites, the Hittites, the Amorites, the Perizzites, the Hivites, and the Jebusites.
> ⁹ And now, behold, the cry of the people of Israel has come to me, and I have also seen the oppression with which the Egyptians oppress them.
> ¹⁰ Come, I will send you to Pharaoh that you may bring my people, the children of Israel, out of Egypt."
> ¹¹ But Moses said to God, "Who am I that I should go to Pharaoh and bring the children of Israel out of Egypt?"

God saw that the Egyptians were oppressing His people. He heard their cry, knew their sorrows, and saw their afflictions. What a portrait of a merciful and compassionate God this is. God told Moses that He appeared to him as the God of Abraham, Isaac, and Jacob and called the afflicted "my people." These statements recall the covenant that God made with Abraham and his seed, including that Abraham's descendants would be God's people and that He would be their God.[1] God came to deliver His people out of the hand of the Egyptians, and He instructed Moses to bring them forth out of Egypt.

According to verse 11 and the balance of chapter three, Moses lacked confidence that he was capable to carry out what God set before him. Moses expressed uncertainty about being sent to the

---

[1]. For more information about the covenant between God and Abraham that extended to the people of Israel, see Genesis 17:1-8; Leviticus 26:11-15; and Jeremiah 11:1-5.

people of Israel. However, God reassured Moses that He would be with him to help in whatever ways were needed. In Exodus 4, Moses continued to express his concerns, saying he was not well spoken. Thus, God provided Aaron to speak what God gave to Moses (God to Moses to Aaron to Pharaoh).

Exodus 3:19 adds an interesting detail.

> Exodus 3:19-20
> [19] But I know that the king of Egypt will not let you go unless compelled by a mighty hand.
> [20] So I will stretch out my hand and strike Egypt with all the wonders that I will do in it; after that he will let you go.

God knew in advance that Pharaoh would not let His people go without a show of might and some time passing. However, He promised that there was deliverance to come.

Closer Context

With this background, we now move on to the closer context of the unusual expression in Exodus 5.

> Exodus 5:1-5
> [1] Afterward Moses and Aaron went and said to Pharaoh, "Thus says the LORD, the God of Israel, 'Let my people go, that they may hold a feast to me in the wilderness.'"
> [2] But Pharaoh said, "Who is the LORD, that I should obey his voice and let Israel go? I do not know the LORD, and moreover, I will not let Israel go."

> ³ Then they said, "The God of the Hebrews has met with us. Please let us go a three days' journey into the wilderness that we may sacrifice to the LORD our God, lest he fall upon us with pestilence or with the sword."
> ⁴ But the king of Egypt said to them, "Moses and Aaron, why do you take the people away from their work? Get back to your burdens."
> ⁵ And Pharaoh said, "Behold, the people of the land are now many, and you make them rest from their burdens!"

This is the first occasion in the records of Exodus 5-12 where God, by way of Moses, made known His Word and will to Pharaoh: "Let My people go," so that His people would be free to worship Him. The people of Israel were in a dark situation. God's request for their release from bondage was a reasonable request. God introduced the light of His Word into this dark situation.

When God's representatives approached Pharaoh, he responded with, "Who is the Lord that I should obey?" In the culture of ancient Egypt, a vast number of deities were revered as sacred; Pharaoh was also considered as having divine authority. However, the God of the Hebrews was not regarded as a god in Pharaoh's eyes. By making light of God's request, Pharaoh showed his lack of regard for the Lord God. According to verses 4 and 5, Pharaoh was alarmed that the Hebrews would cease work. After all, they were a free and plentiful source of labor for his building projects.

2. Moses and an Unusual Expression

Exodus 5:6-9

⁶ The same day Pharaoh commanded the taskmasters of the people and their foremen,

⁷ "You shall no longer give the people straw to make bricks, as in the past; let them go and gather straw for themselves.

⁸ But the number of bricks that they made in the past you shall impose on them, you shall by no means reduce it, for they are idle. Therefore they cry, 'Let us go and offer sacrifice to our God.'

⁹ Let heavier work be laid on the men that they may labor at it and pay no regard to lying words."

The words, which Moses and Aaron spoke to Pharaoh, originated with God, yet Pharaoh called them "lying words." Pharaoh said the people of Israel ought not to pay attention to words from God, but instead pay attention to words from Pharaoh. Thus he set himself in opposition to the Lord God.

Exodus 5:10-16

¹⁰ So the taskmasters and the foremen of the people went out and said to the people, "Thus says Pharaoh, 'I will not give you straw.

¹¹ Go and get your straw yourselves wherever you can find it, but your work will not be reduced in the least.'"

¹² So the people were scattered throughout all the land of Egypt to gather stubble for straw.

> [13] The taskmasters were urgent, saying, "Complete your work, your daily task each day, as when there was straw."
>
> [14] And the foremen of the people of Israel, whom Pharaoh's taskmasters had set over them, were beaten and were asked, "Why have you not done all your task of making bricks today and yesterday, as in the past?"
>
> [15] Then the foremen of the people of Israel came and cried to Pharaoh, "Why do you treat your servants like this?
>
> [16] No straw is given to your servants, yet they say to us, 'Make bricks!' And behold, your servants are beaten; but the fault is in your own people."

The foremen complained to Pharaoh about the extra workload. They reported that Pharaoh's own taskmasters were at fault for the Israelites not being able to meet their daily brick-making quota. They were looking for some sympathy. Do you think Pharaoh was sympathetic?

> Exodus 5:17-21
>
> [17] But he said, "You are idle, you are idle; that is why you say, 'Let us go and sacrifice to the LORD.'
>
> [18] Go now and work. No straw will be given you, but you must still deliver the same number of bricks."
>
> [19] The foremen of the people of Israel saw that they were in trouble when they said, "You shall by no means reduce your number of bricks, your daily task each day."

2. Moses and an Unusual Expression

> [20] They met Moses and Aaron, who were waiting for them, as they came out from Pharaoh;
> [21] and they said to them, "The LORD look on you and judge, because you have made us stink in the sight of Pharaoh and his servants, and have put a sword in their hand to kill us."

Once the appointed foremen realized how bad their situation was, they blamed Moses and Aaron for their troubles.

As we touched on in Exodus chapters three and four, Moses was reluctant to request the release of God's people. However, God encouraged Moses and reassured him that the Lord would be with him. Now with this verbal attack from the foremen, how would Moses respond?

> Exodus 5:22-23
> [22] Then Moses turned to the LORD and said, "O Lord, why have you done evil to this people? Why did you ever send me?
> [23] For since I came to Pharaoh to speak in your name, he has done evil to this people, and you have not delivered your people at all."

Moses admirably responded by turning to the Lord God. However, the words Moses used to express himself sound unusual to our ears. Moses posed a question that *seems* to say God did something contrary to His nature. To understand the unusual expression, the Lord did "evil to this people," let us first address: who was responsible for the evil treatment of God's people? Then we will address: why Moses spoke in this manner?

Additionally, before moving on, let us note an important sequence in verse 23: Pharaoh did evil to the people of Israel *ever since* Moses came to Pharaoh to speak in God's name.

Related Scriptures

The following related verses recount things that had previously happened to Israel—before God sent Moses to redeem His people.

> Numbers 20:15-16
>
> [15] How our fathers went down to Egypt, and we lived in Egypt a long time. And the Egyptians dealt harshly with us and our fathers.
>
> [16] And when we cried to the Lord, he heard our voice…
>
> Deuteronomy 26:6-7
>
> [6] And the Egyptians treated us harshly and humiliated us and laid on us hard labor.
>
> [7] Then we cried to the Lord, the God of our fathers, and the Lord heard our voice and saw our affliction, our toil, and our oppression.

From the context of Exodus 5 we saw that it was Pharaoh and the Egyptians who did evil to the people of Israel. The related passages say that it was the Egyptians' harsh treatment of the people of Israel that prompted God's people to cry to the Lord.

Both before they cried to the Lord, as we see here, and after, as we read in Exodus 5, it was Pharaoh and the Egyptians who treated the

2. Moses and an Unusual Expression

people of Israel harshly and laid on them hard labor. Together these records agree that it was Pharaoh and the Egyptians, and *not* God, who did evil to the people of Israel. Therefore, how do we understand Moses' unusual manner of speech? What is God communicating by this expression?

Ways to Understand the Scriptures

Reading the context and related scriptures is the first step in allowing the Scriptures to interpret themselves. Since the context and related passages have not revealed the meaning of the unusual expression in Exodus 5, we next need to consider additional ways as to how all Scripture interprets itself. Since the Scriptures are pure words from God then the difficulty must be in our understanding. Some additional ways we can address problems—in our understanding of the Scriptures—is by recognizing figures of speech, customs, and manners of speaking of the lands and times of the Bible. Therefore, we will now take the time to consider a little bit about figures of speech, idioms, and biblical culture that will help us to understand the unusual expression, the Lord did "evil to this people."

Figures of Speech

All languages have norms that govern grammatical structure as well as the arrangement and meaning of words and phrases. Departures from language norms result in unusual or nonliteral usage of words, which we call figures of speech. Figures of speech fall into two basic categories: figures of grammar or figures of meaning (or thought).[2]

2. Figures of meaning are also called figures of thought or figures of semantics. Semantics is the branch of linguistics that studies the relationship or arrangement of words and their meaning.

Did God Do It?

God's Word says many things that are clear and understandable right where they are written. However, when words or expressions do not follow the rules or norms of grammar or meaning, then we ought to consider *if* it is a figure of speech.

A figure of meaning is illustrated by the expression, "Joe is a night owl." The normal meaning of "owl" is shifted to a figurative meaning. Joe is not a nocturnal bird of prey but he does stay up late at night. In meaning-based figures of speech, the grammatical construction is not the focus; instead the focus is on how the figurative language has affected the meaning of the expression as a whole.

When figures of speech occur in the Scriptures, these departures from language norms are by divine design and communicate what God authored. Figurative language never lessens God's intended meaning but rather adds depth to the meaning.[3]

In the context of Exodus 5, the Lord did "evil to this people" is not literally true to fact. This word group is a figure of speech based on a shift in meaning (or thought).

> "The Lord did evil to this people" is a figure of meaning (or thought).

Idioms

A commonly-used, meaning-based figure of speech is an idiom. A simple definition of an idiom is a fixed expression typically used in a

---

[3]. E. W. Bullinger, *Figures of Speech Used in the Bible* (Messrs. Eyre and Spottiswoode, London, 1898; Baker Book House, Grand Rapids, Michigan, 1968).

2. Moses and an Unusual Expression

figurative sense. Idioms are "non-literal, culture-specific expressions"[4] with a whole-unit meaning. They are often multi-word expressions. Unless a person is already familiar with the expression, the words do not make sense and cannot be understood at face value. Instead, the whole word unit has its own unique meaning and does not mean what the typical definition of its separate parts would mean. For example, "to pull one's leg" (to tease), or "to hit the books" (to study) are idioms understood by the combination of words and not the separate meaning of each word. However, while idioms are generally fixed expressions, some idioms have a variable pattern.[5] For example, "Joe pulled Sally's leg," may vary by inserting different doers or recipients, such as "Fred pulled Ann's leg."

Many present-day idioms, such as "to pull one's leg" or "to hit the books," express action (by using an active verb). E.W. Bullinger and Robert Young wrote about a pattern of words in the Scriptures that express action. According to Bullinger and Young this pattern of words may be used figuratively in the Scriptures as a biblical idiom. Bullinger added that these active-verb idioms were *not* used to express the actual "doing of the thing." Both Young and Bullinger went on to identify a variety of related things that may be meant by the idiomatic expression. For example: such expressions may mean not the actual doing of it but the announcement of it, or not the actual doing of it but the permission of it, or not the actual doing of it but

---

4. Julia Hans, *Go Figure! An Introduction to Figures of Speech in the Bible* (Merrimack Media, Cambridge, Massachusetts, 2016) p. 241.

5. "'Fixed expression' is not completely accurate if we consider that many of these lexical units are not entirely static." Ana Rojo, *Step by Step: A Course in Contrastive Linguisitics and Translation* (Peter Lang Ltd, International Academic Publishers, 2009), Google Books PDF, p. 133.

the giving of an occasion for it. The central point that these scholars make is that active-verb expressions in the Scriptures are often idioms and therefore do *not* express the actual doing of the thing.[6] Because both the context and related scriptures of Exodus 5:22 show that the Lord did "evil to this people" is not true to fact then we know that it is figurative. It is a biblical idiom with a whole-unit meaning. The pattern of these kinds of idiomatic expressions may be represented as "the Lord God + action + recipient."

> "The Lord did evil to this people" is an example of a biblical idiom that does not express the actual doing of the thing.

E. W. Bullinger labeled some of these expressions an "idiom of permission." This study will *not* use this label. Instead, the intent of this study is to take a fresh look at active-verb expressions that *seem* to say God did something contrary to His nature. In present-day English, some people hear the word "permission" and infer that God permitted evil. This connotation has hindered some people from recognizing God's good nature in records where such expressions occur. Therefore, this study will take a fresh look at these kinds of expressions and will simple call it a particular biblical idiom.[7]

---

6. See E. W. Bullinger, *Figures of Speech Used in the Bible* (Messrs. Eyre and Spottiswoode, London, 1898; Baker Book House, Grand Rapids, Michigan, 1968), p.823. See also Robert Young, *Young's Analytical Concordance to the Bible* (Nashville, TN, Thomas Nelson, Inc., 1982), "Illustrations of Bible Idioms," p. 15.

7. In addition, Bullinger classified the idiom of permission as an idiom of grammar where the active was put for the passive. However, advances in linguistics show that idioms are usually understood on a semantic level from context. This study classifies this particular biblical idiom as an idiom of meaning and not of grammar.

So, how do we go about understanding what God is communicating with this idiom? First, we consider the context! Next, since idioms are culture-specific expressions, we consider how the culture of the lands and times of the Bible influenced the culture-specific meaning of such expressions. We allow the scriptural context and biblical culture to reveal the meaning of this idiom.

Idioms and Context

The importance of context to understand figures of speech, and especially meaning-based figures such as idioms, is widely documented. One source states, "When seeking to identify a figure of speech and when seeking to understand how the figure might bring emphasis to a verse or passage of Scripture, it is paramount to read and to carefully consider the context in which the figure occurs. This might necessitate reading the whole passage or chapter or perhaps reading the entire book to gain an understanding of the context."[8] Another source concludes that idioms can only be fully understood if they are considered in the context of the written texts in which they occur.[9] For example, although well-known idioms such as "to pull one's leg" and "to hit the books" are usually figurative, in certain contexts the words could be literal. For example, if an animated professor took his fist and pounded a stack of books to make a point, then "hit the books" would be literal and not idiomatic. Similarly, "you're pulling my leg" would be literal if two children scampered up a tree and the

---

8. Julia Hans, *Go Figure! An Introduction to Figures of Speech in the Bible* (Merrimack Media, Cambridge, Massachusetts, 2016), pp. 295-296.
9. Rosamund Moon, *Fixed expressions and Idioms in English: A Corpus-Based Approach* (Oxford Studies in Lexicography and Lexicology, 1998).

lower one pulled the higher one's leg. Therefore, a careful consideration of the context is required to determine if an unusual expression is figurative or literal, and if figurative, what is being communicated.

The context of Exodus 5 and the related verses of the expression the Lord did "evil to this people" show that the separate words do not mean what they typically would. Since according to the context these words are not literally true to fact, the expression is figurative. It is a biblical idiom with a whole-unit meaning derived from common usage in the culture of the lands and times of the Bible.

> Idioms require context:
> First, to determine if an unusual expression is figurative or literal.
> Secondly, to understand what the expression means.

Biblical Idioms and the Western Mind

An idiom reflects the local character, history, and mindsets of a language, place, or time and convey an abundance of cultural information. In short, an idiom reflects the culture from which it comes. The Bible describes a culture and time very different from that of present-day Western societies. According to Bishop K. C. Pillai, "The Bible is an Eastern book in the sense that it was written in the East, by the East at that time. They wrote it in the terminologies and phraseologies of the Eastern culture." (That is to say, the culture of the lands and times of the Bible.) Pillai goes on to say, "Eastern people's way of life...is their religion; their religion is their way of life. They're knit together. In the Western world...religion has nothing to do with their way of life. Religion and their way of life are poles apart in the Western world.... In the East, culture and religion are one...."[10] Therefore, we cannot rely on our present-day Western thinking to understand certain Biblical expressions that arose in the culture of the lands and times of the Bible.

The culture of the lands and times of the Bible was a God-centered one. God's commandments, statutes, and judgments were an integral part of the daily life of the Hebrew people. Their daily activities and speech reflected their culture. Thus their idioms also reflected their God-centered culture.

Since idioms are strongly linked with culture, they function as a hybrid of both figures of speech and manners and customs of the Bible. Thus, both the written and the cultural context of a biblical idiom is needed to unlock its meaning.

Let us also note that the Scriptures were recorded in ancient biblical languages with its own speech patterns and idioms. The Scriptures are translated primarily from biblical Hebrew for the Old Testament and biblical Greek for the New Testament.[11] However, after the Babylonian captivity, the common spoken language of the Hebrew people became a form of Aramaic,[12] which continued into New Testament times. Thus Old Testament idioms continued into New

---

10. "Digitized Teachings of Bishop K.C. Pillai" by Word Promotions Limited, recording 038 Side 2, Part 2 and recording 026 Side 1, Part 1; 39:46 to 40:41.

11. There also exist manuscripts of the Old and the New Testament in Aramaic.

12. George M. Lamsa, *Old Testament Light* (Prentice Hall, Inc. Englewood Cliffs, NJ, 1964), p. 393.

Testament times. Hebrew and Aramaic are both Semitic languages and share many similarities. Therefore, biblical scholars call biblical idioms Semitisms or more specifically Hebraisms or Aramaisms depending on the word's root language.[13] These languages communicated idioms in ways unfamiliar to present-day English.

As we seek to understand certain idioms that are not as understandable to us in present times, we must bear in mind the culture and language from which they originated. Biblical idioms reflect the culture, way of life, and thinking patterns of people of the lands and times of the Bible and not present-day Western ones.

Three Important Cultural Influences

So what aspects of the God-centered culture of Old Testament times have bearing on idioms such as the Lord did "evil to this people?" The following three are notable.

- Those who lived in Old Testament times were not to mention the name of other gods.
- Generally, those who lived in Old Testament times did not know nor mention the devil because it was not until the earthly life and ministry of Jesus Christ that the devil and his nature were more fully revealed.
- Those who lived in Old Testament times did mention God Who is the Most High and Most Powerful Lord overall.

The upcoming three sections will consider these three cultural influences. Afterwards, we will pull together our considerations of

---

13. These terms are also applied to any Hebraic or Aramaic language features brought into New Testament Greek.

idioms, context, and cultural influences as they relate to biblical idioms such as the Lord did "evil to this people."

Cultural Influence: Name Not Mentioned

From the time of Moses, the covenant of the law laid the foundation for many aspects of daily living for God's people of that time. Exodus 20 presents the first commandment of the Mosaic Law.

> Exodus 20:1-5
>
> [1] And God spoke all these words, saying,
>
> [2] "I am the LORD your God, who brought you out of the land of Egypt, out of the house of slavery.
>
> [3] You shall have no other gods before me.
>
> [4] You shall not make for yourself a carved image, or any likeness of anything that is in heaven above, or that is in the earth beneath, or that is in the water under the earth.
>
> [5] You shall not bow down to them or serve them…"

Culturally, bowing down was the position of respect or worship. God said to not put any other gods before Him, to not worship other gods, nor to serve them. According to Deuteronomy 6:24, keeping all the law was for the good of God's people always.[14]

Exodus 23 gives another detail concerning the first commandment of the covenant of the law.

---

14. Deuteronomy 6:24: "And the LORD commanded us to do all these statutes, to fear the LORD our God, for our good always, that he might preserve us alive…"

> Exodus 23:13
>
> Pay attention to all that I have said to you, and make no mention of the names of other gods, nor let it be heard on your lips.

The people of Israel were instructed to pay attention to the commandments of the covenant of the law. The first commandment was to have no other gods before the One True God. Keeping this commandment included not even letting the names of other gods be heard on their lips.

> Joshua 23:7
>
> That you may not mix with these nations remaining among you or make mention of the names of their gods or swear by them or serve them or bow down to them.

To mention the name of other gods is associated with serving and bowing down to other gods in worship. Therefore, to mention the name of other gods was not a light thing or a mere slip of the tongue, but to mention the name of other gods was associated with worshipping other gods. To do so would break the first commandment of the covenant of the law.

In chapter one, we saw that God is the source of truth, light, life, and deliverance while the devil is the source of lies, deception, darkness, bondage, and death. In chapter one, we saw that God and the devil are two opposing sources of information. Thus, we might ask: Who is the source of power and information behind other gods? Deuteronomy 32 answers this question.[15]

---

15. See also Leviticus 17:7; II Chronicles 11:15; and Psalm 106:37.

2. Moses and an Unusual Expression

Deuteronomy 32:16-17

¹⁶ They stirred him to jealousy with strange gods; with abominations they provoked him to anger.
¹⁷ They sacrificed to demons [devils,^KJV false gods^NIV] that were no gods, to gods they had never known, to new gods that had come recently, whom your fathers had never dreaded.

To sacrifice to strange gods was to sacrifice to devils.[16] Their source of power and information was and is the devil.

From these verses, we see that according to God's instructions in the covenant of the law, His people were not to mention the names of other gods in their everyday lives. Acknowledging this aspect of the Mosaic Law begins to give us a basis to understand a particular biblical idiom.

Cultural Influence: Not Yet Fully Known

We have already noted that the devil has many names. In the Old Testament, the devil and his activities are mentioned by names other than the devil or Satan—such as the serpent in Genesis 3 and Baal or strange gods throughout the Old Testament.[17] Moreover, men and women in the Old Testament who walked with and for the One True God knew whatever God chose to reveal to them, which may have included information about the devil's activities. However, *generally*

---

16. See also I Corinthians 10:20: "No, I imply that what pagans sacrifice they offer to demons [devils] and not to God...."
17. For the serpent, see Genesis 3:1-19. For examples of Baal or Baalim, see Judges 2:11, 13; I Samuel 7:4 and 12:10; and I Kings 16:31-32. For examples of strange gods, see Genesis 35:2; Deuteronomy 32:12, 16; Joshua 24:20, 23; Judges 10:16; I Samuel 7:3; II Chronicles 14:3 and 33:15; Psalm 44:20 and 81:9.

in the divine narrative of the Old Testament God did not choose to name the devil or Satan.[18] Most notably, it was not until the earthly life and ministry of Jesus Christ that the devil and his nature were more fully revealed.

> John 8:44
>
> You are of your father the devil, and your will is to do your father's desires. He was a murderer from the beginning, and does not stand in the truth, because there is no truth in him. When he lies, he speaks out of his own character, for he is a liar and the father of lies.

Jesus Christ made known the devil and his nature during his earthly life and ministry. Specifically, here Jesus Christ taught that the devil was a murderer from the beginning, his character or nature is to lie, and he does not stand in the truth. The devil is utterly lacking in truth.

In the next verse, the thief represents the devil.

> John 10:10
>
> The thief comes only to steal and kill and destroy. I came that they may have life and have it abundantly.

As Jesus Christ taught the people about himself, he also continued to more fully reveal the nature of the devil and his activities. What Jesus Christ came to do is also seen in the following scripture.

---

18. There are a few exceptions, for example: Job 1:1-2:7; I Chronicles 21:1; and Zechariah 3:1-2.

2. Moses and an Unusual Expression

> I John 3:8
> Whoever makes a practice of sinning is of the devil, for the devil has been sinning from the beginning. The reason the Son of God appeared was to destroy the works of the devil.

Jesus Christ came to destroy the works of the devil; he came to make known and destroy the evil things caused by the devil and those who are of the devil.

Those who learned from Jesus Christ continued to more fully reveal the work of the devil.

> Acts 5:3
> But Peter said, "Ananias, why has Satan filled your heart to lie to the Holy Spirit and to keep back for yourself part of the proceeds of the land?"

Peter made known that Satan was the source of the lie and deception. If this statement was in the Old Testament it might say, "why hath God filled thine heart to lie" because Satan, his nature, and his ways had not yet been more fully revealed by Jesus Christ.

> I Thessalonians 2:17-18
> ¹⁷ But since we were torn away from you, brothers, for a short time, in person not in heart, we endeavored the more eagerly and with great desire to see you face to face,
> ¹⁸ because we wanted to come to you—I, Paul, again and again—but Satan hindered us.

The apostle Paul and those traveling with him were not unsure as to who hindered them; they did not say "but God hindered us" as might have been said in the Old Testament. Instead, here Paul knew and named Satan as the source of the hindrance.

> II Corinthians 2:10-11
>
> [10] Anyone whom you forgive, I also forgive. Indeed, what I have forgiven, if I have forgiven anything, has been for your sake in the presence of Christ,
>
> [11] so that we would not be outwitted [taken advantage of] by Satan; for we are not ignorant of his designs [schemes].

II Corinthians chapter two addresses the need for forgiveness among the brethren. In this context verse 11 warns to not allow oneself to be outwitted or taken advantage of by Satan. Jesus Christ came to render Satan's designs or schemes inactive by making them known. The Old Testament believer did have God's commandments to believe so as to avoid entanglements with Satan's schemes. However, the devil was not openly credited for his evil doings as we see here in II Corinthians 2. Thus the people of the lands and times of the Old Testament did not name the devil and Satan in the idioms that developed in their culture.

> I Peter 5:8-9
>
> [8] Be sober-minded; be watchful. Your adversary the devil prowls around like a roaring lion, seeking someone to devour.
>
> [9] Resist him, firm in your faith [believing]…

2. Moses and an Unusual Expression

Those who lived after Christ's accomplished works were exhorted to be watchful against "your adversary, the devil." They had been taught that the devil's nature was figuratively to prowl about seeking to devour people. The exhortation was to resist the devil; they were to do so by firmly believing God's Word.

We ought never be intimidated by the devil and his activities for the Scriptures repeatedly confirm that God is so much greater than the devil. I John 4:4 declares that those who are born of God have overcome the devil (and his band of devils) because the God of the Scriptures is greater than the god of this world.[19] II Thessalonians 3:3 adds that "the Lord is faithful. He will establish you and guard you against the evil one." We can confidently believe that God is both willing and able to keep us from the evil that the devil intends.

In the lands and times of the Old Testament, God's people were acquainted with other gods from the surrounding nations. However, it was not until the life and ministry of Jesus Christ that the evil nature and wicked purposes of the devil (and his band of devils) were more fully revealed. Even so, Israel did have God's commandments that instructed them to not follow other gods as well as knowledge of the benefits and blessings to their lives when they kept God's commandments. Thus, naming the devil was not a part of the idioms and manner of speech that developed during Old Testament times.

In contrast, the pattern we see from men who walked with God in the times after Christ's accomplished, redemptive work is to note that the source of hindrance, lies, deception, and all manner of evil

---

19. I John 4:4: "Little children, you are from God and have overcome them, for he who is in you is greater than he who is in the world."

is the devil and *not* the Lord God. That is *not* to say we should go around pointing out all that Satan does; doing so might not be words that minister grace or build up.[20] However, words that credit God for things *He does not do* would not encourage the hearer either. II Corinthians 2 exhorts us to not to be ignorant of Satan's schemes. Instead, we are to resist by standing firmly on God's Word.

This section has set forth the second of three important cultural influences that provide a basis to understand a particular biblical idiom. Namely, the devil and his nature were not fully revealed and therefore not generally known until the earthly life and ministry of Jesus Christ.

Cultural Influence: Do Mention the Lord God

We are seeking to understand why certain cultural expressions name the Lord God for something He did not do.

> Psalm 83:18
>
> That they may know that you alone, whose name is the
> Lord, are the Most High over all the earth.

The Lord is the Most High God Who is over all the earth. He is to be made known. God is far above all else on earth and in heaven. God was credited because He is Lord overall.

> Psalm 47:2
>
> For the Lord, the Most High, is to be feared [reverenced], a great king over all the earth.

---

20. See Ephesians 4:29: "Let no corrupting talk come out of your mouths, but only such as is good for building up, as fits the occasion, that it may give grace to those who hear."

2. Moses and an Unusual Expression

God is to be reverenced. The Lord Most High is the great King over all the earth. He is to be reverenced and acknowledged as awesome.

> Genesis 14:18-19
>
> [18] And Melchizedek king of Salem brought out bread and wine. (He was priest of God Most High.)
>
> [19] And he blessed him and said, "Blessed be Abram by God Most High, Possessor of heaven and earth."

> Genesis 17:1
>
> When Abram was ninety-nine years old the LORD appeared to Abram and said to him, "I am God Almighty; walk before me, and be blameless."

In Genesis 14, the priest of the Most High God spoke by divine revelation and blessed Abram (later named Abraham) by the Most High God and proclaimed that this God is the possessor of heaven and earth. Later in Genesis 17, God introduced Himself to Abram as the Almighty God, which may also be rendered the Most Powerful God.[21] God is the Most High and the Most Powerful God Who is the possessor of heaven and earth.

> Psalm 57:2-3[KJV]
>
> [2] I will cry unto God most high; unto God that performeth *all things* for me.
>
> [3] He shall send from heaven, and save me *from* the reproach of him that would swallow me up. Selah...

---

21. The Hebrew word *shaddai* means "almighty" or "most powerful." See Walter J. Cummins, *Scripture Consulting Select Studies* (Scripture Consulting, Franklin, Ohio, 2010), p. 65.

David credited God with performing all things for him because He is the Most High. Psalm 40 is a psalm of David.

> Psalm 40:14-16
>
> [14] Let those be put to shame and disappointed altogether who seek to snatch away my life; let those be turned back and brought to dishonor who delight in my hurt!
> [15] Let those be appalled because of their shame who say to me, "Aha, Aha!"
> [16] But may all who seek you rejoice and be glad in you; may those who love your salvation say continually, "Great is the LORD!"

David lived at a time when all of the covenant of the Mosaic Law was to be kept. Here, as his enemies harassed and afflicted him, David did not mention the name of the god who was the source of affliction but instead exhorted that God's people continually magnify the Lord as he himself did. When faced with affliction, David did not say God caused the affliction but he did speak words that magnified the Lord and emphasized how big God really is in the face of the affliction.

After considering the idiomatic charateristics sometimes present in language and seeing some cultural influences in the Old Testament, we can better understnd Moses' words in Exodus 5:22. Much like David in Psalm 40, Moses was frustrated with the situation and cried out to God in a manner of speech of the land and times of the Bible.

In Exodus 5:23, Moses noted that it was after he spoke words from God to Pharaoh, then Pharaoh did evil to the people of Israel.

2. Moses and an Unusual Expression

Once God's Word was spoken, Pharaoh had a choice. Pharaoh now had information from God and he could either pay attention to God's Word, or not. Pharaoh's response to God's Word was to do evil to God's people. Moses figuratively credited God by asking, "Lord, why have you done evil to this people?" However, the context shows that God did not do evil to His people. God's involvement was that He gave His Word to Pharaoh. Pharaoh's freewill response was to reject the Word of the Lord. God was figuratively credited with the results produced by Pharaoh's choice in relation to information from God.

The God-centered culture of the Old Testament knew and acknowledged that God is the Most High and Most Powerful Lord overall. Therefore, the speech and idioms of those who lived in the lands and times of the Bible did mention God Who is Lord overall. By David's example, we see that idiomatically naming God was not intended to blame God for the affliction, but instead to magnify the Lord in the face of it.[22]

Recap: Idioms, Context, and Culture

To understand idiomatic expressions like the Lord did "evil to this people" let us pull together what we have seen:

- Idioms are nonliteral, culture-specific expressions with a whole-unit meaning.
- Active-verb expressions in the Scriptures are often idioms and do not express the actual doing of the thing.

---

22. We too can magnify God in the face of affliction in our day and time. God is not the source of bad things that happen in our lives, the devil is. When junk happens we can choose to turn to God, magnify Him; we can focus on how big God is!

- Idioms require context. The closer and wider context of the unusual expression determines if the expression is figurative (an idiom) or literal as well as what it means.
- Biblical idioms must be understood in light of the culture of the lands and times of the Bible and not according to present-day cultures and thinking. The vocabulary and idioms of those who lived in Old Testament times reflected their God-centered culture. These cultural expressions were not intended to blame God but instead to magnify Him in the face of affliction.
- Thus, the meaning of a biblical idiom is understood from the context, related scriptures, and biblical culture.[23]

These essential considerations give us a basis to understand a particular idiom found in the Scriptures.

Summary

In this chapter we saw that the unusual expression the Lord did "evil to this people" is not literal but is an example of a biblical idiom. Using a common idiom of his day, Moses *seemed* to say God did evil but God did not do it! The expression is an idiom that does not say what actually happened. The context clarifies that Pharaoh and the Egyptians did evil to God's people.

---

23. The position this study takes is that the idiom, that seems to say God did something that He did not do, is a figure of meaning or thought and not a figure of grammar. That is to say this idiom is not understood by a shift in grammar (active put for the passive) but is understood from the context and related scriptures as well as the culture of Old Testament times.

2. Moses and an Unusual Expression

The context of Exodus 5 shows that God gave His Word to Pharaoh and Pharaoh rejected it. Having rejected information from God, Pharaoh then did evil to God's people. The biblical idiom figuratively credited the Lord with the results produced by Pharaoh's choice in relation to information from God. In this manner, the idiom points to the spiritual cause behind the actions—namely, the rejection of God and His Word. In the culture of the lands and times of the Bible, this biblical idiom was not intended to slander God, but to magnify the Lord in the face of affliction.

> This particular biblical idiom is defined as: An idiom that *seems* to say God acted toward someone in a manner contrary to God's nature or a person's freedom of will, when the context and related passages indicate otherwise.

The following summarizes what we have seen about this biblical idiom in our introductory record of Exodus 5.

- The context along with its related passages often shows who, other than God, was responsible for the action.
- The context and related passages often, but not always, show that someone did not believe information from God.
- The context and related passages often, but not always, show the spiritual causes behind the physical.

- By naming God, this idiom does not focus on people and their freewill choices but does focus on God Who is Lord overall.

In closing, we recognize that expressions that seemingly blame negative actions on the Just God of the Scriptures may potentially be puzzling or unsettling to our understanding of God's goodness. This is very understandable, for the Scriptures declare that God is abundant in goodness and mercy and brings life and deliverance to people.

This study is about our good and just God, which is a very large topic in the Scriptures. Therefore, to provide boundaries and focus to this study, we will only consider records that include expressions that *seem* to say God did something contrary to His nature. To that end, the idiomatic pattern of words under consideration in this study is "the Lord God + action + recipient." This pattern of words is commonly found and usually literal, however when the context shows that it is not true to fact, it is figurative. In the upcoming chapters, as we see records with occurrences of such wording, we will allow the internal integrity of the Scriptures to determine if such expressions are literal or figurative, or if we do not know. While doing so we will keep a firm foundation in knowing that God is light, good, just, and merciful throughout the Scriptures.

3

Pharaoh and the Heart

The God of the Scriptures is the Father of light and the Giver of every good thing. He is just, long-suffering, merciful, gracious, and abundant in goodness. Yet, there is another who opposes God and is unjust, unmerciful, and the opposite of good. The information that God gives is true and leads to life and deliverance. Information from the devil is full of deceit and darkness, and leads to death and destruction. God is just and always allows people to choose which source they will believe. God always has people's best interests in mind.

Chapter two considered that the Lord did not do evil to the people of Israel and introduced an idiomatic pattern found in the Scriptures. We saw that the Lord did "evil to this people" is an example of a biblical idiom that seems to say God acted toward people in a manner contrary to His nature or a person's free will, although the context of Exodus 5 shows that God did not do it. God gives His Word to be believed and people can choose what source of information to believe. God gave His Word to Pharaoh and Pharaoh rejected the Word of the Lord. However, this cultural expression does not

Did God Do It?

focus on people and their freewill choices. Instead, it focuses on God Who is Lord overall.

Who Hardened Pharaoh's Heart?

Next, we will continue in Exodus and consider some seemingly contradictory scriptures regarding who hardened Pharaoh's heart.

> Exodus 9:12
>
> But the LORD hardened the heart of Pharaoh, and he did not listen to them, as the LORD had spoken to Moses.
>
> Exodus 7:22
>
> But the magicians of Egypt did the same by their secret arts. So Pharaoh's heart remained hardened, and he would not listen to them, as the LORD had said.
>
> Exodus 8:32
>
> But Pharaoh hardened his heart this time also, and did not let the people go.

Pharaoh's hard heart is mentioned 18 times in the book of Exodus.[1] Some of these occurrences say the Lord hardened Pharaoh's heart, while others say that Pharaoh hardened his own heart. Several references to the hardening of Pharaoh's heart state only that it was hardened and do not state who did it. Because there are some verses that credit the Lord and some that credit Pharaoh, these verses alone do not make it clear as to who was responsible for the hardening of Pharaoh's heart. It is an apparent contradiction.

---

1. Exodus 4:21; Exodus 7:3, 13, 14, and 22; Exodus 8:15, 19, and 32; Exodus 9:7, 12, 34, and 35; Exodus 10:1, 20, and 27; Exodus 11:10; and Exodus 14:4 and 8.

The Context of these Expressions

We have already considered portions of Exodus 1-5, which also provide background to this chapter. Let us recap. We saw that the people of Israel had been in bondage in Egypt for many years. God sent His prophet, Moses, and his spokesman, Aaron, to Pharaoh to request the release of God's people. Pharaoh responded to information from God by calling God's words lying words. When God, by way of Moses, gave His Word to Pharaoh, he responded by withholding straw yet still demanding that the people of Israel maintain the same daily brick-making quota. Moreover, the Egyptian taskmasters beat the foremen, whom they had set over the Israelites. By these actions the Egyptians chose to do evil to the people of Israel.

We will now pick up the context of the expressions regarding Pharaoh's heart in Exodus 6.

> Exodus 6:1
> But the LORD said to Moses, "Now you shall see what I will do to Pharaoh; for with a strong hand he will send them out, and with a strong hand he will drive them out of his land."

God had a plan for delivering His people.

> Exodus 6:4-7
> ⁴ I also established my covenant with them to give them the land of Canaan, the land in which they lived as sojourners.

> ⁵ Moreover, I have heard the groaning of the people of Israel whom the Egyptians hold as slaves, and I have remembered my covenant.
>
> ⁶ Say therefore to the people of Israel, 'I am the LORD, and I will bring you out from under the burdens of the Egyptians, and I will deliver you from slavery to them, and I will redeem you with an outstretched arm and with great acts of judgment.
>
> ⁷ I will take you to be my people, and I will be your God, and you shall know that I am the LORD your God, who has brought you out from under the burdens of the Egyptians.

God heard the groaning of His people and remembered His covenant with these people.

God's Covenant with His People

Let us briefly digress and look at the covenant mentioned above. This covenant is recorded in Genesis 15. A covenant is a legally binding agreement.

> Genesis 15:13-14
>
> ¹³ Then the LORD said to Abram, "Know for certain that your offspring will be sojourners in a land that is not theirs and will be servants there, and they will be afflicted for four hundred years.
>
> ¹⁴ But I will bring judgment on the nation that they serve, and afterward they shall come out with great possessions.

God informed Abraham that his descendants would be afflicted in a strange land for many years. However, He reassured Abraham that He would bring his descendants out with great substance. As part of the Genesis 15 covenant, God committed Himself to deliver Abraham's descendants from the nation that would afflict them. In Exodus, God remembered His covenant and acted to keep His covenant with Abraham's descendants. The deliverance of God's people and the judgment to those who oppressed His people are two aspects of the same legally binding agreement.

God had a covenant agreement with the people of Israel whereby He committed Himself to the terms of the agreement. On the other hand, Pharaoh and the Egyptians did not have a relationship with God. Instead, they worshipped many other gods. The Egyptians made willful decisions that put them in opposition to the One True God; they were not innocent people who just happened to be in the wrong place at the wrong time. They oppressed God's people. By considering God's covenant with Israel in Genesis 15, we can see that the deliverance of God's people and the execution of judgment to those who oppressed His people are both part of the terms of this covenant. Executing judgment to the oppressors and providing deliverance to God's people are two aspects of the same covenant. It is as if they are two sides of the same coin.

With this digression over, let us return to the context of the unusual expressions.

Continuing in the Context

We were considering what God instructed Moses to say to Pharaoh.

> Exodus 7:2-6
>
> ² You [Moses] shall speak all that I command you, and your brother Aaron shall tell Pharaoh to let the people of Israel go out of his land.
>
> ³ But I will harden Pharaoh's heart, and though I multiply my signs and wonders in the land of Egypt,
>
> ⁴ Pharaoh will not listen to you. Then I will lay my hand on Egypt and bring my hosts, my people the children of Israel, out of the land of Egypt by great acts of judgment.
>
> ⁵ The Egyptians shall know that I am the LORD, when I stretch out my hand against Egypt and bring out the people of Israel from among them."

In Exodus 5:2, Pharaoh said, "I do not know the Lord, and moreover, I will not let Israel go." On the other hand, here God said "the Egyptians shall know that I am the Lord, when I stretch out my hand against Egypt and bring out the people of Israel from among them." God was to produce mighty signs and wonders to deliver His people.

Adding to this, let us consider Mark 16:20: "And they [the apostles] went out and preached everywhere, while the Lord worked with them and confirmed the message by accompanying signs." As the apostles preached God's Word, God worked with them and confirmed His Word with signs. God may choose to confirm His Word with signs following. In Exodus, Moses and Aaron spoke God's Word and will. Afterward, God chose to multiply His signs and wonders and to confirm His Word. By these signs and wonders the Egyptians could know that God is the Lord.

3. Pharaoh and the Heart

It is noteworthy that what God did in support of His people as signs and wonders are also described as great judgments and later as plagues to the enemies of God's people.

> Exodus 7:8-14
>
> [8] Then the LORD said to Moses and Aaron,
>
> [9] "When Pharaoh says to you, 'Prove yourselves by working a miracle,' then you shall say to Aaron, 'Take your staff and cast it down before Pharaoh, that it may become a serpent.'"
>
> [10] So Moses and Aaron went to Pharaoh and did just as the LORD commanded. Aaron cast down his staff before Pharaoh and his servants, and it became a serpent.
>
> [11] Then Pharaoh summoned the wise men and the sorcerers, and they, the magicians of Egypt, also did the same by their secret arts.
>
> [12] For each man cast down his staff, and they became serpents. But Aaron's staff swallowed up their staffs.
>
> [13] Still Pharaoh's heart was hardened, and he would not listen to them, as the LORD had said.
>
> [14] Then the LORD said to Moses, "Pharaoh's heart is hardened; he refuses to let the people go.

By a God-given miracle, Aaron's rod turned into a serpent and ate those of Pharaoh's magicians. Thus, God again confirmed His Word

Did God Do It?

and demonstrated His power. Pharaoh's response to God's manifested power was to harden his heart and to refuse to let God's people go.[2]

> Exodus 7:17-23
>
> [17] Thus says the LORD, "By this you shall know that I am the LORD: behold, with the staff that is in my hand I will strike the water that is in the Nile, and it shall turn into blood.
>
> [18] The fish in the Nile shall die, and the Nile will stink, and the Egyptians will grow weary of drinking water from the Nile."'"
>
> [19] And the LORD said to Moses, "Say to Aaron, 'Take your staff and stretch out your hand over the waters of Egypt, over their rivers, their canals, and their ponds, and all their pools of water, so that they may become blood, and there shall be blood throughout all the land of Egypt, even in vessels of wood and in vessels of stone.'"
>
> [20] Moses and Aaron did as the LORD commanded. In the sight of Pharaoh and in the sight of his servants he lifted up the staff and struck the water in the Nile, and all the water in the Nile turned into blood.
>
> [21] And the fish in the Nile died, and the Nile stank, so that the Egyptians could not drink water from the Nile. There was blood throughout all the land of Egypt.

---

2. Verse 14 states that Pharaoh's heart was hardened but does not credit God with it.

> ²² But the magicians of Egypt did the same by their secret arts. So Pharaoh's heart remained hardened, and he would not listen to them, as the LORD had said.
> ²³ Pharaoh turned and went into his house, and he did not take even this to heart [set his heart[NASB and KJV]].

According to verse 17, the Egyptians would know that God was the Lord when the waters of the Nile turned to blood. By these signs and wonders, they would know He was more powerful than their sorcerers and magicians. Yet when the rods became serpents and when the waters turned to blood, Pharaoh still did not believe the information from the Most High God. On the other hand, Pharaoh paid attention to input from his sorcerers and magicians, and their enchantments. Which source of information do you suppose was behind Pharaoh's sorcerers and magicians? As we have seen, their source of information was the devil.

Thus far in Exodus, we have seen four occurrences concerning Pharaoh's heart being hardened. As we go along, let us pay attention to the context of these occurrences. Exodus 7:14 says Pharaoh refused to let the people go. Exodus 7:23 adds that Pharaoh did not take even these divine signs to heart. This Hebrew phrase indicates that Pharaoh made a willful decision.[3] Thus the context shows that Pharaoh willfully decided to ignore God's Word and refused to let God's people go. God always allows people to choose between

---

3. "The heart is the seat of the will. A decision may be described as 'setting' the heart." See R. Laird Harris, Gleason L. Archer, and Bruce K. Waltke, *The Theological Wordbook of the Old Testament* (Chicago, Illinois: Moody Publishers 1980) p. 467, word number 1071.

Did God Do It?

available sources of information: true and life-giving information from God or deceitful and leading-to-death information from the devil.

> Exodus 8:1-2
> ¹ Then the LORD said to Moses, "Go in to Pharaoh and say to him, 'Thus says the LORD, "Let my people go, that they may serve me.
> ² But if you refuse to let them go, behold, I will plague all your country with frogs.

Again Pharaoh refused to obey God, and God brought to pass His Word.

> Exodus 8:8
> Then Pharaoh called Moses and Aaron and said, "Plead with the LORD to take away the frogs from me and from my people, and I will let the people go to sacrifice to the LORD."

Four times in these Exodus passages, God, by way of Moses, asked Pharaoh to "let my people go that they may serve me." Pharaoh had God's Word in the situation. How would Pharaoh respond and what would Pharaoh's response produce?

> Exodus 8:13-15
> ¹³ And the LORD did according to the word of Moses. The frogs died out in the houses, the courtyards, and the fields.

¹⁴ And they gathered them together in heaps, and the land stank.

¹⁵ But when Pharaoh saw that there was a respite, he hardened his heart and would not listen to them, as the Lord had said.

In ancient Egypt, the frog was deified as a goddess of fertility.[4] Yet the frogs that the Egyptians revered were powerless against the Lord God. Once the immediate problem went away, Pharaoh hardened his own heart and again stubbornly refused to release God's people from bondage.

Exodus 9:1-7

¹ Then the Lord said to Moses, "Go in to Pharaoh and say to him, 'Thus says the Lord, the God of the Hebrews, "Let my people go, that they may serve me.

² For if you refuse to let them go and still hold them,

³ behold, the hand of the Lord will fall with a very severe plague upon your livestock that are in the field, the horses, the donkeys, the camels, the herds, and the flocks.

⁴ But the Lord will make a distinction between the livestock of Israel and the livestock of Egypt, so that nothing of all that belongs to the people of Israel shall die.""'

⁵ And the Lord set a time, saying, "Tomorrow the Lord will do this thing in the land."

---

4. See footnote on Exodus 8:2 in the *New American Standard Bible Study Bible* (Grand Rapids, Michigan: Zondervan, 1999).

> ⁶ And the next day the LORD did this thing. All the livestock of the Egyptians died, but not one of the livestock of the people of Israel died.
> ⁷ And Pharaoh sent, and behold, not one of the livestock of Israel was dead. But the heart of Pharaoh was hardened, and he did not let the people go.

God's Word to Pharaoh was again, "Let my people go, that they may serve me. For if you refuse to let them go..."

Pharaoh did not have to refuse; he had a choice. God gave Pharaoh another opportunity to change his mind and obey God's instructions, but again he refused. These repeated refusals show a willful stubbornness on Pharaoh's part.

Since Pharaoh yet again refused God's request, another plague followed. We will pick up the conversation between Moses and Pharaoh in verse 18.

> Exodus 9:18-22
> ¹⁸ Behold, about this time tomorrow I will cause very heavy hail to fall, such as never has been in Egypt from the day it was founded until now.
> ¹⁹ Now therefore send, get your livestock and all that you have in the field into safe shelter, for every man and beast that is in the field and is not brought home will die when the hail falls on them.'"
> ²⁰ Then whoever feared the word of the LORD among the servants of Pharaoh hurried his slaves and his livestock into the houses,

3. Pharaoh and the Heart

²¹ but whoever did not pay attention to the word of the Lord left his slaves and his livestock in the field.
²² Then the Lord said to Moses, "Stretch out your hand toward heaven, so that there may be hail in all the land of Egypt, on man and beast and every plant of the field, in the land of Egypt."

God mercifully gave instructions to avoid harm to those who would listen. Those servants among Pharaoh's household who feared or reverenced the Word of the Lord and heeded God's instructions avoided that harm. Those who did not regard the Word of the Lord ignored God just as Pharaoh had. Then Moses did as God instructed and the Lord rained hail on the land of Egypt. When the situation became bad enough, Pharaoh finally sought God's help.

Exodus 9:27-30
²⁷ Then Pharaoh sent and called Moses and Aaron and said to them, "This time I have sinned; the Lord is in the right, and I and my people are in the wrong.
²⁸ Plead with the Lord, for there has been enough of God's thunder and hail. I will let you go, and you shall stay no longer."
²⁹ Moses said to him, "As soon as I have gone out of the city, I will stretch out my hands to the Lord. The thunder will cease, and there will be no more hail, so that you may know that the earth is the Lord's.
³⁰ But as for you and your servants, I know that you do not yet fear [respect or reverence] the Lord God."

After the seventh plague Pharaoh seemed to have a momentary change of heart. However, even though the Lord had made Himself known to the Egyptians by signs and wonders Moses recognized that they did not respect or reverence Him.

> Exodus 9:34-35
> ³⁴ But when Pharaoh saw that the rain and the hail and the thunder had ceased, he sinned yet again and hardened his heart, he and his servants.
> ³⁵ So the heart of Pharaoh was hardened, and he did not let the people of Israel go, just as the Lord had spoken through Moses.

God, by way of Moses, continued to make known His Word and will to Pharaoh regarding the release of His people. God confirmed His Word with signs following. God introduced His light into this dark situation. By the hardening of his heart, Pharaoh rejected God and His Word.

We saw in Exodus 3:19-20 that God knew in advance that Pharaoh would not let His people go unless compelled by a mighty hand. However, it was Pharaoh's own freewill responses that necessitated a mighty hand to compel him to release God's people.

By putting together what we have read from the wider context of Exodus 1-9, we see that the unusual expression "the Lord hardened the heart of Pharaoh" is figurative and not literal.

Related Scriptures: Other Hard Hearts

Let us add to our consideration, other scriptures that speak of a hard heart.

3. Pharaoh and the Heart

> Deuteronomy 15:7
>
> If among you, one of your brothers should become poor, in any of your towns within your land that the LORD your God is giving you, you shall not harden your heart or shut your hand against your poor brother.

Who does this verse say is responsible for hardening of the heart?

> Zechariah 7:9 and 11-12
>
> ⁹ "Thus says the LORD of hosts, Render true judgments, show kindness and mercy to one another,
>
> ¹¹ But they refused to pay attention and turned a stubborn shoulder and stopped their ears that they might not hear.
>
> ¹² They made their hearts diamond-hard lest they should hear the law and the words that the LORD of hosts had sent by his Spirit through the former prophets. Therefore great anger came from the LORD of hosts.

These people's refusal to hear God is illustrated with they "turned a stubborn shoulder and stopped their ears that they might not hear." Verse 12 adds that the people themselves made their own hearts as hard as a diamond so that no words from the Lord would get through. Here the hardness of heart was directed against words from the Lord God.

Who Is Responsible for the Heart?

Having considered the context of several occurrences of expressions about Pharaoh's hard heart as well as other accounts of a hard heart in the Scriptures, let us next consider a broader Biblical understanding about a person's heart.

> Luke 6:45
>
> The good person out of the good treasure of his heart produces good, and the evil person out of his evil treasure produces evil, for out of the abundance of the heart his mouth speaks.

The word "treasure" may be used figuratively in the Scriptures to mean "thoughts," as it does here in this verse.[5] Therefore, Luke 6 says the heart can contain either good thoughts or evil thoughts according to the abundance of what is in the heart.

> Deuteronomy 11:16
>
> Take care lest your heart be deceived, and you turn aside and serve other gods and worship them.

> Proverbs 23:12
>
> Apply your heart to instruction and your ear to words of knowledge.

In Deuteronomy 11, the people of Israel were told to take care of their hearts and that doing so would prevent them from being deceived. Proverbs says to apply one's heart to instruction and knowledge. To "take care" and to "apply" point to a person's active responsibility for his or her own heart.

---

5. See Bishop K.C. Pillai, *The Orientalisms of the Bible,* Vol.1 (Munkus Publishing Compansy, Inc. Fairborn, Ohio, 1969), p.2.

3. Pharaoh and the Heart

Proverbs 4:23

Keep your heart with all vigilance [diligence[NASB, KJV, AMP]],
for from it flow the springs of life.

To "keep your heart" is to guard the heart. The Hebrew word rendered "springs" means "goings forth" or "outgoing."[6] The imagery here, again teaches us that each individual is responsible for guarding what comes out of one's own heart. We guard the heart by guarding what we put into it. When we put words of life into the heart then that is what will come out of the heart. It's not automatic; it takes vigilance and diligence.

Psalm 119:112

I incline my heart to perform your statutes forever, to
the end.

Deuteronomy 30:10

When you obey the voice of the LORD your God, to
keep his commandments and his statutes that are written
in this Book of the Law, when you turn to the LORD
your God with all your heart and with all your soul.

To apply, take care, keep, incline or turn one's heart, all indicate willingly choosing what goes into one's heart. God always allows people to choose which source of information they will believe. What a person applies his or her heart to determines what is in the

---

6. See R. Laird Harris, Gleason L. Archer, and Bruce K. Waltke, *The Theological Wordbook of the Old Testament* (Chicago, Illinois: Moody Publishers 1980), p. 893, word number 893e. See also William Wilson, *Wilson's Old Testament Word Studies* (Grand Rapid, Michigan: Kregel Publications, 1978), p. 232 "issue" 4d.

heart—good or evil. What is in the heart determines what comes out of the heart.

> II Corinthians 9:7
> Each one must give as he has decided in his heart, not reluctantly or under compulsion, for God loves a cheerful giver.
>
> Romans 10:10
> For with the heart one believes and is justified, and with the mouth one confesses and is saved.

According to these scriptures, deciding and believing occur in the heart. In II Corinthians 9:7, we see that a person can give according to a decision made in the heart. In Romans 10:10, we learn a person can believe from the heart. Deciding and believing in the heart have associated actions. To keep, apply, incline, turn, choose, or believe all indicate something a person does in his heart according to his or her own freedom of will.

> Proverbs 1:29-30
> [29] Because they hated knowledge and did not choose the fear [reverence] of the LORD,
> [30] [they] would have none of my counsel and despised all my reproof.

When these people chose not to reverence the Lord, it resulted in despising the reproof of God's Word. On the other hand, if the person reverences the Lord God, he may appreciate the reproof of God's Word. From these verses, we see that each person is responsible for:

what he puts in his heart, the thoughts of the heart, and the willing choices from the heart, as well as the resulting actions. Applying one's heart to instruction and knowledge from God enables a person not to be deceived by evil.

To wrap up this section on "who is responsible for the heart," let us pull together some scriptural truths regarding the heart:

- In the Scriptures, thoughts, choices, decisions, believing and associated actions are said to come from the heart.
- Each individual is responsible for what goes into and what comes out of his or her heart.
- According to God's original design, people have freedom of will to choose between available sources of information.
- God always allows people to choose which source of information he or she will put into his or her heart. He never oversteps anyone's free will.
- Thus, each person is responsible for his or her own heart and the thoughts, decisions, believing, and actions that come from the heart.

God's Word says that each individual is responsible for what goes in and what comes out of his or her heart. Yet, our current society is inundated with movies, songs, and commentators who propound that people are somehow not responsible for the directions, actions, and fluctuations of the heart. These opinions do not agree with the Scriptures. According to the Scriptures, each individual *is* responsible for his or her own heart.

Idiomatic Espressions with the Word "Heart"

When we acknowledge these Scriptural truths, then we understand that expressions that seem to say God made someone's heart do something are often figurative and not literal.

Acts 16 provides another example of the idiom with the word "heart" as well as a comparison with the Pharaoh record.

> Acts 16:10
>
> And when Paul had seen the vision, immediately we sought to go on into Macedonia, concluding that God had called us to preach the gospel to them.

The apostle Paul received revelation from God, and immediately Paul and those with him (Silas and Timothy) traveled to Macedonia, to preach the gospel of God to the people of that city.

> Acts 16:13-15
>
> [13] And on the Sabbath day we [Paul, Silas, and Timothy] went outside the gate to the riverside, where we supposed there was a place of prayer, and we sat down and spoke to the women who had come together.
> [14] One who heard us was a woman named Lydia, from the city of Thyatira, a seller of purple goods, who was a worshiper of God. The Lord opened her heart to pay attention to what was said by Paul.
> [15] And after she was baptized, and her household as well, she urged us, saying, "If you have judged me to be faithful to the Lord, come to my house and stay." And she prevailed upon us.

3. Pharaoh and the Heart

Lydia heard and gave attention to God's Word that Paul spoke. The spoken Word assisted her understanding. Just as Pharaoh had God's Word spoken by Moses and Aaron, so Lydia had God's Word spoken by Paul. However, Pharaoh and Lydia's responses to God's Word were quite different. Lydia chose to pay attention to God's Word while Pharaoh chose to ignore them. Lydia responded favorably to information that originated from God while Pharaoh did not. Lydia made a willing decision from her heart for which she was responsible; Pharaoh, too, was responsible for his own willful decisions. When Lydia heard and attended to God's Word, she decided to open her heart to the Lord. On the other hand, Pharaoh's response was to harden his heart and stubbornly refuse information from God. Idiomatically the Scriptures say, "the Lord hardened Pharaoh's heart" and "whose heart the Lord opened." If God literally did as these expressions say, it would be contrary to God's nature. However, God did not, for He never oversteps anyone's freedom of will.

"The Lord hardened Pharaoh's heart" and "whose [Lydia's] heart the Lord opened" are both examples of a particular biblical idiom with the pattern "the Lord God + action + recipient." We recognize that these expressions are figurative because the usual meaning of the separate words in these expressions:

- do not fit with the context and related scriptures, and
- do not agree with what the Scriptures say about who is responsible for the heart.

> This particular biblical idiom is defined as: An idiom that *seems* to say God acted toward someone in a manner contrary to God's nature or a person's freedom of will, when the context and related passages indicate otherwise.

We have seen the following characteristics about this particular biblical idiom:

- The meaning of a biblical idiom is understood from the context, related scriptures, and biblical culture.
- This idiom often, but not always, shows the spiritual cause behind the physical happenings.
- According to the God-centered culture of Old Testament times, the devil was not named. In their culture, this idiom was not intended to blame God, nor did this idiom mean that He did evil. Instead, it acknowledged God, Who is Lord overall and magnified Him in the face of affliction.

Our consideration of who is responsible for the heart adds the following point to this list of characteristics.

- When the unusual expression contains the word "heart" and seems to say God made someone's heart do or believe something, the expression is usually figurative and not literal. The final determination requires an examination of the context and related scriptures.

For more information on idiomatic expressions with the word "heart" see "Appendix C Working List—Figurative."

The records of Pharaoh and Lydia each show that God gave His Word to someone who responded to information from God. Pharaoh rejected the Word of the Lord and Lydia accepted the Word of the Lord. Interestingly, the occurrence of the idiom with Lydia in Acts 16 demonstrates that this idiom may occur in a positive context. Lydia freely opened her heart to God's Word and became a faithful believer. God's involvement in each situation was to make known His Word.

Summary

In this chapter we considered the puzzling words "the Lord hardened Pharaoh's heart." We first examined the context over several chapters in Exodus. We saw that God gave His Word to Pharaoh by way of Moses. Pharaoh responded by rejecting information from God. Next, we considered what the Scriptures say regarding who is responsible for the heart. The Scriptures say that each individual is responsible for his or her own heart and the thoughts, decisions, believing, and actions that come from the heart. By putting these findings together, we see that "the Lord hardened the heart of Pharaoh" is not true to fact; it is an example of a biblical idiom. It is figurative and not literal. Pharaoh was responsible for hardening his own heart.

God's involvement in the records regarding Pharaoh's hard heart was the introduction of His Word. God confirmed His Word to Pharaoh with many signs. He demonstrated His power with many mighty acts. However, Pharaoh and the Egyptians stubbornly opposed God and mistreated God's people. When God gave His

Did God Do It?

Word to Pharaoh, He justly allowed Pharaoh to decide how he would respond. God justly and patiently gave the Egyptians multiple opportunities to decide to respond in a way that would reduce their consequences.

Instead the Egyptians chose to rely on a source of information that did not serve them well. They relied on information from the sorcerers, magicians, and wise men of Egypt. These men and Pharaoh (who listened to them) arrogantly set themselves in opposition to the Lord God. According to the Scriptures the source behind the gods of Egypt along with their sorcerers and magicians was the devil. We saw that deception, lies, wickedness, and death characterize information from the devil. The devil's injustice is based on his nature of evil, arrogance, and darkness. All the advice and enchantments of the sorcerers and magicians of Egypt did not lead Pharaoh toward deliverance. Instead, their advice and enchantments led to the plagues and multiple losses.

On the other hand, God's actions of deliverance to His people and mercy to their enemies were based on His just and good nature. When we see God's justice in the Scriptures, we ought also to look for other characteristics of God's nature. Throughout the records in Exodus, God was merciful, long-suffering, and just to enemies of His people. He is indeed a God of light in Whom there is no darkness at all.

4

Pharaoh and the Passover

We are considering how wonderful our God is throughout the Scriptures. Chapter one of this study was an introductory consideration of the contrasting natures of God and the devil: light versus dark; good versus evil; and just versus unjust. Chapter one also introduced essential background about choices people make and their freedom of will to do so.

Chapters two and three considered two unusual expressions in Exodus: the Lord did "evil to this people" and "the Lord hardened Pharaoh's heart." Chapter two also considered a little bit about figures of speech, idioms, and some aspects of biblical culture helpful to understand the biblical idiom under consideration in this study. Chapter three also considered what the Scriptures say about who is responsible for the heart. We found the unusual expressions in the previous two chapters to both be figurative. Each expression is an occurrence of the biblical idiom that *seems* to say God did something contrary to His nature or a person's freedom of will but, according to the context and related scriptures, He did not. In the Hebrew culture of the lands and times of the Bible, naming God in this idiomatic expression was not intended to blame God nor disparage Him. In their God-centered culture, this idiom acknowledged God as Lord overall and magnified Him in the face of affliction.

Unusual and Seemingly Difficult Wording

We will begin by considering a potentially unsettling verse in Exodus 12.

> Exodus 12:12
>
> For I will pass through the land of Egypt that night, and I will strike all the firstborn in the land of Egypt, both man and beast; and on all the gods of Egypt I will execute judgments: I am the LORD.

Killing all the firstborn people and animals in the land of Egypt does not fit with current concepts of benevolence and justice. More significantly, this verse seems to contradict many clear verses about God's nature of love, light, and justice.

Verse 23, of this same record, brings up something that some people find equally as difficult to understand.

> Exodus 12:23
>
> For the LORD will pass through to strike the Egyptians, and when he sees the blood on the lintel and on the two doorposts, the LORD will pass over the door and will not allow the destroyer to enter your houses to strike you.

The main sticking point of this record for some people has to do with the destroyer. This chapter will address both the unusual

4. Pharaoh and the Passover

expression about the Lord striking all the firstborn of Egypt and the destroyer.

Our approach in this study is to allow the intrinsic evidence of the Scriptures to determine if expressions, such as the Lord striking the firstborn, are literal or figurative, or if we simply do not know. So far, the unusual expressions in the records of Moses and Pharaoh said God did things not supported by other scriptures; the expressions were examples of the idiom. However, each time we are faced with difficult wording in the Scriptures that *seems to* associate God with evil, we must take the necessary time to consider what the Scriptures say. We do not want to assume that if it was figurative in one occurrence, then it will be in another. Instead, we read the context as well as related scriptures. As we consider such difficult wording, let us hold in mind that the God of the Scriptures does not change; He is the God of light, love, mercy, grace, long-suffering, goodness, and truth.

Background

This chapter we will pick up where we left off in Exodus, and will consider portions of Exodus chapters 10-12. Thus what we already handled in the previous two chapters serves as background for this chapter.

In Exodus 1-9, God saw the affliction of His people, remembered His covenant, and worked with Moses to deliver His people. He gave Pharaoh multiple opportunities to release His people from bondage and to stop the need for yet another plague. The Lord God performed many signs and wonders to cause the release of His people from bondage. These signs and wonders plagued the Egyptian enemies. With each God-given opportunity, Pharaoh stubbornly refused to pay attention to the Word of the Lord and the signs that confirmed it.

Let us also take note that the Egyptians were a nation who had arrogantly rejected God. They worshipped strange gods and did abominable acts for the sake of their gods. They were not innocent by-standers.[1]

Context

As we read the context, please hold in mind what we already learned about expressions with the word "heart." Variations of "the Lord hardened Pharaoh's heart" are figurative and not literal. Moreover, Pharaoh's responses necessitated a mighty hand to compel him to release God's people.

> Exodus 10:1-4 and 20
>
> [1] Then the Lord said to Moses, "Go in to Pharaoh, for I have hardened his heart and the heart of his servants, that I may show these signs of mine among them,
>
> [2] and that you may tell in the hearing of your son and of your grandson how I have dealt harshly with the Egyptians and what signs I have done among them, that you may know that I am the Lord."
>
> [3] So Moses and Aaron went in to Pharaoh and said to him, "Thus says the Lord, the God of the Hebrews, 'How long will you refuse to humble yourself before me? Let my people go, that they may serve me.

---

1. For more information, see the subsection entitled "God's People" in chapter five.

> ⁴ For if you refuse to let my people go, behold, tomorrow I will bring locusts into your country.
>
> ²⁰ But the LORD hardened Pharaoh's heart, and he did not let the people of Israel go.

God by way of Moses continued to make known His Word and will, saying, "Let my people go, that they may serve me." God's communications to Pharaoh were consistent and clear. However, Pharaoh refused to humble himself before God. Thus God graciously gave Pharaoh another opportunity to avoid further consequences but once again Pharaoh refused. Pharaoh's ongoing refusal was not God's desire. With each stubborn, deliberate refusal, Pharaoh prolonged misery for Egypt.

From Pharaoh's point of view, the release of his abundant supply of these inexpensive, non-Egyptian laborers may have seemed foolish. But God had made Himself known unto Pharaoh by His spokesmen and in signs and wonders. Which source of information would have best served Pharaoh to believe: information from God or information from his senses influenced by the relationship he chose to have with sorcerers, magicians, and enchantments?

God had said to Abraham in Genesis 15 that He would judge the nation that afflicted His people.[2] Over the course of time, Egypt and their Pharaoh afflicted God's people with bondage and servitude. God gave Pharaoh multiple opportunities to release His people and to minimize the consequences for that nation. With each opportunity God demonstrated His mercy and justness toward Egypt. Since

---
2. Genesis 15:14: "But I will bring judgment on the nation that they serve…"

Did God Do It?

God is faithful to His Word, the release of God's people as promised in Genesis 15 was non-negotiable. Losing their workforce would have been a significant loss to Egypt; however, God offered mercy to His people's oppressors so that the amount of grief the oppressors endured before His people were released could be minimized. For each step along the way, Pharaoh was given the light of God's Word to guide his choices regarding which source of information to believe.

Our God is mighty and awesome, capable of both showing mercy to the Egyptians and bringing to pass deliverance for His people according to His Word.

> Exodus 11:1
> The LORD said to Moses, "Yet one plague more I will bring upon Pharaoh and upon Egypt. Afterward he will let you go from here. When he lets you go, he will drive you away completely.

God demonstrated His might and power with signs and wonders to bring about the release of His people. As Pharaoh repeatedly refused and hardened his heart, the consequences escalated. Each time Moses and Aaron came before Pharaoh, God again gave information so that Pharaoh could choose deliverance for Egypt. But each time, Pharaoh responded by strengthening his refusal and hardness of heart. What was God to do?

Pharaoh's stubborn refusals led to the last plague.

> Exodus 12:1-3, 6-11
> ¹ The LORD said to Moses and Aaron in the land of Egypt,

4. Pharaoh and the Passover

² "This month shall be for you the beginning of months. It shall be the first month of the year for you.
³ Tell all the congregation of Israel that on the tenth day of this month every man shall take a lamb according to their fathers' houses, a lamb for a household.

⁶ And you shall keep it until the fourteenth day of this month, when the whole assembly of the congregation of Israel shall kill their lambs at twilight.
⁷ Then they shall take some of the blood and put it on the two doorposts and the lintel of the houses in which they eat it.
⁸ They shall eat the flesh that night, roasted on the fire; with unleavened bread and bitter herbs they shall eat it.
⁹ Do not eat any of it raw or boiled in water, but roasted, its head with its legs and its inner parts.
¹⁰ And you shall let none of it remain until the morning; anything that remains until the morning you shall burn.
¹¹ In this manner you shall eat it: with your belt fastened, your sandals on your feet, and your staff in your hand. And you shall eat it in haste. It is the LORD's Passover.

This was the first, which is the original, Passover.

Exodus 12:12-13
¹² For I will pass through the land of Egypt that night, and I will strike all the firstborn in the land of Egypt, both man and beast; and on all the gods of Egypt I will execute judgments: I am the LORD.

> ¹³ The blood shall be a sign for you, on the houses where you are. And when I see the blood, I will pass over you, and no plague will befall you to destroy you, when I strike the land of Egypt.

The Hebrew word for "execute judgments" in verse 12 connotes an act of judgment by a just judge.³ God had given Pharaoh multiple opportunities to release His people and avoid further consequences. By following God's instructions the people of Israel would be spared. The firstborn means the first to be born, the eldest, whether young or old. In Bible times the firstborn usually inherited more and was next in line as the head of the family. Many of the firstborn animals were used in worship to the Egyptian gods, who were also being judged. In verse 12, the words, "I am the Lord," remind us that God had repeatedly informed them that in the deliverance of the people of Israel, the Egyptians would know that He is the Lord God Most Powerful.⁴ Furthermore, the people of Israel would know that they were His people and He was their God.

> Exodus 12:23-31
>
> ²³ For the LORD will pass through to strike the Egyptians, and when he sees the blood on the lintel and on the two doorposts, the LORD will pass over the door and will not allow the destroyer to enter your houses to strike you.

---

3. William L. Holliday, *A Concise Hebrew and Aramaic Lexicon of the Old Testament* (Grand Rapids, Michigan: William B. Eerdmans Publishing Company, 1988), p. 380.
4. See Exodus 3:13-15; 6:2-8; 7:5, 17.

4. Pharaoh and the Passover

²⁴ You shall observe this rite as a statute for you and for your sons forever.

²⁵ And when you come to the land that the LORD will give you, as he has promised, you shall keep this service.

²⁶ And when your children say to you, 'What do you mean by this service?'

²⁷ you shall say, 'It is the sacrifice of the LORD's Passover, for he passed over the houses of the people of Israel in Egypt, when he struck the Egyptians but spared our houses.'" And the people bowed their heads and worshiped.

²⁸ Then the people of Israel went and did so; as the LORD had commanded Moses and Aaron, so they did.

²⁹ At midnight the LORD struck down all the firstborn in the land of Egypt, from the firstborn of Pharaoh who sat on his throne to the firstborn of the captive who was in the dungeon, and all the firstborn of the livestock.

³⁰ And Pharaoh rose up in the night, he and all his servants and all the Egyptians. And there was a great cry in Egypt, for there was not a house where someone was not dead.

³¹ Then he summoned Moses and Aaron by night and said, "Up, go out from among my people, both you and the people of Israel; and go, serve the LORD, as you have said.

God said that He would bring one plague more on Pharaoh and the Egyptians after which Pharaoh would let His people go from Egypt. In the final plague, God said that He would pass through the land of Egypt and strike all the firstborn in the land of Egypt. He also said that he would execute judgment against all the gods of Egypt.

God gave His Word to Pharaoh; he chose to not believe information from Him.

God gave His Word to the people of Israel; they chose to believe information from Him.

God was faithful to His Word. His deliverance of the people of Israel was just and His judgment against Egypt was just. In doing so, He demonstrated that He was higher and more powerful than all the gods of Egypt.

The Destroyer and Related Scriptures

Exodus 12:23 says "the Lord will pass over the door and will not allow the destroyer to enter your houses to strike you." The Lord would not allow the destroyer to strike His people when they obeyed His instructions. Evidently, the Lord could allow or not allow the destroyer to act. Thus, for some people, the sticking point of this record has to do with the destroyer.

To begin into this topic, let us pose some oft-asked questions and then consider what the Scriptures say in response. Who was the destroyer? Was the destroyer a separate entity, acting on its own? Is the destroyer of the devil? Did the destroyer represent another and if so who? We are considering such questions about the destroyer to add clarity regarding what God did or did not do in this record. As we

4. Pharaoh and the Passover

do so, let us continue to hold in mind the many clear scriptures about God's nature. In our inquiry about the destroyer, we will continue to allow the intrinsic evidence of the Scriptures to lead the way.[5]

Psalm 78 gives an account of the final plague, which complements the account given in Exodus 12. Psalm 78 adds to our understanding of who the destroyer is.

> Psalm 78:41-48
>
> [41] They [the people of Israel] tested God again and again and provoked the Holy One of Israel.
>
> [42] They did not remember his power or the day when he redeemed them from the foe,
>
> [43] when he performed his signs in Egypt and his marvels in the fields of Zoan.
>
> [44] He turned their rivers to blood, so that they could not drink of their streams.
>
> [45] He sent among them swarms of flies, which devoured them, and frogs, which destroyed them.
>
> [46] He gave their crops to the destroying locust and the fruit of their labor to the locust.
>
> [47] He destroyed their vines with hail and their sycamores with frost.
>
> [48] He gave over their cattle to the hail and their flocks to thunderbolts.

---

5. The "destroyer" has been referred to as the "angel of death" by sources outside of the Scriptures. Since this term is not found in the Scriptures, it is not applicable to our study of what the Scriptures say.

Did God Do It?

Psalm 78 recounts when the people of Israel did not remember when God bared His mighty hand for them as He delivered them from the Egyptian enemy. Verse 43 begins to recount the signs and wonders God wrought in Egypt, which were necessary to compel a very stubborn Pharaoh to let His people go. As we noted in chapter three and see again here: the signs and wonders God did to deliver His people from bondage are also called plagues to the enemies of His people—they are two sides of the same coin. Verse 49 recounts the final plague.

> Psalm 78:49-52
>
> [49] He [God] let loose on them [the foe] his burning anger, wrath, indignation, and distress, a company of destroying angels.
>
> [50] He made a path for his anger; he did not spare them from death, but gave their lives over to the plague.
>
> [51] He struck down every firstborn in Egypt, the firstfruits of their strength in the tents of Ham.
>
> [52] Then he led out his people like sheep and guided them in the wilderness like a flock.

Exodus 12:23 referred to the destroyer and Psalm 78:49 speaks of angels. The context of both terms refers to the same event. Thus Exodus 12 provides some information about the being called "the destroyer" and Psalm 78 provides additional information calling them "angels." A study of angels in the Scriptures does not find creatures with halos and wings; instead the Scriptures testify that angels are messengers. A look at the about 400 combined occurrences of

4. Pharaoh and the Passover

the Hebrew word *mal'ak* translated "angel" or "messenger" and the Greek word *angelos*[6] translated "angel" or "messenger" show that these words can refer to either spirit messengers (angels) or human messengers.[7] Most often when the Scriptures translate these words as "angel" it refers to a spirit messenger from God. In the Scriptures, spirit messengers may be sent by God or by the devil, however more are under God's command.[8]

> Psalm 103:19-21
>
> [19] The LORD has established his throne in the heavens, and his kingdom rules over all.
> [20] Bless the LORD, O you his angels, you mighty ones who do his word, obeying the voice of his word!
> [21] Bless the LORD, all his hosts, his ministers, who do his will!

Other versions render verse 20 as follows: "angels...who perform His word, obeying the voice of His Word,"[NASB] and "angels...who do his bidding, who obey his word."[NIV] God's angels obey God's voice and perform His word or do His bidding. As spirit messengers, angels are ones who are sent to do, say, or perform what the one who sends them commands. Thus, what angels say and do is not of their own making. What angels (spirit messengers) does or says represents the one who sent them.

---

6. The Hebrew word *mal'ak* and the Greek word *angelos* are corresponding words as seen in Joshua 6:25 and James 2:25 that refer to the same event.
7. In I Samuel 19:11-15 and Luke 7:18-24 we see human messengers sent by people. In II Chronicles 36:16 and Haggai 1:13 we see prophets as messengers sent by God.
8. See Revelation 12:9 and Matthew 25:41. In the Scriptures, angels from the devil are often called: devils, demons, unclean spirits, and evil spirits.

Similar to Exodus 12, a record in Psalm 91 refers to angels under God's command at the time of a plague.

> Psalm 91:9-11
>
> ⁹ Because you have made the LORD your dwelling place— the Most High, who is my refuge—
> ¹⁰ no evil shall be allowed to befall you, no plague come near your tent.
> ¹¹ For he will command his angels concerning you to guard you in all your ways.

Psalm 91 refers to an unspecified time when God did not allow a plague to come near the home of His people. God commanded His angels to guard their home. When the angels carried out God's command, their actions represented the One Who sent them. That is to say, their actions represented God.

The Hebrew word rendered "destroyer" is derived from the Hebrew word *shahat* meaning to destroy or to corrupt. The derivative rendered "destroyer" is used four times in the Old Testament. This derivative is used twice in I Chronicles 21 to refer to an angel of the Lord sent to destroy.⁹

Next, let us consider how the following multiple versions render the Hebrew words about the "angel" in Psalm 78:49: a company of destroying angels,^ESV a band of destroying angels,^NIV *a mission of angels of calamity and woe,*^AMP a band of deadly messengers,^HCSB a mission of angels of woes.^DBY These phrases accurately describe what

---

9. The four occurrences of this derivative are: Exodus 12:23: "the LORD...will not allow the destroyer;" I Chronicles 21:12: "with the angel of the LORD destroying throughout;" I Chronicles 21:15: "God sent an angel to Jerusalem to destroy it;" Jeremiah 2:30: "devoured your prophets like a ravening [destroying^KJV] lion."

4. Pharaoh and the Passover

the angels did in Exodus 12. They did bring calamity and woe to enemies who had enslaved God's people for years.[10]

These multiple versions also show that there was more than one angel. There was a band or company of angels sent to perform a single mission.

We have been gathering information from the Scriptures to help us understand who the destroyer is and what God did or did not do. Before we pull it all together, let us add the following two verses that speak of the same event.

> Exodus 13:15
>
> For when Pharaoh stubbornly refused to let us go, the LORD killed all the firstborn in the land of Egypt, both the firstborn of man and the firstborn of animals. Therefore I sacrifice to the LORD all the males that first open the womb, but all the firstborn of my sons I redeem.'

> Numbers 33:4
>
> While the Egyptians were burying all their firstborn, whom the LORD had struck down among them. On their gods also the LORD executed judgments.

These verses agree with information regarding God's actions and Pharaoh's response that we saw in the context of Exodus 1-12.

---

10. The King James Version renders the Hebrew word to describe the angels as "evil angels." The Hebrew word translated "evil" in KJV is the general Hebrew word for "bad" or "evil." This Hebrew word has a range of meanings that must be understood from the context. The phrase in multiple versions above helps us see the range of possible meanings. To describe these angels as "evil" does not accurately represent the context the word occurs in, nor does it accurately represent angels under God's command.

Did God Do It?

Exodus 13 and Numbers 33 along with numerous other verses say that on this passover night, God killed all the firstborn of Egypt.[11] We add to these accounts that Exodus 12 says the destroyer was under God's command and that Psalm 78 says God sent destroying angels. Therefore, by understanding some of the Hebrew words used in the record of the destroyer and by putting together information found in multiple accounts of the same event, we see that, on this passover night, God commanded spirit messengers to act on His behalf. When put together, these accounts also suggest that the destroyer may have been the head of a band or company of God's angels (spirit messengers). The Scriptures say that God gave them charge to execute judgment on the Egyptian enemies and to protect His people. Each account of this event adds to our understanding so that by putting them together we get the whole picture. Thus, God commanded a band of angels, including the destroyer, to carry out the final plague and at the same time to protect His people. God's angels also executed God's judgment against all the false gods of Egypt. These actions by God are in harmony with other scriptures about God Who commands His angels and judges the world.

We started this section with some questions about the destroyer and have seen from the Scriptures that the destroyer did not act on its own nor did it act on behalf of the devil. The destroyer and the band of angels acted on God's command and brought deliverance to His people.[12]

---

11. See also Psalm 78:51, 105:36, 135:8, and 136:10.
12 See Isaiah 37:36 (also found in II Kings 19:35) for another similar example where an angel of the Lord acts on God's behalf to deliver His people from enemies.

4. Pharaoh and the Passover

In the previous plagues, God sent Moses as His messenger to Pharaoh and to carry out the plagues on Egypt (river turned to blood, frogs, pestilence on Egyptian livestock, hail, locust, and darkness). In the final plague, God sent destroying angels as messengers to do His will so that His people could be set free. Neither Moses nor the destroying angels represented their own interests; they represented God's interests. Perhaps this differs with previous teaching about the destroyer, if so we have the privilege of considering the evidence of the Scriptures presented here.

The Scriptures declare that no iniquity dwells in God but that He is light, good, and just. Thus the activities of angels who carried out instructions from God would also be in alignment with the many good things we know about the God of the Scriptures. That is not to say that we automatically or thoughtlessly call it just. Instead, we read the Scriptures, as we are doing here, and let the Scriptures address our sensibilities.

Is it not light that God gave His Word to Pharaoh so that he could have made other choices? Is it not just that God gave the Egyptian enemies multiple opportunities to minimize the plagues? Is it not good that God delivered His people from bondage? Is it not beneficial to all humankind that God saved those in the line of Christ so that the consequences of Adam's sin could one day be reversed?[13]

Our desire in this study is to line our thinking up with what the Scriptures say and to not allow the current cultural thinking to

---

13. For more information see chapter five, in particular, see the subsection, "God's Purpose in Christ."

infiltrate our attitudes toward our very good God. God and His Word define what is good and just, and not current culture.

We have seen that God was faithful to His Word (Genesis 15:13-14) to deliver His people from the nation that enslaved them. He did so by a series of plagues carried out by His messengers: Moses and the band of angels. Moses put into motion the first nine plagues. The destroying angels carried out the final plague. Throughout these events, God was abundantly merciful to a very stubborn Pharaoh and the Egyptian oppressors. Pharaoh could have made choices that improved the Egyptians situation but he did not.

A Consideration for Another Time

Before continuing, let us briefly note the future significance of the passover lamb.

> I Corinthians 5:7
>
> ...For Christ, our Passover lamb, has been sacrificed.
>
> I Peter 1:18-19[WTJ]
>
> [18] Knowing that you were redeemed, not with corruptible *things*...
>
> [19] but [*you were redeemed*] with the precious blood of Christ (as of a lamb without blemish and without spot).

The sacrifice of the passover lamb in Exodus 12 foreshadowed an even greater sacrifice by Christ our Passover. Christ's sacrifice redeemed mankind from Adam's sin and made salvation by grace available. Although we are not handling it here, a study of Christ our Passover would be an enriching study, well worth undertaking.

4. Pharaoh and the Passover

Justice and Mercy

In our day, there are many different standards and ideals of what is just and right that have nothing to do with the God of the Scriptures. Present-day standards and sensibilities may denounce how God administered judgment in this record. However, it is not for man to judge God's actions. As those who love God, we need to be careful to not let present-day standards usurp what God says is just and right.

There are two sources of spiritual information and people decide which they will believe. God is just, and because He is just, He always respects people's freedom of will to decide which source of information they will believe.

The Egyptians relied on information from the wise men, sorcerers, and magicians of Egypt. Information from these advisors proved to be deceptive and deadly. These advisors' influence led the Egyptians down a path to death. God gave them many opportunities to pay attention to words that would improve their situation, but they did not listen.

What the Egyptians believed had resulting actions.

> Exodus 1:13-14
>
> [13] So they ruthlessly made the people of Israel work as slaves
>
> [14] and made their lives bitter with hard service, in mortar and brick, and in all kinds of work in the field. In all their work they ruthlessly made them work as slaves.

The Egyptians ruthlessly made the people of Israel work as slaves and made their lives bitter. The Egyptians were enemies of God's people. God heard the cry of the Israelites and delivered them from their enemies. Even in our day and time, we celebrate a victory against enemies and view it as good. On the world stage today, we see various forms of modern slavery and recognize that it may take strong measures to deliver people from bondage. When people are freed from oppression, we celebrate a victory and call it good. Similarly, in Exodus, Pharaoh's stubbornness necessitated strong measures to secure the release of God's people from their enemies. Was not the Israelites release from many years of bondage a good thing?

God acted justly and rightly in delivering His people from bondage from their enemies. God actions were also just to the Egyptian enemies. He gave them multiple opportunities to minimize the consequences to the nation that enslaved His people. God was repeatedly merciful and long-suffering. In all that God did, He did not overstep anyone's freedom of will. These are characteristics of God's justice. God's standard of justice is based on His nature and reflects Who He is. God introduced the light of His Word to improve the Egyptians situation. Information from God to Pharaoh was clear and intended to benefit the Egyptians. He was not deceitful or mean-spirited. He set forth information worthy of being believed and the Egyptians decided to reject information from God. God was just, merciful, and long-suffering to the enemies of His people.

The deliverance to God's people and mercy to enemies are in stark contrast to the injustice of the devil. There is no mercy in the devil's injustice. Information from the devil brings darkness, affliction, and leads to death. However, God was merciful, He introduced light, His path gave a way to minimize the consequences and save lives even among the enemy. God's actions that led to the deliverance of His people were just and good.

Summary

At the onset of this chapter, we noted that the words "I will strike all the firstborn in the land of Egypt, both man and beast" (Exodus 12:12) may be difficult or unsettling. Even so, we ought not immediately label them as figurative. Instead, we have taken the necessary time to consider the Scriptural context over multiple chapters as well as related scriptures.

We found that the context of the unusual expression showed that Pharaoh was stubborn and arrogant against God and did evil to the Hebrew people. The sorcerers, the wise men, and the gods of Egypt influenced Pharaoh to oppose God. God offered Pharaoh many opportunities to not escalate to the next plague. However, Pharaoh's stubborn refusal required strong measures, which led to the final plague. To carry out the final plague, God sent a band of angels that either included or was led by the destroyer. This was the manner God chose to deliver His people from bondage in Egypt. God kept His covenant to Abraham's descendants; He was faithful to His Word.

We must recognize that our opinions and sympathies about what is just and good are affected by the world around us. Our modern systems of social justice do not determine if what God does is just or good. It is the Scriptures that establish what is good and just and right.

Did God Do It?

> II Corinthians 10:5
> We destroy arguments and every lofty opinion raised agaisnt the knowledge of God, and take every thought captive to obey Christ.

As Christians, we must bring our arguments, our opinions, and even our feelings subject to the knowledge of God. To stand firmly on God's Word requires that we bring every thought captive to obey Christ. If we do not subject our wayward thoughts to God's higher thoughts then we risk not being in a position to trust fully in our very good God.

> Isaiah 5:19-20
> [19] ...Let the counsel of the Holy One of Israel draw near, and let it come, that we may know it!"
> [20] Woe to those who call evil good and good evil, who put darkness for light and light for darkness, who put bitter for sweet and sweet for bitter!

What the God of the Scriptures says is good or evil defines what is good or evil. Judgment to enemies and deliverance for God's people are good. God was faithful to His Word, just in judgment, and powerful on behalf of His people. In all that God did, He did not overstep anyone's freedom of will. He acted in a manner consistent with His nature throughout the Scriptures.

This record reassures us that even in the face of overwhelming odds, God always fulfills His Word and provides for His people. Because God is faithful to His Word we can rely on Him and trust

4. Pharaoh and the Passover

in Him. God fulfilled His Word at that time and He will continue to fulfill His Word at all times.

Did God Do It?

5

More Essential Background: Covenants and Justice

We are seeking to grow in our appreciation of God's good nature even when considering potentially unclear or possibly unsettling expressions about God's actions. Our aim is to determine whether such expressions are figurative or literal, or if we do not know. Chapter one handled essential background about the opposing natures of God and the devil. Chapters two through four each considered an unusual expression from Exodus that seemed to say God did something contrary to His nature or a person's free will. By examining the context and related scriptures, we found two of them to be figurative and one to be literal.

This chapter does not consider a specific unusual expression. Instead, this chapter will look at essential background regarding covenants, time periods, and standards of justice in the Scriptures. The goal of this chapter is to provide some breadth and scope of the Scriptures necessary to understand the upcoming chapters.

Time Periods

God dealt with man in various ways at different times. In the Scriptures, these different time periods are sometimes called administrations.[1] At certain times, God initiated a relationship with an individual; at other times, He initiated a relationship with a group of people. We will begin by looking at the relationship between God and Adam and then at certain covenant relationships that God initiated with Abraham and then with the people of Israel. We will also consider the new covenant and God's standard of justice in Christ.

Recognizing the various time periods or administrations in the Scriptures provides essential background to understand how God's dealings with people have changed over time. Appreciating these changes in God's dealings with mankind will provide essential background as we continue to consider God's goodness in all that He does.

Adam

Adam was the first person that God created.

> Genesis 2:7^{KJV}
>
> And the LORD God formed the man *of* the dust of the ground, and breathed into his nostrils the breath of life; and man became a living soul.

God formed man's body and breathed breath life into him. Breath life made him a living soul. This soul life is also called physical life.

---

1. In Ephesians 3:2 the Greek word for these different time periods is rendered in the following ways: "administration" in NIV, DBY, and WTJ, "stewardship" in ESV and NASB, and "dispensation" in KJV.

5. Covenants and Justice

Genesis 1:26 adds that God created man in His image. According to John 4:24 God's image is Spirit. Thus the image that God created man in is spirit. Spirit life was the basis of God and Adam's relationship. Spirit life gave Adam a superior means to relate to and to communicate with God. With the addition of spirit, we see that Adam had both spirit life and physical life.

Adam lived in a very good environment provided by God. God spoke to Adam and gave him information or instructions to benefit him and to help him be successful. Adam's job was to believe and obey information from God. In Genesis 2:17, God told Adam to not eat of the tree of the knowledge of good and evil because, if he ate of that tree, he would die—that's helpful to know.

Regrettably, Adam disobeyed God's commandment and so he died. What part of Adam died? In Genesis 3, we can read that Adam still walked around in a physical body with breath life. So his physical life did not die. The life that died was his spirit life. Adam lost his spirit connection with God. Spirit provided the best means for God to communicate with man, and man with God. Adam no longer had spirit life; he no longer had the best means of communication with God. This loss was tragic. Moreover, the very good environment that God originally provided was also lost.[2]

Romans 5 adds a great deal to our understanding of the outcomes of Adam's disobedience.

---

2. For further information on God's relationship with Adam and the results of Adam's disobedience, see Walter J. Cummins, *The Acceptable Year of the Lord* (Franklin, Ohio: Scripture Consulting, 2005), Chapter 1, "The World's Need for a Savior."

Did God Do It?

> Romans 5:12-16
>
> ¹² Therefore, just as sin came into the world through one man, and death [loss of spirit life] through sin, and so death spread to all men because all sinned—
>
> ¹³ for sin indeed was in the world before the law was given, but sin is not counted where there is no law.
>
> ¹⁴ Yet death [loss of spirit life] reigned from Adam to Moses, even over those whose sinning was not like the transgression of Adam, who was a type of the one who was to come.
>
> ¹⁵ But the free gift is not like the trespass. For if many died through one man's trespass, much more have the grace of God and the free gift by the grace of that one man Jesus Christ abounded for many.
>
> ¹⁶ And the free gift is not like the result of that one man's sin. For the judgment following one trespass brought condemnation, but the free gift following many trespasses brought justification.

Adam's disobedience brought major consequences into the world. The one man, Adam, caused sin, death, and condemnation to enter the world. The consequences of Adam's disobedience passed to all people. On the other hand, Jesus Christ brought grace and justification for many.

5. Covenants and Justice

Genesis 3:15

I will put enmity between you and the woman, and between your offspring and her offspring; he shall bruise your head, and you shall bruise his heel."

In Genesis 3:15, immediately after Adam sinned, God introduced the solution to the sin, death, and condemnation that Adam's sin brought. God promised that the offspring or seed of the woman would one day bruise the head of the serpent (figuratively put for the devil). Looking back we know that the promised seed would be the coming savior, the Lord Jesus Christ.

Let us return to Romans 5 and the contrast between Adam and Jesus Christ.

Romans 5:17-21

[17] For if, because of one man's trespass, death reigned through that one man, much more will those who receive the abundance of grace and the free gift of righteousness reign in life through the one man Jesus Christ.
[18] Therefore, as one trespass led to condemnation for all men, so one act of righteousness leads to justification and life for all men.
[19] For as by the one man's disobedience the many were made sinners, so by the one man's obedience the many will be made righteous [just].
[20] Now the law came in to increase the trespass, but where sin increased, grace abounded all the more,

> [21] so that, as [Adam's] sin reigned in death [of spirit life], grace also might reign through righteousness leading to eternal life through Jesus Christ our Lord.

By Adam's disobedience, sin, death, and condemnation entered into the world. We already noted that what died was spirit life. Loss of spirit life was a significant loss to the very close relationship God wanted with people. This disruption limited God and man's relationship and caused the need for the restoration of that relationship. Adam's sin also corrupted the perfect environment God intended for people.

Let us be clear, the devil was the villain and source of the disruption. God was and is the hero Who sent His Son to deliver the world. God responded to a situation that He did not make but that He worked tirelessly to remedy. God worked through the ages to remedy the consequences of Adam's sin to all mankind. The hope of the promised seed, the coming savior, led the way. Through it all, God sought to bless people wherever possible, within the bounds of His Word and with respect to man's freedom of will. We will now look at the various steps God took as He worked to restore the relationship between God and man.

Abraham

In Genesis 12, God initiated a relationship with Abraham, also called Abram, that is significant throughout the Scriptures.

5. Covenants and Justice

Genesis 12:1-4 and 7

¹ Now the LORD said to Abram, "Go from your country and your kindred and your father's house to the land that I will show you.

² And I will make of you a great nation, and I will bless you and make your name great, so that you will be a blessing.

³ I will bless those who bless you, and him who dishonors you I will curse, and in you all the families of the earth shall be blessed."

⁴ So Abram went, as the LORD had told him, and Lot went with him. Abram was seventy-five years old when he departed from Haran.

⁷ Then the LORD appeared to Abram and said, "To your offspring I will give this land." So he built there an altar to the LORD, who had appeared to him.

God gave His Word to Abraham, and Abraham believed the Word of the Lord and acted on what God said. God promised several things to Abraham: blessings; a great name; to bless those who blessed Abraham and to curse those who dishonored him; that all families of the earth would be blessed in him; and that a great nation would come from his descendants. God initiated a relationship with Abraham as an individual, and later extended it to his seed, meaning his descendants. God said He would give certain land to Abraham's seed.

Did God Do It?

In Genesis 15, God added to His agreement with Abraham. As we will see, God called their agreement a covenant. A covenant is a legally binding agreement. In our day, we are familiar with signed contracts, lease agreements, notarized documents, etc. These are all present-day legally binding agreements in which two or more parties agree to a number of terms or conditions.

> Genesis 15:4-6
>
> ⁴ And behold, the word of the LORD came to him [Abraham]: "This man [the steward of Abraham's household] shall not be your heir; your very own son shall be your heir."
>
> ⁵ And he [the Lord] brought him outside and said, "Look toward heaven, and number the stars, if you are able to number them." Then he said to him, "So shall your offspring be."
>
> ⁶ And he believed the LORD, and he counted it to him as righteousness [justness].

God promised Abraham that he would have an heir born from his own body and from his own offspring. God further promised that Abraham's descendants would be as innumerable as the stars in heaven. Abraham believed information from God, and the Lord God counted Abraham's believing to him as justness. Believing God was the standard for justice for Abraham and was the basis of God and Abraham's relationship. God's commitment to Abraham was not based on him being of the human race. The relationship between God and Abraham was based on their covenant agreement whereby God was faithful to keep His Word and Abraham believed God's Word. In this manner, God and Abraham sealed the terms of their agreement. When Abraham believed and acted on information from God, he was credited with being just.[3]

Next we will consider Galatians 3 where Genesis 15:6 is quoted. But first, the word "faith" needs some clarification. In current times, "faith" has various connotations that may not be helpful to bring into our reading of the Scriptures.[4] Moreover, the Greek word rendered "faith" may also be accurately rendered "believe" or "believing." Rendering this Greek word in a parallel way throughout a passage can improve our understanding of the passage as a whole.

> Galatians 3:6-8
> [6] Just as Abraham "believed God, and it was counted to him as righteousness"?
> [7] Know then that it is those of faith [believing] who are the sons of Abraham.
> [8] And the Scripture, foreseeing that God would justify the Gentiles by faith [believing], preached the gospel beforehand to Abraham, saying, "In you shall all the nations be blessed."

According to verse 8, God preached the gospel beforehand to Abraham. Romans 1:1-4 identifies the gospel as the gospel of God

---

3. Regarding the word "righteousness," let us recall that both the Hebrew and Greek word families rendered as "right, righteous, righteousness" may also be accurately rendered as "just, justice, justness." This study generally uses: just, justice, and justness.

4. For example, "faith" may mean to belong to a particular religion or church and taking it that way in this verse would add confusion. Abraham had information from God that he received and acted on; that is to say he believed God.

concerning God's Son, Jesus Christ. By putting the accounts of Abraham in Genesis together with Galatians we see that Abraham knew the gospel concerning the coming savior during his lifetime. God later inspired holy men to record in the New Testament what He had previously proclaimed to Abraham. The New Testament often clarifies or completes what we know from the Old Testament.

To continue to add to our understanding of God and Abraham's relationship let us consider verse 16 of Galatians 3.

> Galatians 3:16-17
>
> [16] Now the promises were made to Abraham and to his offspring. It does not say, "And to offsprings," referring to many, but referring to one, "And to your offspring," who is Christ.
>
> [17] This is what I mean: the law, which came 430 years afterward, does not annul a covenant previously ratified by God, so as to make the promise [to Abraham] void.

Galatians refers to the covenant God made with Abraham and says that Christ would come from Abraham's offspring. Although the law came after God's covenant with Abraham, the law did not invalidate what God had already promised to Abraham. Instead the subsequent covenant of the law between God and Abraham's descendants built upon God's promises to Abraham.

What is so very significant in this section of Scripture is the clarification Galatians 3:16 offers: Christ would come from Abraham's offspring and Abraham knew this because God had told him.

Now let us return to Genesis 15.

5. Covenants and Justice

> Genesis 15:7-8
>
> ⁷ And he said unto him, I am the LORD who brought you out from Ur of the Chaldees to give you this land to possess [inherit]."
>
> ⁸ And he said, "O LORD God, how am I to know that I shall possess it?"

God again mentioned the land that He would give Abraham to possess as an inheritance. Abraham asked God how he would know that he would possess it for an inheritance. God responded by having Abraham lay out certain animals, which he did according to God's instructions.

> Genesis 15:17-18
>
> ¹⁷ When the sun had gone down and it was dark, behold, a smoking fire pot and a flaming torch passed between these pieces.
>
> ¹⁸ On that day the LORD made a covenant with Abram...

Smoking firepots and flaming torches were commonly used in the lands and times of the Bible to provide a light in the dark. These lights were symbolically used in the Scriptures to symbolize God's presence. The act of passing the smoking firepot and flaming torch through the sacrificial animal pieces represented that God was present to seal His commitment to the covenant. God and Abraham did not sign a legal document as we might in present times. In the lands and times of the Bible, the symbolic presence of God passing through the animal pieces showed God's commitment. Abraham's believing

Did God Do It?

actions of laying out the animals indicated that God and Abraham agreed to the terms of the covenant.

From Genesis 15 we know that part of God and Abraham's agreement was that an heir would come and would be Abraham's very own son. We also saw that many nations would be blessed in Abraham. In Genesis 17, God continued to talk to Abraham about their covenant agreement and promised more regarding Abraham's heir.

> Genesis 17:3-7
> ³ Then Abram fell on his face. And God said to him,
> ⁴ "Behold, my covenant is with you, and you shall be the father of a multitude of nations.
> ⁵ No longer shall your name be called Abram, but your name shall be Abraham, for I have made you the father of a multitude of nations.
> ⁶ I will make you exceedingly fruitful, and I will make you into nations, and kings shall come from you.
> ⁷ And I will establish my covenant between me and you and your offspring after you throughout their generations for an everlasting covenant, to be God to you and to your offspring after you.

Let us continue in Genesis 17 in verse 15.

> Genesis 17:15-16 and 19
> ¹⁵ And God said to Abraham, "As for Sarai your wife, you shall not call her name Sarai, but Sarah shall be her name.

> ¹⁶ I will bless her, and moreover, I will give you a son by her. I will bless her, and she shall become nations; kings of peoples shall come from her."
>
> ¹⁹ God said, "No, but Sarah your wife shall bear you a son, and you shall call his name Isaac. I will establish my covenant with him as an everlasting covenant for his offspring after him.

Just as Abraham would be a father of a multitude of nations, so Sarah would be a mother of nations. Christ, the promised seed, would come from Abraham's seed with his wife Sarah. God also promised to establish an everlasting covenant with Abraham's son, which extended to his offspring. According to Genesis 17:7 this covenant included "to be God to you and to your offspring after you."

So we see that God initially established a covenant agreement with Abraham as an individual. Then God said He would establish His covenant with Abraham's descendants as a group.

The Mosaic Law and the Nation of Israel

Many years after God initiated a covenant relationship with Abraham He built upon it with another covenant, called the covenant of the law. The Mosaic Law did not invalidate the covenant between God and Abraham, but built upon it. God's covenant with Abraham continued through Isaac and subsequent descendants, known as the people of Israel.

> Exodus 19:5-8
>
> ⁵ Now therefore, if you will indeed obey my voice and keep my covenant, you shall be my treasured possession among all peoples, for all the earth is mine;
>
> ⁶ and you shall be to me a kingdom of priests and a holy nation. These are the words that you shall speak to the people of Israel."
>
> ⁷ So Moses came and called the elders of the people and set before them all these words that the LORD had commanded him.
>
> ⁸ All the people answered together and said, "All that the LORD has spoken we will do." And Moses reported the words of the people to the LORD.

God, by way of Moses, laid before the people of Israel all the words of the covenant of the law. Exodus 19:6 says that as the people of Israel obeyed God's voice and kept their covenant, they would be God's treasured possession among all peoples and they would be to the Lord a kingdom of priests and a holy nation. All the people answered together that they would do all that the Lord had spoken. Fundamental to God and Israel's covenant agreement is that God was to be their God and they were to be His people.

Thus, the Lord God formalized His relationship with the people of Israel collectively, as a group. To God, Israel became a holy nation, set apart as His people. Because all the people of Israel decided together to keep the covenant of the law, then God had more to work with than previously. Up until this time there had not been a whole nation

5. Covenants and Justice

that was willing to work with God. Previously God had worked with individual patriarchs such as Abraham and Noah. And how wonderful it was that these patriarchs believed God and walked with Him. However, what an improvement that God now had a whole nation with which to work. This shift brought about a new administration that was administered according to the Mosaic Law; thus, it may be called the law administration.[5]

> Deuteronomy 6:24 and 25
> [24] And the LORD commanded us to do all these statutes, to fear the LORD our God, for our good always, that he might preserve us alive, as we are this day.
> [25] And it will be righteousness [justness] for us, if we are careful to do all this commandment before the LORD our God, as he has commanded us.'

God gave the covenant of the law as an established standard of justice for the benefit and good of the people of Israel. Doing all the commandments of the covenant of the law was the manner in which the people of Israel were legally made just. They were credited with justness by believingly keeping all the law just as Abraham had been credited with justness by believing information from God. When God's people did not keep all the statutes and commandments, the law provided a way for restoration or atonement and included various sacrifices. Hebrews 8 and 10 speak of how the law with its offerings and sacrifices foreshadowed heavenly things concerning

---

5. See II Corinthians 3:7 "The administration of the Law which was engraved in stone..." from *The New Testament in Modern English* by J. B. Phillips.

Christ.[6] During the time of the law, keeping all the law with its offerings and sacrifices served to point the people of Israel toward the better things Christ would bring. The law along with its offerings and sacrifices provided a way for the people of Israel to be justified and to have fellowship with God. As God worked to restore the things Adam had lost, the Mosaic Law provided a means of a relationship with God and a way to preserve the people of Israel until the coming savior (who would restore the losses Adam caused). In the days, before Christ, the Mosaic Law provided the best available standard for justice.

Galatians 3 adds to our understanding of the purpose and benefit of the covenant of the law.

> Galatians 3:19, 22-25[WTJ]
>
> [19] So why the law? It was added for the sake of transgressions until the seed of whom He had made promise came, and He arranged *it* through messengers in the hand of a mediator.
>
> [22] However, the Scripture enclosed all *things* under sin so that the promise [*what was promised*] by believing concerning Jesus Christ might be given to those who believe.

---

6. Hebrews 8:5: "They [the gift offerings according to the law] serve a copy and shadow of the heavenly things...." Hebrews 10:1: "For since the law has but a shadow of the good things to come instead of the true form..."

See also Luke 24:27: "And beginning with Moses and all the Prophets, he [Jesus Christ] interpreted to them in all the Scriptures the things concerning himself." Here, Jesus Christ declared that the Mosaic Law and the prophets spoke of him.

For more information see David Bergey, *Jesus Christ Our Complete Offering: How the Levitical Offerings Foreshadowed Christ* (Printed in the United States, 2017).

5. Covenants and Justice

> ²³ Before the [*foundation for*] believing came, we were confined under the law, closed off from the [*foundation for*] believing that was to be revealed *later*.
> ²⁴ Wherefore, the law had become our tutor until [*the time of the accomplishments of*] Christ, so that we might be justified by believing.
> ²⁵ However, since the [*foundation for*] believing has come, we are no longer under a tutor.

The Mosaic Law was added for the sake of transgressions until the promised seed could come.[7] By his life, death, resurrection, and ascension, Jesus Christ accomplished God's plan of redemption and salvation for all. When God raised Jesus Christ from the dead He gave the foundation for believing to all people. Anyone can now believe concerning Christ.[8]

However, before this foundation for believing was accomplished, those under the law were closed off from all that Christ would accomplish, because he had not yet come. According to James M. Freemen in his book *Manners and Customs of the Bible* this enclosure was similar to how a trusted servant would watch over the safety and protection of the master's sons until they came of age.[9] Because of Adam's disobedience, God and man's relationship was disrupted. The Mosaic Law and the keeping of it enclosed and preserved God's

---

7. The promised seed is first spoken of in Genesis 3:15 and refers to the coming savior, Jesus Christ.
8. To believe concerning Christ is explained in Romans 10:9: "Because, if you confess with your mouth that Jesus is Lord and believe in your heart that God raised him from the dead, you will be saved."
9. See James M. Freeman, *Manners and Customs of the Bible* (Logos International, Plainfield, New Jersey, 1972), "Galatians, The Pedagogue" p. 462.

people alive until God and Jesus Christ could accomplish redemption for all. This was a very good thing.

Abraham knew and believed information from God concerning the coming savior. Those under the law believed concerning the coming savior when they kept the law, its offerings, and its sacrifices that pointed toward Christ.

We have been considering the purpose and benefits of the Mosaic Law. We have taken the time to do so because sometimes people speak as if God initiated the covenant of the law to punish people. Nothing could be further from the truth. The need for the law came about because of Adam's disobedience. The devil's deception of Eve and Adam's disobedience disrupted God and man's very good relationship as well as the very good world God intended for people. Afterwards, the condition of the world became characterized by sin, death, and judgment to condemnation. God tirelessly worked to restore the losses caused by Adam. The covenant of the law was a step forward that pointed people toward the coming savior. The law was an improvement in that it provided a basis for a whole nation to be justified and to have a relationship with God. Each step forward brought all of humankind closer to the full restoration of the losses caused by Adam.

God's People

In I Chronicles 17, David spoke to the Lord God praising Him for how He had dealt with the nation of Israel.

5. Covenants and Justice

I Chronicles 17:21-22

²¹ And who is like your people Israel, the one nation on earth whom God went to redeem to be his people, making for yourself a name for great and awesome things, in driving out nations before your people whom you redeemed from Egypt?

²² And you made your people Israel to be your people forever, and you, O Lord, became their God.

David posed an interesting question in his prayer to God by which he summarizes some points that we have already read. God redeemed the one nation, Israel, to be His own people; and Him to be their God.

Think for a moment how this came about. All people came from Adam and Eve, and later from those who came off the ark with Noah. These people made choices: some reverenced God and walked with Him, while others hardened their heart to God. Those who rejected God excluded themselves from God's blessings.

Among those who rejected God were the Egyptians. In the previous chapters about Moses, the people of Israel, and Pharaoh, we saw that the Egyptians were not innocents who just happened to be at the wrong place, at the wrong time. Pharaoh and the Egyptians made choices that set them in opposition to God. The following record adds to our understanding of the Gentile nations and why they were not innocent bystanders. In the following, the apostle Paul was speaking to a group of people who needed some instruction about spiritual matters.

> Acts 14:15-17
>
> [15] "Men, why are you doing these things? We also are men, of like nature with you, and we bring you good news, that you should turn from these vain things to a living God, who made the heaven and the earth and the sea and all that is in them.
>
> [16] In past generations he [the living God] allowed all the nations to walk in their own ways.
>
> [17] Yet he did not leave himself without witness, for he did good by giving you rains from heaven and fruitful seasons, satisfying your hearts with food and gladness."

God always allows people to choose which source of information they will believe. God demonstrated His goodness to the Gentiles.[10] They could have chosen to pay attention to God Who was the source of that goodness. Instead they choose vain things.

In Acts 4, the believers praised God and quoted words king David had spoken by revelation.

> Acts 4:25-26
>
> [25] Who through the mouth of our father David, your servant, said by the Holy Spirit, 'Why did the Gentiles [arrogantly] rage, and the peoples plot in vain?
>
> [26] The kings of the earth set themselves, and the rulers were gathered together, against the Lord and against his Anointed' [Christ, the anointed one]—.

---

10. See also Matthew 5:45: "So that you may be sons of your Father who is in heaven. For he makes his sun rise on the evil and on the good, and sends rain on the just and on the unjust."

5. Covenants and Justice

The Gentiles set themselves in opposition to the Lord and His Christ, the coming savior. They arrogantly and vainly plotted against God. In the previous chapter, When God executed judgment on the Egyptians and their gods, He was just and merciful. Despite the fact that they were not innocent, He gave them many opportunities to believe Him and avoid negative consequences.

In contrast to the Gentiles, Abraham was one who reverenced God and walked with Him. God initiated a covenant agreement with Abraham, which was later extended to Abraham's descendants who became the nation of Israel. Therefore, under the Mosaic Law, the nation of Israel was God's people and He was their God. The terms of the covenant included a means of justification, protection, provision, and blessings. God's commitment was to those who chose Him and not to those who rejected Him.

The people of the surrounding Gentile nations chose to not pay attention to information from God; they chose to not have a relationship with God. Instead they worshipped strange gods and did abominable acts for the sake of their gods. In chapter two, we saw that the source of power behind strange gods is the devil. The devil and his host of strange gods oppose the One True God. They are characterized by lies, deceit, bondage, and death. The Gentile nations were primarily people who hated God and enticed God's people away from Him. The Scriptures say that they defiled the land by their abominations.[11] Thus the people of the Gentile nations were not innocents who did nothing to deserve God's just actions. Instead, as

---

11. See Deuteronomy 12:31; Ezra 9:1, 11, 14; I Kings 14:24; Leviticus 18:1-30; and Deuteronomy 7:1-8.

Did God Do It?

God protected His people, those who opposed God and His people were treated as enemies.

The Whole Congregation of Israel

God and Israel had each agreed to enter into a legally binding covenant agreement. This arrangement was between God and the nation of Israel as a group, collectively. Two events in Joshua demonstrate the collective nature of this arrangement.

Joshua 6 recounts the God-given victory of the city of Jericho. The Lord instructed Joshua each step of the way. When they entered Jericho, God instructed the Israelites as follows.

> Joshua 6:18-19
>
> [18] But you, keep yourselves from the things devoted to destruction, lest when you have devoted them you take any of the devoted things and make the camp of Israel a thing for destruction and bring trouble upon it.
> [19] But all silver and gold, and every vessel of bronze and iron, are holy to the LORD; they shall go into the treasury of the LORD."

God's instructions were in the best interest of His people—so that trouble would not come upon Israel.

> Joshua 7:1
>
> But the people of Israel broke faith [committed a trespass[KJV]] in regard to the devoted things, for Achan the son of Carmi, son of Zabdi, son of Zerah, of the tribe of

5. Covenants and Justice

Judah, took some of the devoted things. And the anger of the LORD burned against the people of Israel.

God had lovingly warned that no individual was to take any of the treasures of Jericho. Achan disobeyed God's instructions and stole silver and gold that had been set apart as holy to the Lord. Because of Achan's disobedience, many Israelites died in the battle at the city of Ai. When Joshua cried to God, He instructed Joshua how to find the wrongdoer and to bring an end to the trouble Achan's treacherous act brought upon all Israel. While only one Israelite committed the trespass, many more Israelites died because Achan's sin affected more than himself.[12]

Later on in Joshua 22 refers back to the incident in Joshua 7. The reference provides an informative lesson.

Joshua 22 occurs after God's people had successfully moved into the promised land. Before this time, the tribes of Reuben, Gad, and the half tribe of Manasseh had requested to inherit land on the eastern side of Jordan. However, their armed men were to go before the other Israelites until they occupied the God-given land beyond the Jordan. Once the lands beyond the Jordan were secured, they returned to their inheritance on the eastern side of the Jordan. Upon their return, they built a large altar. When the other Israelites beyond the Jordan heard about it, they questioned the intent of the altar. So they sent representatives to investigate. This is where we pick up the record.

---

12. For more information about Achan and Joshua 7 see appendix B, Working List - Literal.

> Joshua 22:15-16
>
> ¹⁵ And they came to the people of Reuben, the people of Gad, and the half-tribe of Manasseh, in the land of Gilead, and they said to them,
>
> ¹⁶ "Thus says the whole congregation of the LORD, 'What is this breach of faith [trespass^KJV] that you have committed against the God of Israel in turning away this day from following the LORD by building yourselves an altar this day in rebellion against the LORD?

The representatives spoke on behalf of the Israelites who settled beyond the Jordan. Their concern was that the altar was a rebellious and unfaithful act against God.

> Joshua 22:18-20
>
> ¹⁸ That you too must turn away this day from following the LORD? And if you too rebel against the LORD today then tomorrow he will be angry with <u>the whole congregation of Israel</u>.[13]
>
> ¹⁹ But now, if the land of your possession is unclean, pass over into the LORD's land where the LORD's tabernacle stands, and take for yourselves a possession among us. Only do not rebel against the LORD or make us as rebels by building for yourselves an altar other than the altar of the LORD our God.
>
> ²⁰ Did not Achan the son of Zerah break faith [commit a trespass] in the matter of the devoted things, and wrath

---

13. Underlining added for emphasis.

fell upon <u>all the congregation of Israel</u>? And <u>he did not perish alone for his iniquity [wrongdoing]</u>.'"

The representatives were concerned that the actions of the tribes that had returned to the eastern side of the Jordan might affect, not only those who had built the altar but also the other Israelites who had not committed (what seemed to them to be) a sin against God. They referred to the previous incident of Achan when the trespass of one individual caused the death of many Israelites. Their concern was that the wrongdoing of a few would affect the whole congregation.

If we were to read on, we would see that the altar did not represent rebellion or unfaithfulness, and the conflict ended peacefully. However, this record teaches an important lesson: under the covenant of the law, the wrongdoing of one Israelite could affect the whole nation.

This is a hard concept for many of us who live in current times. It is important to acknowledge that God did not establish the Mosaic standard of justice out of cruelty, He did so *out of love,* to improve people's condition. A condition that existed because of the devil's deception and Adam's disobedience. By Adam, the condition of the world was characterized by sin, death, and judgment. God was working to improve the situation. God was working to make a form of justification and a relationship with Him available to more people. God was tirelessly working to preserve people alive until the times of the coming savior.

Understanding the lesson of this subsection will be important to an upcoming chapter. So let us review. The lesson from this subsection is not really about Achan or which side of the Jordan the Israelites settled. The lesson here is that the covenant of the law was to the nation of Israel as a whole. So the wrongdoing of one Israelite or a few could affect the whole. Under the law, the wrongdoing of one Israelite could cause not only the wrongdoer to die, but many more could die.

The covenant of the law improved mankind's situation but it was not able to remove sin. It was not until Christ came and mediated a better covenant that a better standard of justice became available. By Christ's accomplished works, anyone can now be justified in Christ. However, at the times of the Mosaic Law, Christ had not yet come, and the wrongdoing of one individual could cause many to die.

Kings of the Nation of Israel

Regarding the king of Israel, I Samuel 12:12 says that "the Lord your God was your king." The Lord God was the king of Israel.[14] Even so, at a certain point in the nation of Israel's history, the people asked for a human king. In I Samuel 8, the elders of Israel brought the people's request for a king to the prophet Samuel.

> I Samuel 8:5-7
>
> ⁵ And said to him, "...Now appoint for us a king to judge us like all the nations."
>
> ⁶ But the thing displeased Samuel when they said, "Give us a king to judge us." And Samuel prayed to the LORD.

---

14. Regarding the Lord God being Israel's King see Deuteronomy 33:3-5; Judges 8:23; I Samuel 8:7; I Samuel 12:12; and Psalm 47:6-9.

5. Covenants and Justice

> ⁷And the LORD said to Samuel, "Obey the voice of the people in all that they say to you, for they have not rejected you, but they have rejected me from being king over them.

The Scriptures declare that God was king over Israel. God had the best interest of His people in mind but the people rejected His reign and asked for a human king. We saw that God always allows people to choose between available sources of information. God allows people free will. Therefore, Samuel set a king over Israel in the manner that God directed.

Having a king changed the way God could administer His affairs with the people of Israel. According to Deuteronomy 17, the duties of the king included keeping all the words of the covenant of the law and reverencing the Lord God. So the law was still God's standard, but now there was the question of how the king would administer affairs intended to be administered by God as their king. From many Old Testament records, we can see that when the king obeyed God, the nation prospered; when he did not obey God, certain consequences affected the whole nation.[15] It is significant to upcoming chapters of this study to recognize that the king's decisions affected the whole nation. We can also recognize from this record that the shift in God and man's relationship did not originate with God. The people insisted on having a human king like the Gentile nations. God honored their freedom of will and continued to work to preserve His people until the coming savior.

---

15. For examples of when the actions of the king affected the whole nation, consider I Kings 9:4-7; I Kings 14:16; and I Kings 18:18.

The Promise of a New Covenant

The covenant of the law was for the good of the people of Israel. Under the law, justification or righteousness depended on keeping all the commandments of the law. However, over time, certain kings and people of Israel did not keep the covenant of the law. The one nation of Israel split into two nations, named Israel and Judah. Over time, as these nations continued to do evil in the sight of the Lord, each were taken into captivity. Even then, when they had turned against God and had gone into captivity, God graciously and mercifully told them of deliverance to come.

> Jeremiah 31:31-34
>
> [31] "Behold, the days are coming, declares the LORD, when I will make a new covenant with the house of Israel and the house of Judah,
>
> [32] not like the covenant that I made with their fathers on the day when I took them by the hand to bring them out of the land of Egypt, my covenant that they broke, though I was their husband, declares the LORD.
>
> [33] For this is the covenant that I will make with the house of Israel after those days, declares the LORD: I will put my law within them, and I will write it on their hearts. And I will be their God, and they shall be my people.
>
> [34] And no longer shall each one teach his neighbor and each his brother, saying, 'Know the LORD,' for they shall all know me, from the least of them to the greatest,

5. Covenants and Justice

declares the LORD. For I will forgive their iniquity, and I will remember their sin no more."

God promised a new covenant whereby each individual would know the Lord. The new covenant would include forgiveness of iniquity to the end that there was no more remembrance of sin. The sacrifices under the law remembered sin and pointed toward God's solution for sin, namely the coming savior.[16] Since, the new covenant and the new law had not yet come, the remembrance of sin was necessary under the law. The new covenant would bring a time when iniquity would be forgiven and sin would be remembered no more.

Romans 8 provides a contrast between the old Mosaic Law and the new law.

> Romans 8:1-2
>
> ¹ There is therefore now no condemnation for those who are in Christ Jesus.
>
> ² For the law of the Spirit of life has set you free in Christ Jesus from the law of sin and death.

The law of sin and death refers to the Mosaic Law, which we have seen was characterized by sin, death, and judgment to condemnation. Those who are in Christ Jesus, have received God's spirit.[17]

---

16. See Hebrews 10:3: "But in these sacrifices there is a reminder [remembrance] of sins every year." Hebrews 10:12: "But when Christ had offered for all time a single sacrifice for sins, he sat down at the right hand of God." Hebrews 10:17-18: "Then he adds, 'I will remember their sins and their lawless deeds no more.' Where there is forgiveness of these, there is no longer any offering for sin."

17. See Ephesians 1:13 "In him [Christ] you also, when you heard the word of truth, the gospel of your salvation, and believed in him [Christ], were sealed with the promised Holy Spirit." Thus, here, to be in Christ is to believe concerning Jesus Christ.

> Romans 8:3-4
>
> ³ For God has done what the law, weakened by the flesh, could not do. By sending his own Son in the likeness of sinful flesh and for sin, he condemned sin in the flesh, ⁴ in order that the righteous [just] requirement of the law might be fulfilled in us, who walk not according to the flesh but according to the Spirit.

The requirements of the Mosaic Law were just or righteous requirements for that time. The covenant of the law of Moses was the best standard of justice available in its day and time as they awaited the fulfillment of God's plan of redemption and salvation. However, the law was weakened by the flesh and could not accomplish a lasting justness or righteousness. The form of justness under the law required keeping all the law. Under the standard of justice of the law, it was necessary to remember sin and to atone for it. However, in Christ Jesus the old standard of the Mosaic Law has been superseded by a new law of the spirit.

Justified Freely by His Grace

Along with the new covenant and the new law of the spirit of life, came a new standard of justice.

> Romans 3:21-24[WTJ]
>
> ²¹ Now, however, the justice [righteousness] of God without the law has been manifested, being witnessed to by the law and the prophets.
> ²² Yes, the justice of God *is* by the believing of Jesus Christ to all those who believe, for there is no difference.

5. Covenants and Justice

> ²³ In fact, all have sinned and come short of the glory of God,
> ²⁴ being justified freely by His grace through the redemption that *is* in Christ Jesus.

In the Old Testament, the Mosaic Law and the prophets bore witness to the new standard of justice that the coming savior would bring. The new standard of justice is not based on keeping the law but is by believing of Jesus Christ. Believing concerning Jesus Christ is compactly stated in Romans 10:9-10.

> Romans 10:9-10
> ⁹ Because, if you confess with your mouth that Jesus is Lord and believe in your heart that God raised him from the dead, you will be saved.
> ¹⁰ For with the heart one believes and is justified, and with the mouth one confesses and is saved.

All who believe concerning Jesus Christ have been judged and found not guilty—they are justified and saved. This new kind of justice of God was initiated by God's grace and accomplished by Christ's redemptive work.

> Ephesians 3:2 [NIV]
> Surely you have heard about the administration of God's grace that was given to me for you.

Because of Christ's redemptive work, a shift has occurred in how God can deal with people. In this administration of God's grace, all who believe concerning Christ are justified freely by God's grace.

Did God Do It?

How thankful we can be to live in these times of the wonderful grace of God.

The following chart provides a summary.

Times before Christ	*Times after Christ*
Characterized by sin, death, and judgment to condemnation	Characterized by grace
Guilty because of Adam	Not guilty because of Christ
Justified by keeping all the law	Justified by Christ's accomplishments
Loss of spirit	Spirit within
The nation of Israel were God's people	Anyone who believes concerning Christ is born of God and is God's child

God's Purpose In Christ

Throughout the ages, God worked to restore the losses to mankind due to Adam's disobedience. God's solution to Adam's disobedience was to send a savior to redeem mankind.

> Ephesians 1:7-9
>
> ⁷ In him [the Christ] we have redemption through his blood, the forgiveness of our trespasses, according to the riches of his grace,
>
> ⁸ which he [God] lavished upon us, in all wisdom and insight
>
> ⁹ Making known to us the mystery of his [God's] will, according to his purpose which he set forth in Christ.

> Ephesians 3:11
>
> This was according to the eternal purpose that he [God] has realized [accomplished] in Christ Jesus our Lord.

God's gracious plan of redemption and salvation was accomplished by the life, death, resurrection, and ascension of Jesus Christ. God's purpose across the ages was set forth and accomplished in Christ Jesus our lord. God would never work against His own stated purpose. Therefore, along the way God protected and preserved His people who believed regarding Christ. In the Old Testament times, God protected and provided for people in the line of Christ from whom Christ would come. Ever since Genesis 3:15, God has performed His Word to His people in light of His eternal purpose in

Christ Jesus our lord. This is a very important point to grasp in order to rightly understand many sections of the Scriptures.

God's Eternal Perspective

We started this chapter in Genesis and briefly considered that Adam originally had spirit life as well as physical life. Therefore, he had two life forms. Adam lost spirit when he disobeyed God. However, by Christ's redemptive work a person can once again have spirit life by believing concerning Jesus Christ.

I John 5:11 says, "God gave us eternal life, and this life is in his Son." John 3:16 adds that "whoever believes in him [God's Son] should not perish but have eternal life."

> Hebrews 2:14-15^{NASB}
>
> ¹⁴ ...That through death He [Jesus Christ] might render powerless [ineffective] him who had the power of death, that is, the devil,
> ¹⁵ and might free those who through fear of death were subject to slavery [bondage] all their lives.

Jesus Christ triumphed over the devil and his power over death. He did so by making eternal life spirit available. Eternal life spirit does not die. By the death, resurrection, and ascension of Jesus Christ, the devil's power over death has been rendered ineffective. God's eternal purpose in Christ relates to His eternal perspective and the ultimate victory over death that Christ's work made possible. Without the perspective of these eternal realities, death seems so finite and final. However, when we keep our eyes on God's eternal realities we can put the weight of death in its proper perspective.

5. *Covenants and Justice*

Summary

We saw that God dealt with man in various ways, over different periods of time to restore the very good things mankind lost because of Adam's sin. For that reason, God's dealings with man have changed over time. God deals with people according to the best standard of justice at the time. He always works with people within the bounds of His Word and with respect to freedom of will.

The Mosaic Law was the standard for justice during a time characterized by sin, judgment to condemnation, and death due to Adam's sin. And yet the law was for the good of the people of Israel. The law provided a means to be justified when keeping all the law and thus a basis for fellowship with God. The legal standard of justice of the law preserved them alive until the time of Christ's redeeming work. The law and its sacrifices pointed the way to Christ.

As God dealt with people in various ways over different time periods, it was always with a view to providing the greatest blessings possible. Each shift was to bring mankind closer to God's solution for Adam's sin, namely the promised seed, Christ. It will be important to remember these things as we consider various records in upcoming chapters of this study.

The grace administration is a time period characterized by abounding grace, justice by believing concerning Christ, and the hope of eternal life. The old covenant judgments are no longer applicable. A far better standard of justice is now available in Christ. The new law of the spirit provides a far better basis for God and man's relationship than was available under the covenant of the law. Moreover, in the coming ages, God will display the exceeding riches of His grace in kindness toward us in Christ Jesus.

God has acted faithfully to bring greater blessings to mankind than have been available since the fall of Adam. In our day, we are blessed to live after Christ came and fulfilled God's plan of redemption and salvation. We live in a time of grace and we have God's promise of many good things yet to come.

6

Abraham

In this study, we have seen that God is the God of light, truth, goodness, mercy, and deliverance. God is always just, loving, and merciful; He is always faithful to His Word. He gives the light of His Word to benefit people. In this study we are seeking to let the Scriptures define what is good and just and not current culture.

Chapters two through four each considered unusual expressions from Exodus that seemed to say God did something contrary to His nature or a person's free will. We found two to be figurative and one to be literal. In chapter two, the Lord did not do evil to His people in Egypt. Instead, Moses and Aaron spoke information from God to Pharaoh; Pharaoh responded by commanding that evil be done to God's people. In chapter three, the Lord did not harden Pharaoh's heart; Pharaoh hardened his own heart. The Scriptures say each person is responsible for his or her own heart and the resulting actions that come from the heart. Therefore, expressions that say God made a person's heart do something are usually figurative. In chapter four, God sent angels to carry out the final plague and free His people from decades of bondage in Egypt. Although the Egyptians arrogantly opposed God and His people, He was abundantly merciful and long-suffering to the nation that enslaved His people.

Chapter five considered more essential background about covenants and justice. This chapter will consider two more unusual and possibly difficult expressions.

Two Unusual Expressions

Two records from the life of Abraham have an unusual expression that some may find puzzling.

> Genesis 12:17
>
> But the LORD afflicted Pharaoh and his house with great plagues because of Sarai, Abram's wife.

> Genesis 20:18
>
> For the LORD had closed all the wombs of the house of Abimelech because of Sarah, Abraham's wife.

Each verse seems to say the Lord God did something that may sound evil to our modern ears. Causing plagues and closing up wombs does not appear to be in harmony with God's nature of love, light, and justice. We have an apparent contradiction.

As we will see, when put together, these two accounts of Abraham's encounters with two different kings provide an interesting contrast of the character of the two kings. Much of the same background material is needed to understand each record. Therefore, they are presented together.

In this study, it is our goal to allow the intrinsic evidence of the Scriptures to provide an answer. As we have in each previous chapter, we will consider the context of each unusual and potentially difficult expression to gain an understanding of God's intended meaning. We will also consider related passages to allow the Scriptures to determine if this unusual expression is literal or figurative, or if we do not know.

Review

Chapter five considered a covenant relationship that God initiated with Abraham and later extended to the people of Israel. The covenant God made with Abraham included distinct promises. Those promises pertained to and rested on the one pivotal promise concerning Christ coming from Abraham's offspring.[1] We saw that God communicated the gospel concerning the coming savior to Abraham and Abraham walked believingly on that information.

Let us also review what God said regarding Abraham's wife Sarah.

> Genesis 17:15-16 and 19
>
> [15] And God said to Abraham, "As for Sarai your wife, you shall not call her name Sarai, but Sarah shall be her name.
>
> [16] I will bless her, and moreover, I will give you a son by her. I will bless her, and she shall become nations; kings of peoples shall come from her."
>
> [19] God said, "No, but Sarah your wife shall bear you a son, and you shall call his name Isaac. I will establish

---

1. See Galatians 3:16: "Now the promises were made to Abraham and to his offspring. It does not say, 'And to offsprings,' referring to many, but referring to one, 'And to your offspring,' who is Christ."

> my covenant with him as an everlasting covenant for his offspring after him.

In Genesis 17, God added to the covenant he had established with Abraham and confirmed that his wife, Sarah, would bear him a son. Moreover, God said that He would establish an everlasting covenant with Abraham and Sarah's son, Isaac.

Putting together the scriptures we have considered, we know that God told Abraham that Christ would come from his body and from his offspring. God further informed Abraham that Sarah would be the mother of his heir. Thus we know from the Scriptures that Christ would come through the lineage descending from the child Abraham and Sarah would have together.

Background

The unusual expressions in Genesis 12 and in Genesis 20 occurred when Abraham left his homeland and journeyed into foreign lands. In current times people may move from one location to another for a better job, to be near family, or for many other reasons. However, in Abraham's day, people generally lived and died where their families had been for generations. Abraham's hometown was Ur of the Chaldees in Mesopotamia. So we might ask: What motivated Abraham to journey into foreign lands?

> Genesis 12:1-5
>
> ¹ Now the LORD said to Abram, "Go from your country and your kindred and your father's house to the land that I will show you.

6. Abraham

² And I will make of you a great nation, and I will bless you and make your name great, so that you will be a blessing.

³ I will bless those who bless you, and him who dishonors you I will curse, and in you all the families of the earth shall be blessed."

⁴ So Abram went, as the LORD had told him, and Lot went with him. Abram was seventy-five years old when he departed from Haran.

⁵ And Abram took Sarai his wife, and Lot his brother's son, and all their possessions that they had gathered, and the people that they had acquired in Haran, and they set out to go to the land of Canaan....

The Lord approached Abraham and instructed him to journey into a land that God would show him. Many people today relocate for human reasons. However, Abraham relocated because God instructed him to do so. Abraham journeyed through foreign lands because he believed information from God.[2]

While we are in Genesis 12:1-5, let us also note that God made several promises to Abraham. He promised that He would bless those who blessed Abraham and curse those who dishonored him. In Genesis 12:3, the Hebrew word translated "curse" is used in a different sense than present-day English might imply. In the phrase

---

2. Hebrews 11:8-9 says that Abraham moved because he believed and obeyed God. Complementary information in Acts 7:2-6 shows that God instructed Abraham to move when Abraham was in Mesopotamia. Therefore, the instructions recorded in Acts 7 preceed Genesis 12.

that is translated "I will curse," the basic meaning is "to bind" in the sense of to prevent from doing something.[3]

God also promised that all families of the earth would be blessed in Abraham, that he would have a great name, and that a great nation would come from his descendants. To all these promises, Abraham responded by believing the Lord God.

It is also noteworthy that the Scriptures call Abraham a friend of God three times.[4] Moreover, Genesis 20:7 says that Abraham was a prophet. A true prophet speaks what God gives him to speak; he speaks for God. Thus the Scriptures show that God and Abraham had an active and successful working relationship.

More Background: Related Scripture

In Genesis 12, God made several promises to Abraham. I Chronicles 16 expands on some of those promises and provides information that complements what we saw in Genesis 12:1-5.

> I Chronicles 16:15-23
>
> [15] Remember his covenant forever, the word that he commanded, for a thousand generations,
>
> [16] the covenant that he made with Abraham, his sworn promise to Isaac,

---

3. See R. Laird Harris, Gleason L. Archer, and Bruce K. Waltke, *Theological Wordbook of the Old Testament* (Chicago, Illinois: Moody Publishers 1980), p. 75, number 168, which states "...Hebrew '*arar* means to 'to bind..., hem in with obstacles, render powerless to resist.'" See also Herbert Chanan Brichto, *The Problem of "Curse" in the Hebrew Bible* (Society of Biblical Literature and Exegesis, Philadelphia, Pennsylvania 1963, reprinted in the Journal of Biblical Literature Monograph Series, volume XIII); and William Wilson, *Old Testament Word Studies* (Grand Rapids, Michigan: Kregel Publications, 1978), p. 105, "curse" meaning number 2.

4. See II Chronicles 20:7; Isaiah 41:8; and James 2:23.

> ¹⁷ which he confirmed to Jacob as a statute, to Israel as an everlasting covenant,
>
> ¹⁸ saying, "To you I will give the land of Canaan, as your portion for an inheritance."
>
> ¹⁹ When you were few in number, of little account, and sojourners in it,
>
> ²⁰ wandering from nation to nation, from one kingdom to another people,
>
> ²¹ he allowed no one to oppress [wrong] them [those with whom God had a covenant relationship]; he rebuked kings on their account,
>
> ²² saying, "Touch not my anointed ones, do my prophets no harm!"
>
> ²³ Sing to the LORD, all the earth! Tell of his salvation from day to day.

In this passage, God promised to protect His people with whom He had a covenant relationship. God specifically did not allow anyone of the nations through which they journeyed to do any wrong to those with whom he had a covenant agreement. God protected them to the end that He reproved kings for their sakes.

I Chronicles 16:22 adds another promise from God: God would not allow anyone to harm His prophets. As noted before, we know from Genesis 20:7 that Abraham was one of God's prophets.[5]

---

5. We ought to clarify that while the phrase, "touch not my anointed ones" is also in I Chronicles 16:22, there is no scriptural evidence that Abraham was an anointed one. Thus, "touch not my anointed ones" does not appear to be applicable to Abraham.

By this complementary information, we see God made promises regarding Abraham's protection that were not recorded in Genesis but were later recorded in I Chronicles 16. God promised to not allow any of the nations through which Abraham journeyed to do wrong or harm to Abraham.

Genesis 12:17 Context

With this background, we are now ready to consider the context of the first unusual expression.

> Genesis 12:9-10
>
> ⁹ And Abram journeyed on, still going toward the Negeb.
> ¹⁰ Now there was a famine in the land. So Abram went down to Egypt to sojourn there, for the famine was severe in the land.

The Bible as History by Werner Keller says that in times of famine Egypt was a place of refuge for nomads. Abraham began his journeys away from his homeland because he obeyed information from God. When there was a severe famine in the land, he journeyed to Egypt to find refuge from the famine. In *The Bible as History*, Keller explains that the Egyptians had a chain of forts and watchtowers to protect against unwelcomed invaders and to retain foreign visitors. He states, "Certainly there were no passports, but formalities and officialdom made life difficult for foreign visitors." Messages would be sent back and forth between the frontier officers and administrative officers at the court of Pharaoh to decide whether an entrance permit would be granted.⁶ So Abraham entered into Egypt with caution.

> Genesis 12:11-13
>
> ¹¹ When he was about to enter Egypt, he said to Sarai his wife, "I know that you are a woman beautiful in appearance,
>
> ¹² and when the Egyptians see you, they will say, 'This is his wife.' Then they will kill me, but they will let you live.
>
> ¹³ Say you are my sister, that it may go well with me because of you, and that my life may be spared for your sake."

One scholar on biblical culture adds to Abraham's concerns for his life saying, "Abraham had heard that many men had lost their lives on account of their beautiful wives."⁷ Another source states, "If Pharaoh were to add Sarai to his harem while knowing that she was Abram's wife, he would have to kill Abram first."⁸

> Genesis 12:14-16
>
> ¹⁴ When Abram entered Egypt, the Egyptians saw that the woman was very beautiful.

---

6. Werner Keller, *The Bible as History* (William Morrow and Company, New York, New York, 1956), pp. 66-67.

7. George M. Lamsa, *Old Testament Light* (Prentice Hall, Inc. Englewood Cliffs, New Jersey, 1964), p.41. Lamsa states, "The Chaldean women were noted for being fair and beautiful." Abraham and Sarah were from Ur of Chaldeans.

8. *New American Standard Bible Study Bible*, (Grand Rapids, Michigan: Zondervan, 1999), p. 22.

Did God Do It?

> ¹⁵ And when the princes of Pharaoh saw her, they praised her to Pharaoh. And the woman was taken into Pharaoh's house.
> ¹⁶ And for her sake he dealt well with Abram; and he had sheep, oxen, male donkeys, male servants, female servants, female donkeys, and camels.

So Sarah was taken into Pharaoh's house, that is to say, his harem. The women of a harem were groomed and readied for the king's pleasure. Let us bring forward a verse from the next record in Genesis 20 that will help us recognize the significance of Sarah, in particular, being taken into Pharaoh's harem.

> Genesis 20:6
> ...It was I [the Lord God] who kept you [the king] from sinning against me. Therefore I did not let you touch her.

From this we see that had the king touched Sarah, as a king would likely touch a woman in his harem, it would have been sinning against the Lord. Remember, it was with Sarah that Abraham would have a son to carry on God and Abraham's covenant agreeement and through whom the line to Christ would come.

Regarding Abraham and Sarah's agreement to only say that she was his sister, some have proposed that Abraham lied or lacked integrity. First, Genesis 20:12 states that Sarah was Abraham's half-sister. Thus, saying she was his sister, was not a lie. Abraham was entering a foreign land whose population did not respect the Lord God; he was unsure of his welcome. As he approached potential enemies, Abraham truthfully stated that Sarah was his sister. He did not add that she was also his wife. God and Abraham had a close, active, working relationship. Abraham obeyed information from God and sojourned into foreign lands. The wider context would lead us to understand that Abraham walked with wisdom as he sought to avoid a dangerous situation.

According to verse 16, Pharaoh treated Abraham well "for her sake." Perhaps the biblical custom of gift giving was involved. One resource says, "In biblical days it was customary to give gifts of all kinds for a myriad of reasons: to win a bride, to pay a dowry, to bind a friendship, to appease an enemy, to feed someone hungry, to express love, and many more."[9]

How would God fulfull His promises to Abraham? There is no scriptural indication that Pharaoh had any respect toward Abraham's God. How would God get Pharaoh's attention? How would God make Himself known?

> Genesis 12:17-20
>
> [17] But the LORD afflicted Pharaoh and his house with great plagues because of Sarai, Abram's wife.
>
> [18] So Pharaoh called Abram and said, "What is this you have done to me? Why did you not tell me that she was your wife?
>
> [19] Why did you say, 'She is my sister,' so that I took her for my wife? Now then, here is your wife; take her, and go."

---

9. James M. Freeman, rewritten and updated by Harold J. Chadwick, *The New Manners and Customs of the Bible* (Alachua, FL: Bridge-Logos, 1998), p. 65, "Giving Gifts."

Did God Do It?

> ²⁰ And Pharaoh gave men orders concerning him, and they sent him away with his wife and all that he had.

God got Pharaoh's attention with a plague. Pharaoh responded by calling Abraham in for questioning. Genesis 12:12 told us that Abraham feared for his life had they known Sarah was his wife. However, Pharaoh did not genuinely listen for the answer to his question. More importantly, God made Himself known in the demonstration of His power. Although, Pharaoh recognized that a power mightier than him had intervened for Abraham, he did not seek to engage with this mighty God. Instead, Pharaoh had Abraham and Sarah abruptly sent away.

In verse 17, the Hebrew word for "afflicted" means to touch, to strike, or produce effect.[10] This Hebrew word is translated: plagued,^KJV struck,^NASB afflicted.^ESV In Genesis 12:3, God promised that He would bless those who blessed Abraham and curse those who dishonored him. We saw that the Hebrew word for "curse" means to bind in the sense of to prevent from doing something. Putting together the Hebrew understanding of these words, we can see that God plagued, struck, or afflicted Pharaoh in order to prevent the Egyptians from harming Abraham. Pharaoh and the Egyptians dishonored Abraham. However, of greater significance, it would have been a sin against God had Pharaoh touched Sarah in the way a king would touch a woman from his harem. The emphasis of this record is not on the

---

10. Francis Brown, Samuel Rolles Driver, Charles Augustus Briggs, *A Hebrew and English Lexicon of the Old Testament* (Oxford, England, UK: Clarendon Press, 1906). See the Hebrew word, *nagha*, rendered "afflicted" in ESV, as offered in the e-lexicon on Parallel Plus by TheBible.org ©2017. To access click on the word "plagued" in KJV.

consequences the Egyptian enemies brought on themselves. Instead, what is significant is that Abraham walked with God and God fulfilled His promises to His prophet Abraham.

We need to hold in mind that Pharaoh and the Egyptians were not innocents that just happened to be at the wrong place at the wrong time. Both from history and the Scriptures, we know that the Egyptians worshipped many gods and set themselves in opposition to the One True God.[11] They made decisions time and again that put them in opposition against the One True God; they did not choose to have a relationship with the Lord God. Thus, God was not committed to take care of them.

On the other hand, God was committed to not allow any harm or wrong to come to His prophet, Abraham, with whom He had a covenant agreement. God was faithful to His promises to Abraham and acted to protect Abraham. Soon after, Abraham, Sarah, and the rest of his household were removed from the difficult situation. In the face of God's great power to protect His people, Pharaoh and the Egyptians still did not soften their hearts to God but instead, Pharaoh gave orders for his men to send away Abraham, Sarah, and all with them.

Genesis 20:18 Context

Holding in mind the background information about Abraham, we will now consider the context of the second unusual expression.

---

11. See Exodus 12:12: "...all the gods of Egypt..." Historical accounts of the gods of ancient Egypt are numerous. For example, see Richard H. Wilkinson, *The Complete Gods and Goddesses of Ancient Egypt*, (Thames and Hudson, New York, NY 2017).

Did God Do It?

> Genesis 20:1-2
>
> ¹ From there Abraham journeyed toward the territory of the Negeb and lived between Kadesh and Shur; and he sojourned in Gerar.
>
> ² And Abraham said of Sarah his wife, "She is my sister." And Abimelech king of Gerar sent and took Sarah.

Similar to Genesis 12, Abraham truthfully stated that Sarah was his sister but did not tell potential enemies that she was also his wife. Abraham continued to walk with God and wisely handled a dangerous situation.

> Genesis 20:3-11
>
> ³ But God came to Abimelech in a dream by night and said to him, "Behold, you are a dead man because of the woman whom you have taken, for she is a man's wife."
>
> ⁴ Now Abimelech had not approached her. So he said, "Lord, will you kill an innocent people?
>
> ⁵ Did he not himself say to me, 'She is my sister'? And she herself said, 'He is my brother.' In the integrity of my heart and the innocence of my hands I have done this."
>
> ⁶ Then God said to him in the dream, "Yes, I know that you have done this in the integrity of your heart, and it was I who kept you from sinning against me. Therefore I did not let you touch her.
>
> ⁷ Now then, return the man's wife, for he is a prophet, so that he will pray for you, and you shall live. But if you do not return her, know that you shall surely die, you

and all who are yours."

⁸ So Abimelech rose early in the morning and called all his servants and told them all these things. And the men were very much afraid.

⁹ Then Abimelech called Abraham and said to him, "What have you done to us? And how have I sinned against you, that you have brought on me and my kingdom a great sin? You have done to me things that ought not to be done."

¹⁰ And Abimelech said to Abraham, "What did you see, that you did this thing?"

¹¹ Abraham said, "I did it because I thought, 'There is no fear of God at all in this place, and they will kill me because of my wife.'

God chose to communicate, with this unbelieving king, by way of a dream. In the dream, God informed Abimelech that continuing to keep Sarah in his harem was not in his own best interest and that touching Sarah would be a sin against Him. Abimelech engaged in the conversation that God initiated. The king claimed that the people of Gerar were an innocent people, and that he had acted in the integrity of his heart and the innocence of his hands. God responded to Abimelech's claims of innocence and said, "Yes, I know that you have done this in the integrity of your heart, and it was I [the Lord God] who kept you from sinning against me. Therefore I did not let you touch her" (Genesis 20:6).

God gave Abimelech true and reliable information that he could believe or not. Abimelech decided to pay attention to information from God. In so doing, Abimelech refrained from sinning against God and refrained from dishonoring Abraham. In this manner, God prevented Abimelech from causing harm to Abraham and fulfilled His promises to Abraham. God was faithful to His Word.

Let us continue in Genesis 20.

> Genesis 20:12-16
> [12] Besides, she is indeed my sister, the daughter of my father though not the daughter of my mother, and she became my wife.
> [13] And when God caused me to wander from my father's house, I said to her, 'This is the kindness you must do me: at every place to which we come, say of me, "He is my brother."'
> [14] Then Abimelech took sheep and oxen, and male servants and female servants, and gave them to Abraham, and returned Sarah his wife to him.
> [15] And Abimelech said, "Behold, my land is before you; dwell where it pleases you."
> [16] To Sarah he said, "Behold, I have given your brother a thousand pieces of silver. It is a sign of your innocence in the eyes of all who are with you, and before everyone you are vindicated."[12]

---

12. The last phrase of verse 16 in KJV says, "thus she was reproved." Saying Sarah was "reproved" does not fit with the scriptural context. See NASB: "To Sarah he said, 'Behold, I have given your brother a thousand pieces of silver; behold, it is your vindication before all who are with you, and before all men you are cleared.'"

6. Abraham

Abimelech was receptive to God and received God's instructions. Thus the king acted according to God's instructions and returned Abraham's wife to him untouched. To Abraham, the king offered land saying, "Behold, my land is before you; dwell where it pleases you." On Sarah's behalf, Abimelech gave gifts to Abraham before witnesses. This public gift-giving cleared Sarah of any suspicion for the time she spent in the king's harem. It was a sign of her innocence before everyone. In this manner, Abimelech showed honor to Abraham and to Abraham's God.

> Genesis 20:17-18
>
> [17] Then Abraham prayed to God, and God healed Abimelech, and also healed his wife and female slaves so that they bore children.
>
> [18] For the LORD had closed all the wombs of the house of Abimelech because of Sarah, Abraham's wife.[13]

God had promised Abimelech that once Abraham's wife was returned, His prophet would pray for him. God fulfilled His promise to Abimelech and Abraham prayed for Abimelech. God answered Abraham's prayer and healed all those of Abimelech's household so that they bore children. Abimelech and his household received God's deliverance. The Lord God protected and delivered Abraham and those with him, while at the same time showing abundant mercy to

---

13. On the topic of God and closing wombs, the reader may be encouraged to consider two additional unusual expressions about closing wombs that are not literal but are figurative. These two figurative expressions are handled in appendix C, subsection "Idiom without Wrongdoing." See "Sarah–Genesis 16:2" and "Hannah–I Samuel 1:5-6." The Hannah record is also handled in chapter eleven of this study.

their potential enemy. God made a way for deliverance, both for His prophet Abraham and for Abimelech's household.

Promises Fulfilled

Let us review some of what God had promised Abraham (as applicable to the records in Genesis 12 and 20). God promised:

- He would bless Abraham and bind anyone who dishonored Abraham to the end they could not cause the intended harm.
- He would not allow anyone of the nations through which they (those with whom he had a covenant agreement) journeyed to do any wrong to them.
- He would protect them (those with whom he had a covenant agreement) to the end that He would reprove kings for their sakes.
- He would not allow anyone to harm His prophets, including Abraham.

From Pharaoh and Abimelech's points of view they may have done nothing wrong. However, from God's point of view, His covenant with Abraham had been breached by their actions. God reproved the kings, Pharaoh and Abimelech, for Abraham's sake. The Lord God kept His covenant with Abraham and fulfilled His promises. He was faithful to His Word.

Comparing Pharaoh and Abimelech

Having considered the context of each unusual expression, some differences between Pharaoh and Abimelech become apparent.

- Pharaoh and Abimelech were very different people going into their encounter with Abraham. God confirmed that Abimelech was innocent and had acted with integrity. No such words were said about Pharaoh.
- The Scriptures give no indication that Pharaoh had any respect for Abraham or his God. It took a plague to get Pharaoh's attention. Once the plague had his attention, he did not seek to right the wrong done to this man for whom God intervened. In contrast, Abimelech was receptive to God; he obeyed instructions from God to right the wrong.
- Once God got Pharaoh's attention, he had them abruptly sent away. On the other hand, Abimelech invited Abraham to dwell in the land of Gerar where he pleased.

Because of Abimelech's response, the whole situation turned out much differently for the nation of Gerar than it did for Pharaoh and the Egyptians.

Summary

In this chapter, we considered two accounts in the life of Abraham that contain two unusual expressions: "the Lord afflicted Pharaoh and his house with great plagues " (Genesis 12:17) and "the Lord had closed all the wombs of the house of Abimelech"(Genesis 20:18). By putting together the context and related passages, we see that both of these expressions are not figurative but are literal. God prevented both Pharaoh and Abimelech from causing harm to Abraham. In

Genesis 12, God made Himself known to Pharaoh by the plague. Therefore, the Egyptians released Sarah and disaster was averted. In Genesis 20, God chose to initiate a conversation with Abimelech by way of a dream; Abimelech listened and obeyed trustworthy information from God, which ended with favorable results for all.

As we near the end of this chapter let us revisit the topic of fairness. We ought to recognize that people hold many different points of view regarding what is fair and just, or conversely, what is unfair or unjust. In our current cultural times, there are many social movements that advocate for things like animal rights, judicial reforms, or fair trade that define justice and fairness according to the standards of those movements. People have different criteria, values, or moral standards that give them a frame of reference from which they interpret justice and judgment. However, these standards often do not consider what the Scriptures say.

This study is careful not to mix in standards from outside the Scriptures. Instead, we are vitally concerned with appreciating God's point of view from the Scriptures. What God and His Word say is just and good, *is* just and good. We have seen from the Scriptures that Abraham had an active, working relationship with God and that he walked with wisdom to avoid entanglement with potential enemies. God's protection of His prophet, Abraham, was in alignment with His nature throughout the Scriptures.

God's Eternal Purpose in Christ

We saw in Galatians 3:16 that the pivotal promise God gave to Abraham was "and to your offspring, who is Christ." All the other promises and covenant terms between God and Abraham set upon the one promise concerning his offspring, who is Christ. Moreover, we saw that Abraham's heir would be with his wife, Sarah. Thus, the line to Christ was to come from the descendants of Abraham with his wife Sarah.

> Ephesians 3:11
> This was according to the eternal purpose that he has realized [accomplished] in Christ Jesus our Lord.

God's eternal purpose was accomplished in Christ Jesus our lord. Abraham and Sarah were part of the line to Christ.

Both in Genesis 12 and Genesis 20, God kept His promises to Abraham, with whom He had a covenant relationship. God was faithful to His Word. God did not allow anyone to do wrong or harm to Abraham. He protected Sarah who would be the mother of Abraham's heir. By protecting Abraham and Sarah in this situation, God also provided for the lineage through whom Christ would come. Moreover, protecting Abraham and Sarah provided a way forward in God's plan of redemption and salvation for all mankind. Throughout the Scriptures, God protected and preserved His people who believed concerning Christ. In this manner, He provided for His eternal purpose in Christ. By doing so, a way was made for greater blessings in Christ than had been available since Adam's fall. God has and will continue to perform His Word to His people in light of His eternal purpose in Christ Jesus our lord. God's plan and purpose in Christ is in the best interest of all mankind for all times.

Did God Do It?

7

Saul

In chapter one, we saw that God introduces the light of His Word to bring life and deliverance to people. Chapters two, three, and four extended across records in Exodus 1-12. We saw that God heard the cry of affliction of His people, remembered His covenant, and delivered them out of bondage in Egypt with many signs and wonders.

In the previous chapters, we have seen that certain wording that *seems* to say God did something contrary to His nature or a person's freedom of will may be figurative or literal depending on the context and related passages. In all that God did we have seen that He gives His Word to benefit people. However, He never imposes His best intentions on anyone. God always allows people to choose between available sources of information.

An Unusual Expression

Saul was the first king of Israel. This chapter will consider an unusual expression about the death of Saul.

> I Samuel 31:4
>
> ...Therefore Saul took his own sword and fell upon it.
>
> I Chronicles 10:4
>
> ...Therefore Saul took his own sword and fell upon it.

These two accounts agree that Saul killed himself. Then ten verses later in I Chronicles we read the following.

> I Chronicles 10:14
>
> ...Therefore the LORD put him [Saul] to death and turned the kingdom over to David the son of Jesse.

We have an apparent contradiction. The two records that say Saul fell on his sword and killed himself cause us to question if the phrase, "the Lord put him to death" is figurative or literal?

Background

God had a covenant relationship first with Abraham and later with the nation of Israel, who were Abraham's descendants. The covenant relationship between God and the nation of Israel included that the Lord was their God and the Israelites were His people. God's promises to Abraham concerning Christ—that Christ would come from Abraham's offspring—continued to the nation of Israel. Thus the Israelites were in the line of Christ.

> Psalm 44:4[NIV]
>
> You are my King and my God, who decrees victories for Jacob.

7. Saul

To understand the unusual expression, we must recognize that the Lord God was King of Israel and had Israel's best interest in mind.[1]

> Deuteronomy 17:14-15
>
> [14] When you come to the land that the LORD your God is giving you, and you possess it and dwell in it and then say, 'I will set a king over me, like all the nations that are around me,'
>
> [15] you may indeed set a king over you whom the LORD your God will choose....

God knew in advance that there would come a time when the Israelites would forget His constant care and provision for them, and would imagine that they would be better off with a human king. It must have grieved God to anticipate their request. However, He responded by instructing the people of Israel on how to best handle the non-ideal situation, when the time came. God's first instruction was that He would choose the king.

> Deuteronomy 17:18-20
>
> [18] And when he sits on the throne of his kingdom, he shall write for himself in a book a copy of this law, approved by the Levitical priests.
>
> [19] And it shall be with him, and he shall read in it all the days of his life, that he may learn to fear [reverence] the LORD his God by keeping all the words of this law and these statutes, and doing them,

---

1. Regarding the Lord God being Israel's King see Deuteronomy 33:3-5; Judges 8:23; I Samuel 8:7; 10:19; 12:12; and Psalm 47:6-9.

[20] that his heart may not be lifted up above his brothers, and that he may not turn aside from the commandment, either to the right hand or to the left, so that he may continue long in his kingdom, he and his children, in Israel.

The future kings of Israel were to write a copy of the law and read it daily; they were to reverence the Lord God. Kings of Israel were to keep and do all the words of the law and its statutes. Saul was the first king of Israel. God foretold that a king's heart would not be lifted up above his brethren or turn aside from God's commandments when he kept the words of the law. Deuteronomy 17 records what God told the Israelites in advance in preparation for a coming time. That time came in I Samuel 8.

> I Samuel 8:4-5 and 22
>
> [4] Then all the elders of Israel gathered together and came to Samuel at Ramah
>
> [5] and said to him, "Behold, you are old and your sons do not walk in your ways. Now appoint for us a king to judge us like all the nations."
>
> [22] And the LORD said to Samuel, "Obey their voice and make them a king." Samuel then said to the men of Israel, "Go every man to his city."

The elders of Israel asked Samuel, the prophet, to appoint a king to judge over them like all the nations. The "nations" refers to the surrounding Gentile nations who did not believe God. God always

7. Saul

allows people to choose, therefore, He selected the best available human king and set him over Israel.

We are building background and a wider context to understand the unusual expression. Next, let us consider the anointing of Saul as the new king.

> I Samuel 10:1
>
> Then Samuel took a flask of oil and poured it on his head and kissed him and said, "Has not the Lord anointed you to be prince over his people Israel? And you shall reign over the people of the Lord and you will save them from the hand of their surrounding enemies. And this shall be the sign to you that the Lord has anointed you to be prince over his heritage.

Samuel then instructed Saul about what would occur next. The instruction in verse 6 is pertinent to this chapter.

> I Samuel 10:6 and 9-10
>
> ⁶ Then the Spirit of the Lord will rush upon you, and you will prophesy with them and be turned into another man.
>
> ⁹ ...And all these signs came to pass that day.
> ¹⁰ When they came to Gibeah, behold, a group of prophets met him, and the Spirit of God rushed upon him, and he prophesied among them.

The spirit of the Lord came upon Saul. This new spirit upon Saul was evidenced when Saul prophesied. The evidence of spirit

Did God Do It?

demonstrated that Saul not only had physical life but also life associated with God's spirit. Therefore, he was called "another man." God equipped Saul with spirit as a means of communication with Him. God's spirit upon Saul equipped him to succeed as king.

Saul now had information from God both by the written covenant of the law and by way of spirit. In addition, Saul received information from God spoken by the prophet Samuel.

Context: Complementary Accounts

We will now consider the context of the unusual expression from the two complementary accounts of the end of Saul's life.

> I Samuel 31:1-6
>
> ¹ Now the Philistines were fighting against Israel, and the men of Israel fled before the Philistines and fell slain on Mount Gilboa.
>
> ² And the Philistines overtook Saul and his sons, and the Philistines struck down Jonathan and Abinadab and Malchi-shua, the sons of Saul.
>
> ³ The battle pressed hard against Saul, and the archers found him, and he was wounded by the archers.
>
> ⁴ Then Saul said to his armor-bearer, "Draw your sword and thrust me through with it, lest these uncircumcised come and thrust me through, and mistreat me." But his armor-bearer would not, for he feared greatly. Therefore Saul took his own sword and fell upon it.
>
> ⁵ And when his armor-bearer saw that Saul was dead, he also fell upon his sword and died with him.

7. *Saul*

⁶ Thus Saul died, and his three sons, and his armor-bearer, and all his men, on the same day together.

Next, I Chronicles 10 records the same event.

I Chronicles 10:1-6

¹ Now the Philistines fought against Israel, and the men of Israel fled before the Philistines and fell slain on Mount Gilboa.

² And the Philistines overtook Saul and his sons, and the Philistines struck down Jonathan and Abinadab and Malchi-shua, the sons of Saul.

³ The battle pressed hard against Saul, and the archers found him, and he was wounded by the archers.

⁴ Then Saul said to his armor-bearer, "Draw your sword and thrust me through with it, lest these uncircumcised come and mistreat me." But his armor-bearer would not, for he feared greatly. Therefore Saul took his own sword and fell upon it.

⁵ And when his armor-bearer saw that Saul was dead, he also fell upon his sword and died.

⁶ Thus Saul died; he and his three sons and all his house died together.

These two accounts give an almost identical report of Saul's death.[2] An archer's arrow wounded Saul. Saul asked his armor bearer

---

2. II Samuel 1:1-10 records an account of Saul's death giving to David by an Amalekite. Having already read the divine narrative in the two complementary accounts, we ought to question the accuracy of the Amalekite's account. See ESV Study Bible p. 542 and NASB Study Bible p. 403, which say that the Amalekite lied to David in hopes of his appreciation and a reward.

to thrust his sword through his body so that he would die and not be mistreated by the enemy. His armor bearer would not kill Saul, so Saul took a sword, fell on it, and thereby killed himself.

I Chronicles 10 explains that the next day the Philistines found Saul and his sons dead on the battlefield. As Saul had feared the Philistines did mistreat his dead body. However, the unusual expression that we are trying to understand has to do with how Saul died, which is again addressed in verse 13.

> I Chronicles 10:13-14
>
> [13] So Saul died for his breach of faith. He broke faith with the LORD in that he did not keep the command of the LORD, and also consulted a medium, seeking guidance.
>
> [14] He did not seek guidance from the LORD. Therefore the LORD put him to death and turned the kingdom over to David the son of Jesse.

I Chronicles 10:13 states that the cause of Saul's death was twofold:

- Saul did not keep the command of the Lord (he did not keep the word of the Lord[NIV, NASB]).
- Saul consulted a medium, seeking guidance.

To understand these causes and to reconcile the contradictory account, we need to consider some related scriptures.

7. *Saul*

Related Scripture

A pivotal occasion in Saul's life, when he "did not keep the command of the Lord," occurred not long after Saul was made king.

> I Samuel 15:1-3 and 9-11
>
> [1] And Samuel said to Saul, "The LORD sent me to anoint you king over his people Israel; now therefore listen to the words of the LORD.
>
> [2] Thus says the LORD of hosts, 'I have noted what Amalek did to Israel in opposing them on the way when they came up out of Egypt.
>
> [3] Now go and strike Amalek and devote to destruction all that they have. Do not spare them, but kill both man and woman, child and infant, ox and sheep, camel and donkey.'"
>
> [9] But Saul and the people spared Agag and the best of the sheep and of the oxen and of the fattened calves and the lambs, and all that was good, and would not utterly destroy them. All that was despised and worthless they devoted to destruction.
>
> [10] The word of the LORD came to Samuel:
>
> [11] "I regret that I have made Saul king, for he has turned back from following me and has not performed my commandments." And Samuel was angry, and he cried to the LORD all night.

So what had Amalek done? Many years before as God's people journeyed away from bondage in Egypt, Amalek set himself against

Did God Do It?

God's people and attacked the weary Israelites from behind. Throughout the history of Israel, the Amalekites repeatedly scorned the Lord God and showed contempt for His people.[3] In I Samuel 15, God gave clear and specific instructions to smite the Amalekite enemies and to utterly destroy all that they had, but verses 9-19 point out that Saul did not do as God instructed. Instead, Saul made several excuses for his choices, including blaming others, when it was Saul who had explicit instructions from God, and it was Saul who was responsible for carrying out those instructions.

We will consider the lessons of verses 10 and 11 after the next passages. For now, let us consider the Word of the Lord to Saul, spoken by the prophet Samuel picking up the record in verse 19.

> I Samuel 15:19-21
>
> [19] Why then did you not obey the voice of the LORD? Why did you pounce on the spoil and do what was evil in the sight of the LORD?"
>
> [20] And Saul said to Samuel, "I have obeyed the voice of the LORD. I have gone on the mission on which the LORD sent me. I have brought Agag the king of Amalek, and I have devoted the Amalekites to destruction.
>
> [21] But the people took of the spoil, sheep and oxen, the best of the things devoted to destruction, to sacrifice to the LORD your God in Gilgal."

Did Saul actually go "on the mission on which the Lord sent [him]," as Saul claimed in verse 20? He did not. Even when Samuel

---

3. See Deuteronomy 25:17-19; Exodus 17:8-16; and Judges 3:13; I Samuel 15:2-3.

confronted Saul with his disobedience, Saul continued to lie, deny, and make excuses for his choices. Again, let us recognize that it was Saul who had explicit instructions from God and it was Saul who chose to disobey God. Continuing to speak for God, the prophet, Samuel, summarized Saul's transgression to his face:

> I Samuel 15:22-26
>
> ²² And Samuel said, "Has the LORD as great delight in burnt offerings and sacrifices, as in obeying the voice of the LORD? Behold, to obey is better than sacrifice, and to listen than the fat of rams.
>
> ²³ For rebellion is as the sin of divination, and presumption is as iniquity and idolatry. Because you have rejected the word of the LORD, he has also rejected you from being king."
>
> ²⁴ Saul said to Samuel, "I have sinned, for I have transgressed the commandment of the LORD and your words, because I feared the people and obeyed their voice.
>
> ²⁵ Now therefore, please pardon my sin and return with me that I may bow before the LORD."
>
> ²⁶ And Samuel said to Saul, "I will not return with you. For you have rejected the word of the LORD, and the LORD has rejected you from being king over Israel."

In this encounter with Samuel, Saul continued to blame others and make excuses for his actions. Although in verse 24, he said, "I have sinned" he ended with another excuse by which he dodged responsibility for his own choices.

Let us summarize what Saul did: he turned away from following God and did not perform God's commandments (verse 11), he did evil in the sight of the Lord (verse 19), he was rebellious and stubborn against God (verse 23), and he rejected the command of the Lord. In short, Saul transgressed against God and His Word.

Shortly after this event, the following occurred.

> I Samuel 16:14
> Now the Spirit of the LORD departed from Saul, and a harmful spirit from the LORD tormented him.

Having looked at Saul's transgression against God and His Word, the first part of this verse is understandable. When Saul rejected God and His Word, he lost his spirit connection with God. However, saying what then tormented Saul was "a harmful spirit from the Lord" does not make sense. The Scriptures show that God would not give a harmful spirit but that the devil would. The second half of this verse is not true to fact; it is figurative. A further discussion of this verse is offered in the section of appendix C entitled "Saul and the Harmful Spirit."

We are considering the evidence of the Scriptures regarding the two spiritual causes of Saul's death as recorded in I Chronicles 10:13. The second cause given is that Saul "consulted a medium, seeking guidance." A "medium" is a person influenced by a spirit messenger from the devil. Information from the devil, and therefore from a medium, is full of lies, deceit, wickedness, and injustice, and it leads to bondage and death. The covenant of the law addressed mediums in Leviticus 19:31: "Do not turn to mediums or necromancers; do not seek them out, and so make yourselves unclean by them." The people of Israel were instructed to not turn to, nor seek information from mediums or those who practiced wizardry. These practices were and are associated with the devil and his evil darkness. These instructions in Leviticus 19 were for the good of God's people. God's good intention was that those under the devil's influence would not defile His people.

It is important to note that the prophet Samuel had died before the following occurred. Samuel was not alive to speak with Saul.

> I Samuel 28:3-7
>
> ³ Now Samuel had died, and all Israel had mourned for him and buried him in Ramah, his own city. And Saul had put the mediums and the necromancers out of the land.
>
> ⁴ The Philistines assembled and came and encamped at Shunem. And Saul gathered all Israel, and they encamped at Gilboa.
>
> ⁵ When Saul saw the army of the Philistines, he was afraid, and his heart trembled greatly.
>
> ⁶ And when Saul inquired of the LORD, the LORD did not answer him, either by dreams, or by Urim, or by prophets.
>
> ⁷ Then Saul said to his servants, "Seek out for me a woman who is a medium, that I may go to her and inquire of her." And his servants said to him, "Behold, there is a medium at En-dor."

Did God Do It?

Many years before this time, Saul had removed from Israel anyone who practiced wizardry, that is to say anyone who was a medium. At this time, when the Philistines gathered their armies to fight against Israel, Saul was afraid and his heart trembled greatly. He wanted information about the impending battle, however, he had rejected God and His Word and he had lost his spirit connection with the One True God. In addition, Saul's choices had led him to being influenced by a harmful spirit. So verse 6 ought to stand out.

Moreover, we ought to consider whether Saul genuinely inquired of the Lord or not. II Chronicles 7:14 says that if God's people humbly seek Him, He will answer. These verses state what God's response would be if His people genuinely and humbly turned to Him.[4] Therefore, all that we have read about Saul ought to cause us to question whether he genuinely sought information from God, or did he only appear to do so.

So, after going through the motions of seeking the Lord, Saul asked his servants to find a woman who is a medium. Interestingly, his servants knew right where to find one.

> I Samuel 28:8-10
>
> [8] So Saul disguised himself and put on other garments and went, he and two men with him. And they came to the woman by night. And he said, "Divine for me by a spirit and bring up for me whomever I shall name to you."

---

[4]. II Chronicles 7:14: "If my people who are called by my name humble themselves, and pray and seek my face and turn from their wicked ways, then I will hear from heaven and will forgive their sin and heal their land."

⁹ The woman said to him, "Surely you know what Saul has done, how he has cut off the mediums and the necromancers from the land. Why then are you laying a trap for my life to bring about my death?"

¹⁰ But Saul swore to her by the LORD, "As the LORD lives, no punishment shall come upon you for this thing."

According to verses 9 and 10, the woman of Endor knew that a person who was a medium was forbidden in Israel. Saul acknowledged that it was so, but assured the woman that he would not allow her to be punished for this thing. Thus, Saul knowingly and willingly disobeyed God's Word.

I Samuel 28:11-14

¹¹ Then the woman said, "Whom shall I bring up for you?" He said, "Bring up Samuel for me."

¹² When the woman saw Samuel, she cried out with a loud voice. And the woman said to Saul, "Why have you deceived me? You are Saul."

¹³ The king said to her, "Do not be afraid. What do you see?" And the woman said to Saul, "I see a god coming up out of the earth."

¹⁴ He said to her, "What is his appearance?" And she said, "An old man is coming up, and he is wrapped in a robe." And Saul knew that it was Samuel, and he bowed with his face to the ground and paid homage [respect-ᴬᴹᴾ].

Was this really Samuel? No, the medium is speaking information from the devil intended to deceive and harm.

After Saul rejected God in I Samuel 15, there is no scriptural evidence that he ever again paid his respects to God's prophet while he was living. Without such evidence, we might question how genuine Saul is here in the respect he seems to show.

> I Samuel 28:15-17
>
> [15] Then Samuel said to Saul, "Why have you disturbed me by bringing me up?" Saul answered, "I am in great distress, for the Philistines are warring against me, and God has turned away from me and answers me no more, either by prophets or by dreams. Therefore I have summoned you to tell me what I shall do."
> [16] And Samuel said, "Why then do you ask me, since the LORD has turned from you and become your enemy?
> [17] The LORD has done to you as he spoke by me, for the LORD has torn the kingdom out of your hand and given it to your neighbor, David.

Samuel was dead; he was not able to speak for God. The words the medium spoke were not from dead Samuel; they were false and deceptive words. Therefore, we should recognize that it was *not* God Who had become Saul's enemy, but rather it was Saul who had turned away from God.

As to tearing the kingdom from Saul's hands, let us recall that the kings of Israel were to obey God and to keep the covenant of the law. When Saul chose to disobey God and reject the covenant of the law, he then disqualified himself from being king over Israel. Saul's freewill decision had consequences for himself and for Israel. Because of his own choices, he was no longer qualified to be king. In that sense, Saul tore the kingdom out of his own hands. God responded by providing someone who was qualified to be king of Israel, David, in Saul's stead. God works with those who turn to Him. He did not overstep Saul's freedom of will, but God continued to provide for His people, Israel.

By reading on in I Samuel 28, we can see that soon after Saul received false counsel from the medium he was wounded in battle and killed himself. In chapter one we learned that information from the devil leads to bondage and death; the record of the end of Saul's life is an example of this scriptural pattern.

Next, I Samuel 15:11 is repeated for our consideration.

> I Samuel 15:11
> "I regret that I have made Saul king, for he has turned back from following me and has not performed my commandments." And Samuel was angry [distressed[NASB]] and he cried to the LORD all night.

When Saul turned away from following God, Samuel was angry because of Saul's disobedience. Samuel was also distressed and cried unto the Lord all night. Samuel was God's prophet; how it must have grieved Samuel to see Saul turn his back on God. From a human point of view, one could sympathize with Saul. But what about God? When the people requested a king, Saul was well able to succeed as king. Saul had God's Word in the covenant of the law; he had God's profitable instructions. He also had God's spirit upon him, giving him a communication line with God. God set Saul up for success. However, God does not control what a person does with what he is given. When Saul turned his back on God, it was a sad loss for God and for God's people, Israel.

Summary

God gave information and instructions to Saul to benefit him as king and to benefit His people, Israel. Saul had the Word of the Lord from the covenant of the law, by God's spirit upon him, and from God's prophet, Samuel. Thus, God gave His Word to Saul and Saul rejected the Word of the Lord. When Saul rejected the Word of the Lord, he started on a path that led to his own harm and eventual death.

Samuel and Chronicles each record that Saul took his own sword, fell upon it, and died. I Chronicles adds that Saul died because Saul did not keep the Word of the Lord and for consulting a medium.

Because God is just, He allowed Saul to choose between available sources of spiritual information. God's involvement in Saul's choices was the giving of His Word. God did not do anything contrary to Saul's freedom of will.

Therefore, by reviewing background scriptures, two complementary contexts, and related scriptures, we see that "the Lord put Saul to death" is not true to fact. Physically, Saul killed himself. Spiritually, Saul brought deadly consequences upon himself. Although it is not literally true, according to the manner of speech of Old Testament times the Scriptures figuratively say, the Lord put Saul to death. The unusual expression is an idiom that *seems* to say God did something that He did not do. We have seen that the context and related scriptures of this idiom often show the spiritual cause behind the physical. This characteristic is seen especially well regarding Saul's death as it is recorded in Samuel and Chronicles.

The books of Samuel, Kings, and Chronicles give the history of the people and kings of Israel and cover many of the same events, but with different details. Just as the four gospels recount the life of Jesus Christ from four different perspectives, with distinct emphases and word usage; so the historical books of Samuel, Kings, and Chronicles often cover the same events from different perspectives. Samuel and Kings often give man's point of view with a focus on the physical, human aspects of an event. On the other hand, the books of Chronicles often add the spiritual cause behind the physical, from God's point of view. Each account is needed to see the whole picture.[5]

The physical cause of Saul's death is recorded in both Samuel and Chronicles, while the spiritual causes of Saul's death are only recorded in I Chronicles 10. Together the complementary accounts of Saul's death show both the physical cause of Saul's death as well as the spiritual causes behind the physical. Thus, the complementary accounts combine in such a way so that the reader has a more complete and accurate picture of what occurred.

Review: A Particular Biblical Idiom

The context and related scriptures show that "the Lord put Saul to death" is not true to fact; it is figurative. The unusual expression regarding Saul's death fits the characteristics of the particular biblical

---

5. See E. W. Bullinger, *The Companion Bible* (Zondervan Bible Publishers 1964), Appendix 56, "The Parallel Passages of the Historical Books."

idiom this study is considering. Let us review:
- Active-verb expressions in the Scriptures with the pattern of "the Lord God + action + recipient" are idiomatic when the context and related scriptures show that the words are not true to fact.
- This particular biblical idiom *seems* to say God did something contrary to His nature or a person's freedom of will but according to the context and related scriptures He did not.
- When the unusual expression has the word "heart" (as seen in chapter three) and seems to say God made someone's heart do or believe something, the expression is usually figurative and not literal.
- The idiom's meaning is understood from biblical culture, context, and related scriptures.[6]
- According to the God-centered culture of Old Testament times, the devil was not named. In their culture, this idiom was not intended to blame God, nor did this idiom mean that He did evil. Instead, they acknowledged God, Who is Lord overall and magnified Him in the face of affliction.

Furthermore the related scriptures and context of this idiom often, but not always, show the following:
- Who, other than God, was responsible for the action credited to God.

---

6. The position this study takes is that the idiom, that seems to say God did something He did not do, is a figure of meaning (or thought) and not a figure of grammar. That is to say this idiom is not understood by a shift in grammar (active put for the passive) but is understood from the context and related scriptures as well as the culture of Old Testament times.

- The spiritual cause behind the physical.
- That someone had information or instructions from God that he or she did not believe.

The unusual expression, "the Lord put Saul to death," is a particular biblical idiom that *seems* to say God did something that He did not actually do.

A Closing Note

In this study we are considering certain unusual expressions that may be figurative or literal depending on the context. We have found that these unusual expressions often occur in a context where a person made choices that led to negative consequences. Please do not misconstrue a characteristic of these unusual expressions to be generally applicable to present day life. In other words, we ought never think that every affliction in life is because somebody did something wrong. This would not be based in the Scriptures, and this is not what this study is saying. Instead, let us acknowledge that we live in an evil world in which the devil, as the god of this world, causes bad things to happen. We can take comfort knowing that Christ has triumphed over the devil—both now and in the future. As Jesus Christ said in John 16:33, "...take heart; I have overcome the world."

We recognize that hearing the unusual expression, "the Lord put Saul to death," may be hard to hear. This is understandable because there are so many clear scriptures about how good and wonderful the God of the Scriptures is. In the biblical culture of Old Testament times, such expressions were not intended to blame God but did

Did God Do It?

acknowledge the Lord Who is the Most High, Most Powerful Lord overall.

Although the elders of Israel foolishly requested a human king, God graciously and mercifully selected the best king possible; then He equipped him for success. As Saul ruled the nation of Israel, God allowed Saul to choose which source of information he would believe. Regrettably, Saul chose to reject God and His Word and made decisions that ultimately led to his death. The Lord was good and just in all that He did to help Saul succeed and to provide for His people. God was true to His nature as set forth in the Scriptures; He was gracious, merciful, just, and faithful to His Word.

8

David

We are considering God's goodness throughout the Scriptures and certain unusual expressions regarding His actions. In chapter five of this study, we looked at certain covenant relationships and their associated standards of justice. We started with the devil's deception[1] and Adam's disobedience in Genesis 3. Sin, death, and judgment to condemnation entered the world because of Adam's sin. However, God promised the seed of the woman as the savior for the world.[2] God did not introduce sin, death, and judgment to condemnation into the world, but He did tirelessly work to provide a solution to the sin Adam introduced. God worked with people to provide the best standard of justice possible to allow humankind to move toward ultimate deliverance. God initially worked with individuals such as Noah, Abraham, and Isaac. When the Israelites collectively agreed to keep all the covenant of the law, God had a greater capacity to bless a whole nation. However, by the time of the prophet Samuel, the people of Israel unwisely requested to have a human king instead

---

1. In Genesis 3, the devil is figuratively represented as the serpent.
2. Looking back, we know the coming savior would be Jesus Christ.

Did God Do It?

of the Lord God being their king. The first king, Saul, disqualified himself from being king, so God selected David to be the second king of Israel. Kings of Israel were meant to walk with God and obey His commandments. When the king of Israel listened to God, the nation prospered. When the king of Israel did not rely on the Lord God, the whole nation was subject to the consequences.

In chapter five, we saw that Christ would come from Abraham's offspring and that Abraham knew this because God had told him. This chapter focuses on an event in the life of David. David was the second king of Israel and he was a descendant of Abraham.

> Matthew 1:1
> The book of the genealogy of Jesus Christ, the son of
> David, the son of Abraham.

Jesus Christ was called both the son of David and the son of Abraham. It is significant that both Abraham and David's descendants were of the line to Christ.

Two Sets of Unusual Expressions

There is a troublesome event in the life of king David that is recorded both in II Samuel 24 and I Chronicles 21. The two accounts add to each other and provide complementary information that when put together provides a more complete and accurate account. First, we will address the apparent contradiction in the opening verse of each account. Then we will address the unusual expression in the potentially more difficult portions of these corresponding accounts.

In the opening verses, the term "to number" means "to count" and is similar to taking a census.

8. David

> II Samuel 24:1
>
> Again the anger of the LORD was kindled against Israel, and he [the Lord] incited David against them, saying, "Go, number Israel and Judah."

> I Chronicles 21:1
>
> Then Satan stood against Israel and incited David to number Israel.

These verses agree that David was prompted to number the men of Israel. However, the opening verses disagree as to *who* incited David to number Israel. We have an apparent contradiction.

The other unusual and potentially difficult expression occurs about 14 verses later in each account.

> II Samuel 24:15
>
> So the LORD sent a pestilence on Israel from the morning until the appointed time. And there died of the people from Dan to Beersheba 70,000 men.

> I Chronicles 21:14-15
>
> [14] So the LORD sent a pestilence on Israel, and 70,000 men of Israel fell.
>
> [15] And God sent the angel to Jerusalem to destroy it...

The unusual expressions in the two complementary accounts are similar and equally troublesome. It is difficult to read that God destroyed 70,000 Israelites. Up to this point in this study, we have seen that God brought calamity to enemies of His people. Because the calamity in this chapter is not to enemies but to God's own people, it

Did God Do It?

is understandable that some people find this record to be extremely difficult. However, even when we do not comprehend a record, God's nature has not changed. To gain understanding, we must continue to approach the Scriptures with reverence. We ought to expect to see characteristics of God's nature in this record. We look for His mercy. We look for His justness and His ever-present light.

Background: To Number Israel

This chapter addresses a time when David was prompted to number Israel. At that time, the covenant of the law was the standard of justice. The covenant of the law did not contain any general, ongoing instructions to take a census of Israel.

However, while there were no general commandments to number Israel, there were occasions when God gave specific instructions to number the people of Israel for a specific situation.[3] Thus, taking a census of Israel was on a case-by-case basis as God gave instructions to do so. At the time recorded in II Samuel 24 and I Chronicles 21, *there is no indication* that God gave specific instructions to David to number Israel.

So David did not have information from God to number Israel either from the covenant of the law or by specific instructions from God. Thus, God did not authorize David's actions in either a general or specific way.

---

3. For examples of times God gave specific instructions to take a census of Israel, see Numbers 1:1-4 and 49; 2:32-34; 3:14-16; 26:2; and Exodus 30:11-16.

8. David

Unusual Expressions in the Opening Verses

We saw that the opening verses disagree about *who* incited David to number Israel. II Samuel states that the Lord incited David and I Chronicles states that Satan incited David. The Hebrew word "to incite" means, "to instigate in a bad sense"[4] and has "the underlying idea of cunning deception."[5] Therefore, let us begin to address this apparent contradiction by recalling some of the contrasting characteristics of God and the devil.

God gives information that is light, delivering, true, just, and merciful. In contrast, the devil gives information that is full of lies and deceit, and which leads to calamity and death. We saw in Revelation 12:9-10 that the devil is the "deceiver of the whole world" and "the accuser of our brothers," that is to say, God's people.

Secondly, God and the devil deal very differently with a person's freedom of will. The Lord God never causes anyone to do or think something contrary to his or her own free will. God always allows people to choose between available sources of information. In contrast, the devil does not honor free will; but instead, he seeks to deceive and influence people to not believe and benefit from information from God.

Thus, saying that Satan stood against Israel and incited David to act on information intended to cause harm to God's people fits with

---

4. See the Hebrew word, *suth*, (rendered "he incited" in ESV) in Francis Brown, Samuel Rolles Driver, Charles Augustus Briggs, *A Hebrew and English Lexicon of the Old Testament* (Oxford, England, UK: Clarendon Press, 1906), as offered in the e-lexicon on Parallel Plus by TheBible.org ©2017.

5. See R. Laird Harris, Gleason L. Archer, and Bruce K. Waltke, *The Theological Wordbook of the Old Testament* (Chicago, Illinois, Moody Publishers, 1980), p. 621, word number 1481.

many clear scriptures about the devil's nature. On the other hand, cunning deception does not fit with God's nature.

Continuing to build on what we have learned previously in this study, let us also recall how the historical books of Samuel, Kings, and Chronicles complement each other. Samuel and Kings often report an account primarily from a earthly point of view with a focus on the physical, human aspects of an event. On the other hand, the books of Chronicles often add the spiritual cause behind the physical from God's point of view. Thus these opening verses state *who* influenced David from two different points of view.

I Chronicles 21:1 states what literally and spiritually happened, "Satan stood against Israel and incited David to number Israel." On the other hand, II Samuel 24:1 figuratively states, "he [the Lord] incited David against Israel and Judah." The unusual expression in II Samuel 24:1 is not true to fact. This figurative expression is an example of the biblical idiom that *seems* to say God did something contrary to His nature or a person's freedom of will but He did not. Instead, Satan deceived David to cause harm to God's people. How was God to respond?

Before moving on, we ought to note that while the two complementary accounts in this chapter record a low point in David's life, there are many passages that speak well of David. For example, I Samuel 13:14 says that David was a man after God's own heart. Many other passages show that David sought information from God and was obedient to it.[6] When King David acted on information from God the nation of Israel benefitted.

---

6. For example, see I Chronicles 14:9-16.

Digression: The Anger of the Lord

Although, we have already seen that Satan, not God, incited David, II Samuel 24:1 includes another possibly troublesome expression that raises questions.

> II Samuel 24:1
> Again the anger of the LORD was kindled against Israel, and he incited David against them, saying, "Go, number Israel and Judah."

We will briefly digress to consider what the Scriptures say about "the anger of the Lord." The basic meaning of the Hebrew word for anger is nostril and gives the mind picture of one's nostrils flaring in anger. The anger of the Lord is related to the sin of God's people. The use of this Hebrew word personifies God's displeasure with sin. When His people sin, it displeases God but it also causes Him grief and sorrow. God deals with sin according to the established standard of justice of the time.

From a human point of view, anger often has a negative connotation because humans often misbehave when angry. However, to rightly understand the Scriptures, we cannot import this negative association with God's anger. "The anger of the Lord is not sinful, evil, or the source of capricious attitudes or deeds."[7] Humans may misbehave when angry but God does not. Even in His anger, God is just.

---

7. R. Laird Harris, Gleason L. Archer, and Bruce K. Waltke, *The Theological Wordbook of the Old Testament* (Chicago, Illinois: Moody Publishers 1980), p. 58, word number 133a.

Did God Do It?

Context: I Chronicles 21:14

With this background, we are now ready to address the potentially more difficult portions of these corresponding accounts. After the opening verses, the accounts given in II Samuel 24 and I Chronicles 21 are very similar. Therefore, we will read the remaining portion only from I Chronicles.

> I Chronicles 21:2
>
> So David said to Joab and the commanders of the army, "Go, number Israel, from Beersheba to Dan, and bring me a report, that I may know their number."

The Hebrew word for "know" comes from a word meaning "knowledge gained by the senses."[8] In this situation, David was not seeking information from God.

> I Chronicles 21:3-7
>
> ³ But Joab said, "May the LORD add to his people a hundred times as many as they are! Are they not, my lord the king, all of them my lord's servants? Why then should my lord require this? Why should it be a cause of guilt for Israel?"
>
> ⁴ But the king's word prevailed against Joab. So Joab departed and went throughout all Israel and came back to Jerusalem.
>
> ⁵ And Joab gave the sum of the numbering of the people to David. In all Israel there were 1,100,000 men who

---

8. See R. Laird Harris, Gleason L. Archer, and Bruce K., *The Theological Wordbook of the Old Testament* (Chicago, Illinois, Moody Publishers 1980), p. 366, word number 848.

drew the sword, and in Judah 470,000 who drew the sword.

⁶ But he did not include Levi and Benjamin in the numbering, for the king's command was abhorrent to Joab.

⁷ But God was displeased with this thing, and he struck Israel.

David asked Joab, the captain of the army, to number all the men of Israel, but Joab resisted the king's order and reminded him that the Lord would add a hundred times more people as needed. Joab exhorted David to trust in God more than in numbers. David could have relied on God but he did not.

Joab was aware that this choice by David was not in Israel's best interest. Joab implored David to stop. Regrettably, David did not rescind the command.

In I Chronicles 21:3, Joab asked King David why he would require something that would bring guilt to the people of Israel. The Hebrew word for "guilt" in I Chronicles 21:3 can be rendered "sin to the becoming guilty of the people."⁹ Because of the collective nature of the covenant of the law, David's sin spread to the people of Israel. The standard of justice under the Mosaic Law was to the nation of Israel as a group. We have seen that because of this collective nature, the wrongdoing of one Israelite could cause many

---

9. See the Hebrew word, *ashmah,* rendered "a cause for trespass" in KJV and "a cause for guilt" in ESV. Francis Brown, Samuel Rolles Driver, Charles Augustus Briggs, *A Hebrew and English Lexicon of the Old Testament* (Oxford, England, UK: Clarendon Press, 1906) as offered in the e-lexicon on Parallel Plus by TheBible.org ©2017.

Did God Do It?

to die.[10] Moreover, David was king over Israel. As king, David was responsible for the welfare of the nation of Israel. Regrettably, when David sinned, his decision affected the whole nation of Israel.

David had God's Word in the covenant of the law and often walked with God. In I Chronicles 17:8-10 God made several promises to David, which included that He would subdue David's enemies.[11] However, in this situation, David acted on deceptive information from Satan instead of seeking help from God. Thus, David sinned against God. The king was responsible for the welfare of the nation and his decisions could affect the whole nation, as it did here.

> I Chronicles 21:8-10
> [8] And David said to God, "I have sinned greatly in that I have done this thing. But now, please take away the iniquity of your servant, for I have acted very foolishly."
> [9] And the LORD spoke to Gad, David's seer, saying,
> [10] "Go and say to David, 'Thus says the LORD, Three things I offer you; choose one of them, that I may do it to you.'"

David said, "I have sinned greatly" and "I have acted very foolishly." Thus he began the process of acknowledging his sin and seeking God's deliverance. David beseeched God to take away his iniquity. He knew that the covenant of the law required atonement to stop the consequences of his iniquity. God heard his plea and graciously provided three options to fulfill the necessary atonement.

10. See the subsection entitled "The Whole Congregation of Israel" in chapter five of this study.
11. See I Chronicles 17:8-10 and II Samuel 7:9-11, which give corresponding accounts of promises God made to David.

8. David

I Chronicles 21:11-15

¹¹ So Gad came to David and said to him, "Thus says the Lord, 'Choose what you will:

¹² either three years of famine, or three months of devastation by your foes while the sword of your enemies overtakes you, or else three days of the sword of the Lord, pestilence on the land, with the angel of the Lord destroying throughout all the territory of Israel.' Now decide what answer I shall return to him who sent me."

¹³ Then David said to Gad, "I am in great distress. Let me fall into the hand of the Lord, for his mercy is very great, but do not let me fall into the hand of man."

¹⁴ So the Lord sent a pestilence [plague] on Israel, and 70,000 men of Israel fell.

¹⁵ And God sent the angel to Jerusalem to destroy it, but as he was about to destroy it, the Lord saw, and he relented from the calamity. And he said to the angel who was working destruction, "It is enough; now stay your hand." And the angel of the Lord was standing by the threshing floor of Ornan the Jebusite.

The choice of consequences that God offered were three years of famine in the land, three months of devastation by their enemies, or three days of the sword of the Lord by plague and the angel (spirit messenger) of the Lord. Although three choices were given, according to verse 13, David saw the choices as twofold: fall into the hands of men or rely on God's great mercy. Choosing famine or enemies represented possible solutions by human efforts. The third choice represented complete reliance on God—and God alone. David chose to place himself entirely at the mercy of God. David chose to trust in God's great mercies.

Review: Angels and Cost to God

We have previously considered two things that are applicable to this chapter. So, let us recall what we learned about the angel of the Lord and the importance of God's people.

Angels are spirit messengers. All spirit messengers act on behalf of whomever sends them. Spirit messengers may be sent from God or from the devil. Spirit messengers that God sends are generally called angels. Spirit messengers do not act on their own behalf; they act on behalf of the one who sends them. Thus, what they say and do represents the one who sends them. The angel in I Chronicles 21:12 is called an "angel of the Lord" and verse 15 says "God sent the angel." Thus this angel of the Lord is a spirit messenger sent by God to do His will.

As we read this really tough record, let us keep in mind that God had a vested interest in keeping the people of Israel alive. They were His people and He was their God. Christ would come from the lineage of David. The Israelites were the people through whom Christ would come.

> Psalm 116:15[NIV]
> Precious in the sight of the LORD is the death of his
> faithful servants.

8. David

The death of God's people is precious in His sight. The Hebrew word for "precious" means costly and highly valued. It is no light matter when one of God's people dies. It cost God. The people of Israel were God's people. The life of even one Israelite was valuable and important in the sight of the Lord. It grieved God that so many of His people died because of Satan's deception and David's decision. God could not and would not cast aside His covenant with Israel. His faithfulness relies on God keeping His Word. So we ask: How could God and His people get through this difficult situation? One can only imagine that keeping their eyes on the coming savior and the better covenant the savior would bring, would be of help. Meanwhile, it was important to God to deliver and preserve as many Israelites as possible.

Continuing in the Context

Now, let us pick up the context in verse 15.

> I Chronicles 21:15-22
>
> ¹⁵ And God sent the angel to Jerusalem to destroy it, but as he was about to destroy it, the Lord saw, and he relented from the calamity. And he said to the angel who was working destruction, "It is enough; now stay your hand." And the angel of the Lord was standing by the threshing floor of Ornan the Jebusite.
> ¹⁶ And David lifted his eyes and saw the angel of the Lord standing between earth and heaven, and in his hand a drawn sword stretched out over Jerusalem. Then David and the elders, clothed in sackcloth, fell upon

their faces.

¹⁷ And David said to God, "Was it not I who gave command to number the people? It is I who have sinned and done great evil. But these sheep, what have they done? Please let your hand, O Lord my God, be against me and against my father's house. But do not let the plague be on your people."

¹⁸ Now the angel of the Lord had commanded Gad to say to David that David should go up and raise an altar to the Lord on the threshing floor of Ornan the Jebusite.

¹⁹ So David went up at Gad's word, which he had spoken in the name of the Lord.

²⁰ Now Ornan was threshing wheat. He turned and saw the angel, and his four sons who were with him hid themselves.

²¹ As David came to Ornan, Ornan looked and saw David and went out from the threshing floor and paid homage to David with his face to the ground.

²² And David said to Ornan, "Give me the site of the threshing floor that I may build on it an altar to the Lord—give it to me at its full price—that the plague may be averted [restrained] from the people."

God sent an angel to Jerusalem to take away the iniquity. Then He mercifully paused and proceeded to instruct David how to complete the atonement. In verse 16, God opened David's eyes to see the angel of the Lord with his hand stayed. Afterwards David acknowledged that it was he who had sinned and done evil against God. Perhaps, this time was more heartfelt than David's initial response. Next, David prayed with earnest: "Please let your hand, O Lord my God, be against me and against my father's house. But do not let the plague be on your people."

It is notable that David referred to the people of Israel as sheep. As a youth, David had shepherded his father's flocks and knew that a good shepherd would protect the sheep by putting himself between harm and the sheep. David used the imagery of people as sheep to show his willingness to intercede for the people not only in prayer but also with his life. David's transgression had caused judgment and consequences that affected all Israel, but now he interceded for the people with prayer and his willingness to die on their behalf.

God then instructed David to build an altar to restrain the plague from the people.

> I Chronicles 21:23-28
>
> [23] Then Ornan said to David, "Take it, and let my lord the king do what seems good to him. See, I give the oxen for burnt offerings and the threshing sledges for the wood and the wheat for a grain offering; I give it all."
> [24] But King David said to Ornan, "No, but I will buy them for the full price. I will not take for the LORD what is yours, nor offer burnt offerings that cost me nothing."
> [25] So David paid Ornan 600 shekels of gold by weight for the site.

> ²⁶ And David built there an altar to the LORD and presented burnt offerings and peace offerings and called on the LORD, and the LORD answered him with fire from heaven upon the altar of burnt offering.
> ²⁷ Then the LORD commanded the angel, and he put his sword back into its sheath.
> ²⁸ At that time, when David saw that the LORD had answered him at the threshing floor of Ornan the Jebusite, he sacrificed there.[12]

David presented burnt offerings and peace offerings upon the altar to God. Leviticus 1-7 cover these offerings in detail. From Leviticus we learn that burnt and peace offerings were sweet-savor incense offerings, as was the meal offering. David Bergey, in his book, *Jesus Christ Our Complete Offering* says, "the burnt, meal, and peace offerings were offered up to God as incense. They served as prayer and intercession with a fragrance of quiet acquiescence unto God." Bergey further states "The primary point of the burnt, meal, and peace offering was to approach God in intercession and prayer, turning away wrath.... In essence, these incense offerings were intercessory offerings unto God, which turned away wrath."[13]

King David obeyed God's instructions and built an altar. He then presented burnt and peace offerings. These offerings served to approach God in prayer and intercession for Israel. They stood in the gap between the hand of judgment and the people. When David

---

12. This location became the site of Solomon's temple. See II Chronicles 3:1.
13. David Bergey, *Jesus Christ Our Complete Offering: How the Levitical Offerings Foreshadowed Christ* (Printed in the United States of America, 2017). pp.178-184.

8. David

approached God in prayer and intercession by way of these offerings, God answered with fire from heaven. Fire from heaven upon the altar showed God's acceptance of the offering.[14] The sweet-savor offerings restrained the plague from the people.

Although God had stopped the angel in verse 15, the angel still stood in midair with his sword drawn. After God accepted David's intercessory offerings, the angel then sheathed his sword. Atonement for David's iniquity was complete.

More Review: Just Standards

To accurately handle this potentially difficult record, we must consider it against the backdrop of its own historical times and its own standards of justice. In chapter five, we considered the purpose and benefits of the Mosaic Law. God did not offer a covenant agreement to the nation of Israel to punish them, but rather it was an improvement for the condition of the world at that time. The need for the law came about because of Satan's deception and Adam's disobedience. By Adam's disobedience, sin, death, and judgment to condemnation entered the world. God tirelessly worked to restore the losses caused by Adam. The covenant of the law was a step forward. The sacrifices and offerings of the law pointed people toward the coming savior. The law was an improvement in that it provided a basis for a whole nation to be justified and to have a relationship with God. Because the covenant of the law was to the nation of Israel as a group, its collective nature could either spread benefit or consequences to the Israelites. While, the covenant of the law improved mankind's

---

14. God's acceptance by fire from heaven can be seen in Leviticus 9:22-24 and II Chronicles 7:1-3.

situation, it was not until Christ came and mediated a better covenant that a better justification became available.

Under the law, David's wrongdoing affected all Israel. When David acted on deceptive information from Satan, he caused guilt to spread to all the people of Israel. In these Old Testament times, David's sin required atonement to right the wrong and stop the consequences. God graciously gave David three choices. David chose the sword of the Lord and by that choice he chose to rely solely on God and His mercy. In the midst of the necessary judgment, God mercifully stalled the hand of the destroying angel and instructed David to build an altar for intercessory offerings. David followed God's instructions and interceded for Israel. The Lord answered David's intercessory offerings with fire from heaven and commanded the angel to sheath his sword. Atonement was finished and many were delivered.

Let us be clear, it was Satan who instigated the need for atonement in this situation. God worked within the bounds of David's freewill decision and within the bounds of the standard of justice at that time to deliver as many as possible.

Because God acted quickly to provide the necessary justice, a far greater calamity was prevented. God's prompt administration of justice brought both immediate relief for those who lived as well as far-reaching benefit for all people of all times. By God's just and merciful actions, many survived and thereby continued the line to Christ. When Christ came, he brought a better justification from sin

8. David

than was available at the time of David. However, this very notable improvement had not yet come to pass when David numbered Israel.[15]

God's Plan for Life

The difficulty in this chapter is that many Israelites died. This subsection is included to offer some comfort and a higher perspective.

> Ezekiel 18:32
>
> For I have no pleasure in the death of anyone, declares the Lord GOD; so turn, and live.

God has no pleasure in the death of anyone. God always provides a way for people to turn to Him and live.

In Deuteronomy 30, God presented the people of Israel with choices: life or death; good or evil; blessing or cursing. God set up the people of Israel for success. His Word was near and not far; it was accessible and doable. God exhorted them to choose life by choosing to believe His Word. However, as we have seen throughout this study, God is not the only source of information available in the world. Satan instigated David with deceptive information and people died. Satan's nature is to deceive and devour people. Satan, the devil, is the source of darkness, affliction, and death.

So what hope do the Scriptures offer? God's hope is eternity. Ever since God introduced the coming savior by the seed of the woman, believing concerning this savior is the way to eternity. We have seen that Abraham knew about Christ and anticipated his coming. Under

---

15. For more on how swift justice benefits people, see Ecclesiastes 8:11 and Jeremiah 21:12 in appendix A.

the covenant of the law, the sacrifices pointed toward the coming Christ so that all Israel could anticipate his coming. The Scriptures speak of future times when all that have believed concerning Christ will live again. At the time of David's transgression, many people in the line of Christ did not die but were preserved because of God's merciful and quick justice. However, many Israelites did die at that time. God's comfort is to consider eternity. All the Israelites who died while believing concerning the coming Christ will live again at a future time.[16] That is God's eternal perspective. When we keep our eyes on God's eternal realities we can put the weight of death in its proper perspective.

Summary

In this chapter we have considered three unusual expressions. We found that two are literal and one is figurative.

In the opening verses of the two complementary accounts one is figurative and one is literal. I Chronicles 21:1 "Then Satan stood against Israel and incited David to number Israel" is literal. While, II Samuel 24:1 "and he [the Lord] incited David" is figurative. Satan, and not God, is responsible for inciting the numbering of Israel. Ultimately Satan is the one responsible for the many who died that day.

The second literal expression may seem more difficult and occurs in II Samuel 24:15 and I Chronicles 21:14. Together they say, the Lord sent a pestilence on Israel, and 70,000 men of Israel died. This is a tough, tough record. What are we to do? We read the Scriptures

---

16. See Romans 11:26; John 5:23-25 and 28-29; Acts 24:14-15.

with reverence. We ask God to teach us. Therefore, we have faced these difficult verses by honestly considering what the Scriptures say. For God's perspective on these matters ought to be more important to us than our initial reaction or how we feel about these accounts. We search the Scriptures to see God's grace and mercy even when faced with difficult verses. We must hold our minds to the standard of the Scriptures.[17]

In this chapter, Satan's deception caused many to die. God intervened with quick justice and great mercy. God demonstrated His mercy when He instructed David and accepted his offerings. God set up the covenant of the law to include a way for restoration and atonement. Moreover, God worked with David and made a path for the deliverance of many. This does not diminish those who died, for they were precious to God and will one day live again. So as we consider this truly tough record, let us take comfort from the hope of God's eternity.

A New Standard of Justice in Christ

Old Testament believers looked forward to a time when the coming savior would bring a new and better standard of justice.

---

17. For more about God's perspective on David's wrongdoing, see I Kings 15:5: "Because David did that which was right in the eyes of the LORD, and turned not aside from any thing that he commanded him all the days of his life, except in the matter of Uriah the Hittite."

What is interesting in I Kings 15:5 is what they do not say. It does not say "except in the matter of numbering Israel." Once atonement was made, David and all Israel were justified according to the standard of justice of that time. Thus, David was "right in the eyes of the Lord." God did not associate David's actions and the necessary judgment with doing evil—neither should we.

Did God Do It?

> Romans 3:21-23^{WTJ}
>
> ²¹ Now, however, the justice [righteousness] of God without the law has been manifested, being witnessed to by the law and the prophets.
> ²² Yes, the justice of God *is* by the believing of Jesus Christ to all those who believe, for there is no difference.
> ²³ In fact, all have sinned and come short of the glory of God.

The law spoke to those who were under the law, during a time in which there were direct consequences for not keeping all the law and when certain consequences were applicable to the nation of Israel as a whole. However, by Christ's redemptive work justification is not according to keeping all the law but by believing concerning Christ.

> Romans 3:24-25^{WTJ}
>
> ²⁴ Being justified freely by His grace through the redemption that is in Christ Jesus,
> ²⁵ whom God set before Himself *to be* the place of expiation and conciliation [the place of atonement] in his blood through believing. *This He did* with a view to a demonstration of His justice by the passing over of the previously committed sins in the forbearance of God.

In our day, we no longer need to make atonement for sin according to the covenant of the law. Jesus Christ became the place of atonement for us by his shed blood. We are justified freely by God's grace through the redemption that is in Christ Jesus.

8. David

As we continue to consider the Scriptures, we are coming to appreciate all the more how very blessed we are to live during times when the justice of God is no longer according to keeping all the law. As God dealt with mankind in various ways over different time periods, it was always with a view to providing the greatest blessings possible. In our day, we are blessed to live after Christ came and fulfilled God's plan of redemption and salvation for all. Because of Christ's redemptive work, we can now live in a time when the justice of God is according to God's super-abounding grace.

Throughout the Scriptures, God's nature is one of light, love, mercy, grace, long-suffering, goodness, and truth. God's nature does not change. He is the same loving God in the Old Testament as He is in the New Testament.

Did God Do It?

9

II Thessalonians 2 and God's Enduring Mercy

We are considering how faithful, just, merciful, and good our God is throughout the Scriptures. Up to this point in this study, we focused our attention on Old Testament wording that credits action to the just God of the Scriptures. We found some occurrences of seemingly difficult wording to be literal and some to be figurative. Of the records we have considered, the figurative ones were occurrences of a biblical idiom. This biblical idiom *seems* to say God acted toward someone in a manner contrary to God's nature or a person's freedom of will but the context and related passages indicate otherwise.

So a question may arise: does this idiomatic pattern that developed within the biblical culture of Old Testament times occur in the New Testament too? To answer, let us review the following.

> II Peter 1:20-21
>
> [20] Knowing this first of all, that no prophecy of Scripture comes from someone's own interpretation.

> ²¹ For no prophecy [of Scripture] was ever produced by the will of man, but men spoke from God as they were carried along by the Holy Spirit.

The Word of God did not come by the will of men. The prophecy of the Scripture came by the will of God and God is the Author. God, Who is Spirit, told holy men of God what to write and they wrote what God told them to write. These men wrote in a language, vocabulary, and idioms known to them. Biblical Hebrew is primarily the language of the Old Testament and Biblical Greek is primarily the language of the New Testament. However, after the Babylonian captivity, a form of Aramaic became the common spoken language of the Hebrew people, even into New Testament times. Thus Aramaic influences are also seen in the language of the Scriptures. Both Hebrew and Aramaic are Semitic languages and share many similarities.

In the times of the New Testament, Hebrew was primarily used in the Temple writings and was best understood by those who studied those writings. However, "scholars agree that although the New Testament is written in Greek, many of its idioms are Hebraic or Semitic in nature."[1] Regarding New Testament idioms, E. W. Bullinger adds, "The fact must ever be remembered that, while the language of the New Testament is Greek the agents and instruments employed by the Holy Spirit were Hebrew.... While therefore, the words are Greek, the thoughts and idioms are Hebrew."[2]

---

1. Michael D. Marlowe, "New Testament Semitisms" *The Bible Translator Journal* (Sage Publications, April 1988), p. 215-223. See also Julia Hans, *Go Figure! An Introduction to Figures of Speech in the Bible* (Merrimack Media, Cambridge, Massachusetts, 2016, first edition), p. 243-244.

2. E. W. Bullinger, *Figures of Speech Used in the Bible* (Messrs. Eyre and Spottiswoode, London, 1898; and Baker Book House, Grand Rapids, Michigan, 1968), p. 819.

9. II Thessalonians 2 and God's Enduring Mercy

So we conclude that the answer is yes; idioms that arose out of the biblical culture of Old Testament times may also be found in the New Testament.

Review: Acts 16:14

In fact, we saw an occurrence of this idiom in the New Testament in chapter three of this study. Let us take a moment to review.

> Acts 16:10 and 13-14
>
> [10] And when Paul had seen the vision, immediately we [Paul, Silas, and Timothy] sought to go on into Macedonia, concluding that God had called us to preach the gospel to them.
>
> [13] And on the Sabbath day we went outside the gate to the riverside, where we supposed there was a place of prayer, and we sat down and spoke to the women who had come together.
>
> [14] One who heard us was a woman named Lydia, from the city of Thyatira, a seller of purple goods, who was a worshiper of God. The Lord opened her heart to pay attention to what was said by Paul.

God instructed Paul to preach the gospel in Macedonia. Once in Macedonia, Paul spoke the gospel of God to a group of women gathered to pray. Having heard God's Word, Lydia favorably responded to it. The Lord worked in the situation as Paul spoke information that originated from God. Lydia willingly paid attention. The unusual expression, "the Lord opened her heart" is figurative. It is the biblical idiom that seems to say God did something contrary to His nature or a person's free will but the context shows He did not. To understand this idiom with the word "heart," chapter three explored "who is responsible for the heart" from the Scriptures. We saw that:

- In the Scriptures, thoughts, choices, decisions, believing and associated actions are said to come from the heart.
- Each individual is responsible for what goes into and what comes out of his or her heart.
- According to God's original design, people have freedom of will to choose between available sources of information.
- God always allows people to choose which source of information he or she will put into his or her heart. God never oversteps anyone's free will.
- Thus, each person is responsible for his or her own heart and the thoughts, decisions, believing, and actions that come from the heart.

Therefore, expressions that seem to say God made someone's heart do or say something are often figurative and not literal. God did not control Lydia's response to the gospel Paul preached. Lydia freely believed the gospel. The Scriptures idiomatically say "the Lord opened her heart." Thus, this biblical idiom does occur in the New Testament.

9. II Thessalonians 2 and God's Enduring Mercy

An Unusual Expression
With this review, let us consider another unusual expression in the New Testament.

> II Thessalonians 2:11
> Therefore God sends them a strong delusion, so that they may believe what is false.

To read that God will send strong delusion so that some people may believe what is false may be unsettling and may not seem to be in harmony with other scriptures about God's good nature. However, we cannot automatically decide that a negative action credited to God is figurative without first considering the context and the related passages. We must allow the evidence of the Scriptures to determine if this unusual expression is figurative or literal, or if we do not know.

Wider Context
The great subject of the books of Thessalonians is introduced in the first chapter of I Thessalonians.

> I Thessalonians 1:5-10
> ⁵ Because our gospel came to you not only in word, but also in power and in the Holy Spirit and with full conviction. You know what kind of men we proved to be among you for your sake.
> ⁶ And you became imitators of us and of the Lord, for you received the word in much affliction, with the joy of the Holy Spirit,

⁷ so that you became an example to all the believers in Macedonia and in Achaia.

⁸ For not only has the word of the Lord sounded forth from you in Macedonia and Achaia, but your faith [believing] in God has gone forth everywhere, so that we need not say anything.

⁹ For they themselves report concerning us the kind of reception we had among you, and how you turned to God from idols to serve the living and true God,

¹⁰ and to wait for his Son from heaven, whom he raised from the dead, Jesus who delivers us from the wrath to come.

As we have seen before, the "gospel" refers to the gospel of God concerning God's Son, Jesus Christ. Paul and those with him spoke the gospel of God to the Thessalonians. These Thessalonians responded to Paul's preaching of the gospel by turning away from the idols they had been worshipping and instead serving the living and true God. Many Thessalonians received and believed the gospel of God concerning Jesus Christ to the end that they became examples of believing God. Verse ten introduces the great subject of the books of Thessalonians: the coming of God's Son from heaven. Paul taught the Thessalonians about the hope of Christ's return. They were to serve and to wait with the confident expectation that they had been delivered from the wrath to come.

As we see, the books of Thessalonians are primarily speaking to and addressed to people who had believed the gospel of God concerning Jesus Christ. This brings us to an important key in how to understand the Scriptures. Namely, we need to pay attention to whom a passage of Scripture is speaking or addressed. For example, is it speaking to the people of Israel who lived when the covenant of the law was the standard of justice? Is it addressed to people who lived after Christ accomplished God's plan of redemption and salvation? Is it addressed to people who will live at a future time? We need to ask to whom is a verse or a passage applicable. We also want to recognize that there may be verses within a larger passage that are for instruction only and are not directly applicable to the same people to whom the larger passage applies.

Essential Background: Three Terms

II Thessalonians 2:11 says, "God sends them a strong delusion, so that they may believe what is false." To begin to determine whether this unusual expression is figurative or literal, we need to understand three essential terms in its context. These terms relate to the timing of certain events which will then help us determine to whom the expression in II Thessalonians 2:11 is applicable.

> II Thessalonians 2:1-3
> ¹ Now concerning the coming of our Lord Jesus Christ and our being gathered together to him, we ask you, brothers,
> ² not to be quickly shaken in mind or alarmed, either by a spirit or a spoken word, or a letter seeming to be from us, to the effect that the day of the Lord has come.

> ³ Let no one deceive you in any way. For that day will not come, unless the rebellion [Greek: *apostasia*] comes first, and the man of lawlessness is revealed, the son of destruction.

Paul spoke to the brethren concerning the coming of our Lord Jesus Christ and being gathered together to him. Thus the subject of the coming of God's Son from heaven is continued. It is also noteworthy that the brethren's gathering together unto him is associated with the coming of our Lord Jesus Christ.

The purpose of this digression is to understand how the Scriptures use the terms: *apostasia*, the gathering together, and the Day of the Lord. Understanding what the Scriptures say about these three terms will provide necessary background to determine whether the unusual expression is figurative or literal.

First let us consider the Day of the Lord. It is a large topic and we will only consider the barest portion essential to understand the context of the unusual expression in II Thessalonians 2:11.

> Zephaniah 1:14-15
> ¹⁴ ...The sound of the day of the LORD is bitter; the mighty man cries aloud there.
> ¹⁵ A day of wrath is that day, a day of distress and anguish, a day of ruin and devastation, a day of darkness and gloom, a day of clouds and thick darkness.

The Day of the Lord will be a time of wrath, distress, ruin, and darkness.

9. II Thesalonians 2 and God's Enduring Mercy

Isaiah 2:11-12

¹¹ The haughty looks of man shall be brought low, and the lofty pride of men shall be humbled, and the LORD alone will be exalted in that day.

¹² For the LORD of hosts has a day against all that is proud and lofty, against all that is lifted up—and it shall be brought low.

Those who are lifted up with pride and haughtiness against God are some of the people to whom the Day of the Lord is applicable. Isaiah 13 continues about the Day of the Lord.

Isaiah 13:9 and 11

⁹ Behold, the day of the LORD comes...

¹¹ I will punish the world for its evil, and the wicked for their iniquity; I will put an end to the pomp of the arrogant, and lay low the pompous pride of the ruthless.

We again see that the Day of the Lord will be applicable to those who are full of pride and arrogance against God. It will be a time, in the future, when God will put an end to the showy arrogance and pompous pride of wicked and ruthless people.

I Thessalonians 5:2-5

² For you yourselves are fully aware that the day of the Lord will come like a thief in the night.

³ While people are saying, "There is peace and security," then sudden destruction will come upon them as labor pains come upon a pregnant woman, and they will not escape.

> [4] But you are not in darkness, brothers, for that day to surprise you like a thief.
> [5] For you are all children of light, children of the day. We are not of the night or of the darkness.

We noted already that the books of Thessalonians are primarily true of and applicable to those who have believed concerning Jesus Christ but that portions may be for instruction and not applicable to them. According to verses 4 and 5, the information about the Day of the Lord is not applicable to the brethren who are children of light.

In I Thessalonians 5, we see that the Day of the Lord will come stealthily unannounced similar to a thief in the night. When it does come some people will still say, "peace and security" to assert that all is well; however, the destruction of the Day of the Lord will be inescapable for those to whom it applies. According to Isaiah 2 and 13 this destruction will be applicable to wicked, ruthless, prideful, and arrogant people. The Day of the Lord will be characterized by sudden destruction, darkness, distress, and ruin.

Let us continue in I Thessalonians 5 about the children of light and of the day.

> I Thessalonians 5:8-9
> [8] But since we belong to the day, let us be sober, having put on the breastplate of faith and love, and for a helmet the hope of salvation.
> [9] For God has not destined us for wrath, but to obtain salvation through our Lord Jesus Christ.

9. II Thessalonians 2 and God's Enduring Mercy

The children of light and of the day are people who have obtained salvation by our Lord Jesus Christ. The requirement to obtain salvation is expressed in Romans 10:9, "if you confess with your mouth that Jesus is Lord and believe in your heart that God raised him from the dead, you will be saved." Salvation by believing concerning Jesus Christ delivers a person from the wrath associated with the future times of the Day of the Lord. What else do the Scriptures tell us about this exclusion from the Day of the Lord?

> Romans 5:9-10
> ⁹ Since, therefore, we have now been justified by his blood, much more shall we be saved by him from the wrath of God.
> ¹⁰ For if while we were enemies we were reconciled to God by the death of his Son, much more, now that we are reconciled, shall we be saved [from wrath] by his life.

Through the redemptive work of Jesus Christ all who have believed concerning him have been justified, reconciled, and saved from the future wrath of the Day of the Lord.

Together these verses assure us that the wrath and destruction of the Day of the Lord are absolutely not applicable to anyone who obtains salvation by believing concerning Jesus Christ. The Day of the Lord is a future time period that will be applicable to people who are wicked and ruthless, and are prideful and arrogant toward God.

We are considering three terms to better understand the unusual expression about God's actions in II Thessalonians 2:11. Next, we will consider what the Scriptures say regarding the gathering

Did God Do It?

together. According to II Thessalonians 2:1, the gathering together is associated with the coming of God's Son from heaven. This coming is detailed in I Thessalonians 4 and is speaking of those who have believed concerning Christ.

> I Thessalonians 4:14-18
>
> [14] For since we believe that Jesus died and rose again, even so, through Jesus, God will bring with him those who have fallen asleep.
>
> [15] For this we declare to you by a word from the Lord, that we who are alive, who are left until the coming of the Lord, will not precede those who have fallen asleep.
>
> [16] For the Lord [Jesus Christ] himself will descend from heaven with a cry of command [cry of summons[AMP]], with the voice of an archangel, and with the sound of the trumpet of God. And the dead in Christ will rise first.
>
> [17] Then we who are alive, who are left, will be caught up together with them in the clouds to meet the Lord in the air, and so we will always be with the Lord.
>
> [18] Therefore encourage one another with these words.

A comparison is made in verse 14. We have seen that salvation is obtained when a person believes that God raised Jesus from the dead. Since we believe and have obtained the result of salvation, we can confidently believe that God will raise the dead in Christ. In fact, the dead in Christ will be raised from the dead first. Then both the previously dead in Christ and the alive in Christ will be caught up together into the clouds to meet the lord in the air. This being caught

9. II Thessalonians 2 and God's Enduring Mercy

up together into heaven is what II Thessalonians 2:1 calls the gathering together. The coming of Christ to gather the brethren was future at the time Thessalonians was written and it is still future today.

When the gathering together does occur, Christ will descend from heaven to gather the brethren. At that time, three joyful sounds will signal his arrival: a cry of summons, the voice of an archangel, and the trumpet of God. Verse 18 exhorts the brethren to encourage one another by speaking words that anticipate the gathering together. Once Christ gathers all who have believed concerning Christ (the dead and the alive at the time), they will no longer be on the earth but will be forever with the lord.

The final term that needs to be clarified is the Greek word, *apostasia* as seen in II Thessalonians 2:3: "For that day [the Day of the Lord] will not come, unless the rebellion [*apostasia*] comes first." This Greek word is rendered in the following ways: a falling away,[KJV and YLT] apostasy,[NASB] a rebellion,[ESV and NIV] the departure.[WTJ]

The Liddell and Scott Greek Lexicon defines *apostasia* first as "defection, revolt" and secondly as "departure, disappearance."[3] The question is, which rendering best fits the context?

We already saw that the coming of Christ is the overall theme of the books of Thessalonians. The closer context in II Thessalonians 2:1 speaks of the part of the coming of Christ called the gathering together. I Thessalonians 4 describes the gathering together as a time when both the dead in Christ and the alive in Christ will be snatched up together to depart from the earth and meet the lord in the air.

---

3. Henry George Liddell and Henry Scott, *A Greek-English Lexicon*, revised with a supplement (1968) by Sir Henry Stuart Jones and Roderick McKenzie (Oxford University Press; Oxford, England, 1940), p. 218.

Next, let us consider a related word form, which occurs three times in the Gospels (Matthew 5:31; 19:7; and Mark 10:4).[4] In each occurence, the related word is used in the sense of to let loose from a legal obligation. Each of the occurrences of this related word has to do with a divorce situation that required the wife be put away to the end that she departed.

The context of II Thessalonians 2:2 Paul asked the Thessalonians to not be soon shaken in mind or be alarmed. Rendering this word as "apostasy" or "rebellion," offers very little encouragement to help the Thessalonians not be alarmed. If this word is rendered "departure" or "disappearance" (according to the second definition of Liddell and Scott), the Thessalonians could have been very encouraged. Why so? Reminding the Thessalonians that they would have departed from the earth before the time of the distress, darkness, and destruction of the Day of the Lord would indeed be encouraging. The Scriptures say that those who have believed concerning Christ will not be present at the time of the Day of the Lord; they absolutely will be saved from the wrath to come. Therefore, encouragement that aligned with these truths more appropriately fits the wider context.

So far, we see that rendering *apostasia* as "departure" would fit both the wider and closer context as well as the usage of the related Greek word. Lastly, in our consideration of how to render the Greek word, *apostasia,* let us consider *who* the Scriptures says will

---

4. Matthew 5:31: "It was also said, 'Whoever divorces his wife, let him give her a certificate of divorce [Greek: *apostasion*].'" Matthew 19:7: "They said to him, 'Why then did Moses command one to give a certificate of divorce [Greek: *apostasion*] and to send her away?'" Mark 10:4: "They said, 'Moses allowed a man to write a certificate of divorce [Greek: *apostasion*] and to send her away.'"

9. II Thessalonians 2 and God's Enduring Mercy

determine the timing of the gathering together. We will start with a verse we saw earlier.

> I Thessalonians 4:14
>
> For since we believe that Jesus died and rose again, even so, through Jesus, God will bring with him those who have fallen asleep.

The context of I Thessalonians 4 says that both those who are asleep and those alive in Christ will be caught up together by Jesus Christ to meet the lord in the air. God is the One Who raised Jesus Christ from the dead. It will be God, by means of Jesus Christ, Who will bring with him the dead in Christ at the time of the gathering together.

> I Corinthians 6:14-15
>
> [14] And God raised the Lord and will also raise us up by his power.
> [15] Do you not know that your bodies are members of Christ?...

It is by God's power that the dead are raised. The raising of the dead in Christ at the time of the gathering together will be according to God's power. This truth again shows that "departure" is a more apt translation than "rebellion." That which comes before the man of lawlessness and the Day of the Lord will not come to pass based on rebellion by people but this shift will be according to God's power and determination.

The departure of those who believe concerning Christ will come *before* the man of lawlessness is revealed and before the Day of the

Lord. All who are justified by Christ's redemptive work are saved from the wrath of the Day of the Lord. The manner in which God will save people from the wrath to come is by sending Christ to gather them together into the clouds to meet the lord in the air. They will have departed from the earth before the events of the Day of the Lord begin. So we see that "departure" fits with many clear scriptures about the same event. By considering these terms: *apostasia*, the gathering together, and the Day of the Lord, we have a better understanding of the timing of events in the context of II Thessalonians.

The Context

We are now ready to reread the opening verses of the context of the unusual expression. As we do so we bring with us a better understanding of the Day of the Lord, the gathering together, and the *apostasia*, which we have seen is best rendered, the departure.

> II Thessalonians 2:1-3
> ¹ Now concerning the coming of our Lord Jesus Christ and our being gathered together to him, we ask you, brothers,
> ² not to be quickly shaken in mind or alarmed, either by a spirit or a spoken word, or a letter seeming to be from us, to the effect that the day of the Lord has come.
> ³ Let no one deceive you in any way. For that day will not come, unless the rebellion [departure] comes first, and the man of lawlessness is revealed, the son of destruction.

9. II Thessalonians 2 and God's Enduring Mercy

Apparently at the time of the writing of II Thessalonians, certain people were saying that the Day of the Lord was presently occurring rather than still future. However, verse 3 informs us that the man of lawlessness will not be revealed until *after* the gathering together occurs. Since the gathering together had not yet happened then neither had the events that come after it. However, having briefly looked at the Day of the Lord, we can understand how claims saying the Day of the Lord had arrived would cause the listeners to be shaken in mind or alarmed. Therefore, Paul reassured the Thessalonian believers that first they would depart from the earth in the gathering together, they would be forever with the lord, safely removed from the man of lawlessness. With these words, Paul exhorted the Thessalonian believers to not be shaken in mind, alarmed, or deceived by such false information even if that information seemed to come from Paul himself.

> II Thessalonians 2:3-6
>
> ³ ...And the man of lawlessness is revealed, the son of destruction,
>
> ⁴ who opposes and exalts himself against every so-called god or object of worship, so that he takes his seat in the temple of God, proclaiming himself to be God.
>
> ⁵ Do you not remember that when I was still with you I told you these things?
>
> ⁶ And you know what is restraining him [the man of lawlessness] [from being revealed] now so that he may be revealed in his time.

Verse 3 says, "and the man of lawlessness is revealed." Verse 6 adds that the man of lawlessness will be revealed when what is restraining him is removed. There is an ellipsis in verse 6 that legitimately adds the words "from being revealed." Doing so, helps the reader see that when whatever is restraining the man of lawlessness is removed, then he will be revealed.

> II Thessalonians 2:7-9
>
> [7] For the mystery of lawlessness is already at work. Only he who now restrains it will do so until he is out of the way.
>
> [8] And then the lawless one will be revealed, whom the Lord Jesus will kill with the breath of his mouth and bring to nothing by the appearance of his coming.
>
> [9] The coming of the lawless one is by the activity of Satan with all power and false signs and wonders.

The destruction, the opposition to God, the efforts to steal worship due to God, the lawlessness, and the deception as seen in these verses are each associated with the Day of the Lord and the coming wrath. The ellipsis highlights that something is holding back the man of lawlessness from being revealed but that when the restraint is removed he will be revealed. God, not man or the man of lawlessness, will determine when the restraint will be removed; it will be according to God's determination and God's power. Until then, the revealing of the man of lawlessness and the Day of the Lord are held back—they are still future, and they will not occur until those who have believed concerning Christ depart to be with the lord in the air.

9. II Thessalonians 2 and God's Enduring Mercy

In the upcoming verses, the word "delusion" is used in the sense of "a seduction from the truth."[5]

> II Thessalonians 2:9-12
>
> [9] The coming of the lawless one is by the activity of Satan with all power and false signs and wonders,
>
> [10] and with all wicked deception for those who are perishing, because they refused to love the truth and so be saved.
>
> [11] Therefore God sends them a strong delusion, so that they may believe what is false,
>
> [12] in order that all may be condemned [judged] who did not believe the truth but had pleasure in unrighteousness.

Verse 11 seems to assign an action to God that appears contrary to His nature and contrary to a person's freedom of will. To understand this unusual expression, let us consider what these scriptures tell us about those who will be deluded. Verse 10 describes these future people as ones who will be wickedly deceived because they refused to accept the love of the truth. Contextually the truth is the gospel of God concerning His Son Jesus Christ. For these future people to reject the Word of truth, it must be available. Verse 12 describes these future people as the ones who will not believe the truth. The Greek word rendered "condemned" means "to judge." In

---

5. E. W. Bullinger, *A Critical Lexicon and Concordance to the English and Greek New Testament* (Longmans, Green and Company, London, 1895). Offered in the e-lexicon on Parallel Plus by TheBible.org ©2017. "Delusion" is the Greek word *plane*, the root of the English word planet. Its basic meaning is wandering. In the Scriptures it is used of being led astray from the truth.

the context, the judgment is based on those people's choices. This judgement of people is not based on an arbitrary standard. It is based on decisions that each person will make.

Review

Let us review what we know from the surrounding context of the unusual expression.

- The future lawless one will be one who opposes God, is the son of destruction, and exalts himself to steal worship due only to the Most High God (vv. 3-4).
- The future coming of the lawless one will be according to the activity of Satan (vv. 8-9).
- The activity of Satan will include: power, false signs, lying wonders, and all sorts of wicked and unjust deception (vv. 9-10).
- Those who will be deluded are ones who will refuse to accept the love of the truth and will not believe the truth (vv. 10-12).

Earlier in this chapter we reviewed who is responsible for the heart and the believing that comes from the heart and saw that each individual is responsible for his or her own heart and believing. Thus, these future people will be responsible for their decisions and believing. God will offer His Word but they will refuse to accept and believe. In addition, these people will be wickedly deceived. God does not and will not deceive people, nor will He in any way control what a person believes. On the other hand, Satan or the devil does and will deceptively blind people's eyes from the truth.[6] Satan's nature is

6. See also II Corinthians 4:4 and Luke 8:12.

9. II Thessalonians 2 and God's Enduring Mercy

unjust. Because he is unjust, Satan will deceive people to believe false information that leads to bondage and death. The context and the opposing nature of God and Satan show that at that future time of II Thessalonians 2, Satan will be the source of the deception and not God. Satan will send strong delusion so that some future people will believe what is false.

Summary

This chapter considered the unusual expression, "God sends them a strong delusion, so that they may believe what is false." The context and related scriptures show that the unusual words are not true to fact. The unusual expression is not literal but is figurative. The expression, "God sends them a strong delusion, so that they may believe what is false" is an example of a biblical idiom. Let us review what we have previously seen about this particular biblical idiom:

- This particular biblical idiom *seems* to say God did something contrary to His nature or a person's freedom of will but according to the context and related scriptures He did not.
- The unusual expression is not true to fact; it is an idiomatic active-verb expression with the pattern of "the Lord God + action + recipient."
- When the unusual expression contains the word "heart" and seems to say God made someone's heart do or believe something, the expression is usually figurative and not literal.

- By naming God, this idiom does not focus on people and their freewill choices but does focus on God Who is Lord overall.
- According to the God-centered culture of Old Testament times, the devil was not named. In their culture, this idiom was not intended to blame God, nor did this idiom mean that He did evil. Instead, they magnified Him in the face of affliction.

Furthermore the context and related scriptures of this idiom often, but not always, show the following:
- Who, other than God, was responsible for the action credited to God.
- The spiritual causes behind the physical.
- That someone had information from God that he or she did not believe.

These future people could receive the Word of the Lord available at that time. They could be saved and delivered. However, these future people's response to the Word of the Lord will be to not receive nor believe the truth.

Thus we have seen that the unusual expression in II Thessalonians 2:11 is not literal but is an occurrence of the biblical idiom. It is an idiom that arose out of the biblical culture of Old Testament times. This idiomatic expression was still used by men who wrote words from God in the New Testament writings.

So we see that, although the books of Thessalonians are primarily addressed to and speak to the Thessalonian believers, these portions of II Thessalonians about the lawless one and the Day of the Lord do not apply to, nor are they true of *anyone* who believes concerning Christ.

God's Enduring Mercy

God is good throughout the Scriptures, even in future times.

> Psalm 86:5
>
> For you, O Lord, are good and forgiving, abounding in steadfast love [mercy[KJV]] to all who call upon you.

God's steadfast love, which includes His mercy, is abounding to all who call upon Him. Joel 2 adds to our understanding of those who will call on Him during the times of the Day of the Lord.

> Joel 2:31-32
>
> [31] The sun shall be turned to darkness, and the moon to blood, before the great and awesome day of the LORD comes.
>
> [32] And it shall come to pass that everyone who calls on the name of the LORD shall be saved....

In the future period of time called the Day of the Lord, all who call on the name of the Lord will be saved. We saw that the requirement for salvation in the grace administration is expressed in Romans 10:9, "if you confess with your mouth that Jesus is Lord and believe in your heart that God raised him from the dead, you will be saved." In the future time of the Day of the Lord, believing concerning the Lord Jesus Christ will still be a requirement for salvation. What wonderful truth these verses uncover: even in that future time of darkness and destruction God will continue to offer His Word so that people still on the earth might believe concerning Jesus Christ and be saved. This truth demonstrates God's nature of grace and mercy toward all people even in the future times of the Day of the Lord.

10

Nehemiah 9 and God's Great Mercy

We are considering scriptures in which God introduced His light into dark situations and brought deliverance to people. Each record that we have looked at contains a potentially difficult expression that appears to credit God with seemingly negative actions. We found some to be literal while others were occurrences of a biblical idiom. This biblical idiom *seems* to say God did something contrary to His nature or a person's free will but the context and related scriptures show that He did not. In each passage, whether figurative or literal, God acted true to His nature—He was just, loving, merciful, good, and faithful to His Word.

Nehemiah 9

At the beginning of the book of Nehemiah, Israel had been in captivity for over seventy years. Then a remnant of survivors was granted permission to return to Jerusalem to rebuild the wall. In Nehemiah 9, the people gathered to pray and to recommit themselves to God. Their prayer honors God's power and mercy on behalf of Israel. It also recounts God and Israel's relationship over the years before captivity.

> Nehemiah 9:7-8
>
> ⁷ You are the Lord, the God who chose Abram and brought him out of Ur of the Chaldeans and gave him the name Abraham.
>
> ⁸ You found his heart faithful before you, and made with him the covenant to give to his offspring the land of the Canaanite, the Hittite, the Amorite, the Perizzite, the Jebusite, and the Girgashite. And you have kept your promise, for you are righteous [just].

God gave many promises to Abraham; those promises pertained to and rested on the pivotal promise that Christ would come from Abraham's offspring.[1] Building upon His covenant with Abraham, God made another covenant with the nation of Israel. This covenant included that they would be His people and He would be their God.[2] When they kept God's statutes and commandments the people of Israel were counted just.[3] God initiated these covenant agreements so He could better help and care for His people. God's covenant with Abraham, and then with the nation of Israel, was a stepping stone toward God's redemptive work in Christ.

> Nehemiah 9:9-15
>
> ⁹ And you saw the affliction of our fathers in Egypt and heard their cry at the Red Sea,

---

1. Galatians 3:16: "Now the promises were made to Abraham and to his offspring. It does not say, 'and to offsprings,' referring to many, but referring to one, 'and to your offspring,' who is Christ."

2. See Leviticus 11:45; 22:31-33; 25:38; 26:11-12; and Jeremiah 11:4.

3. Deuteronomy 6:25: "And it will be righteousness [justness] for us, if we are careful to do all this commandment before the Lord our God, as he has commanded us."

10. Nehemiah 9 and God's Great Mercy

¹⁰ and performed signs and wonders against Pharaoh and all his servants and all the people of his land, for you knew that they acted arrogantly against our fathers. And you made a name for yourself, as it is to this day.

¹¹ And you divided the sea before them, so that they went through the midst of the sea on dry land, and you cast their pursuers into the depths, as a stone into mighty waters.

¹² By a pillar of cloud you led them in the day, and by a pillar of fire in the night to light for them the way in which they should go.

¹³ You came down on Mount Sinai and spoke with them from heaven and gave them right rules and true laws, good statutes and commandments,

¹⁴ and you made known to them your holy Sabbath and commanded them commandments and statutes and a law by Moses your servant.

¹⁵ You gave them bread from heaven for their hunger and brought water for them out of the rock for their thirst, and you told them to go in to possess the land that you had sworn to give them.

At Sinai, God and Israel formalized their covenant relationship, out of which came the Mosaic Law. Keeping all God's commandments in the covenant of the law was for the good of the people always. God lovingly informed them of the blessings they would receive for doing all the law. He also told them the consequences they could avoid if they kept their covenant agreement. In each situation, God was faithful to what He said He would do. He was good to the people of Israel. He led them, taught them, and gave them many good things.

> Nehemiah 9:16-19
>
> [16] But they and our fathers acted presumptuously and stiffened their neck and did not obey your commandments.
>
> [17] They refused to obey and were not mindful of the wonders that you performed among them, but they stiffened their neck and appointed a leader to return to their slavery in Egypt. But you are a God ready to forgive, gracious and merciful, slow to anger and abounding in steadfast love, and did not forsake them.
>
> [18] Even when they had made for themselves a golden calf and said, "This is your God who brought you up out of Egypt," and had committed great blasphemies,
>
> [19] you in your great mercies did not forsake them in the wilderness. The pillar of cloud to lead them in the way did not depart from them by day, nor the pillar of fire by night to light for them the way by which they should go.

In return for God's goodness and help, the people of Israel refused to obey God and rebelled against Him. Even so, God was still gracious, full of mercy, and kind. God's mercies were numerous and great. He never forsook His people. God provided light and guidance for them as He led them with the pillar of cloud by day, and the pillar

10. Nehemiah 9 and God's Great Mercy

of fire by night. He consistently provided for them in ways that He could, without overstepping their free will. God was ready to forgive them and did not forsake them. Being ready to forgive is part of God's nature. Psalm 103:10 adds that "He does not deal with us according to our sins, nor repay us according to our iniquities." Although they forsook Him many times and in many ways, He did not repay them according to their iniquities. He withheld what they deserved and instead was gracious, merciful, and abounding in steadfast love.

> Nehemiah 9:20-25
>
> [20] You gave your good Spirit to instruct them and did not withhold your manna from their mouth and gave them water for their thirst.
>
> [21] Forty years you sustained them in the wilderness, and they lacked nothing. Their clothes did not wear out and their feet did not swell.
>
> [22] And you gave them kingdoms and peoples and allotted to them every corner. So they took possession of the land of Sihon king of Heshbon and the land of Og king of Bashan.
>
> [23] You multiplied their children as the stars of heaven, and you brought them into the land that you had told their fathers to enter and possess.
>
> [24] So the descendants went in and possessed the land, and you subdued before them the inhabitants of the land, the Canaanites, and gave them into their hand,

Did God Do It?

> with their kings and the peoples of the land, that they might do with them as they would.
>
> ²⁵ And they captured fortified cities and a rich land, and took possession of houses full of all good things, cisterns already hewn, vineyards, olive orchards and fruit trees in abundance. So they ate and were filled and became fat [well nourished] and delighted themselves in your great goodness.

God fed, clothed, and prospered the descendants of Abraham as He had promised. He gave into their hands well-provisioned land and homes. The people became well-nourished with all the abundant goodness God provided. Yet the people of Israel did not remain faithful to God and their covenant agreement.

> Nehemiah 9:26-28
>
> ²⁶ Nevertheless, they were disobedient and rebelled against you and cast your law behind their back and killed your prophets, who had warned them in order to turn them back to you, and they committed great blasphemies.
>
> ²⁷ Therefore you gave them into the hand of their enemies, who made them suffer. And in the time of their suffering they cried out to you and you heard them from heaven, and according to your great mercies you gave them saviors who saved them from the hand of their enemies.

10. Nehemiah 9 and God's Great Mercy

> ²⁸ But after they had rest they did evil again before you, and you abandoned them to the hand of their enemies, so that they had dominion over them. Yet when they turned and cried to you, you heard from heaven, and many times you delivered them according to your mercies.

God graciously sent prophets who warned the people of Israel of impending troubles. The prophets spoke information that originated with God. However, the people responded by killing the prophets. God wanted to bless His people but they continued to disobey and rebel. They continued to turn their backs on God and His Word. When trouble arose yet again and the people of Israel did return to God, almost unbelievably, He was ready to forgive. God once again would deliver them not according to their iniquities but according to His very great mercies.

> Nehemiah 9:29-31
>
> ²⁹ And you warned them in order to turn them back to your law. Yet they acted presumptuously and did not obey your commandments, but sinned against your rules, which if a person does them, he shall live by them, and they turned a stubborn shoulder and stiffened their neck and would not obey.
> ³⁰ Many years you bore with them and warned them by your Spirit through your prophets. Yet they would not give ear. Therefore you gave them into the hand of the peoples of the lands.

> ³¹ Nevertheless, in your great mercies you did not make an end of them or forsake them, for you are a gracious and merciful God.

For many years, God sent prophets who spoke what He gave them to speak. In this manner, God repeatedly gave timely warnings with a view toward restoration and deliverance. He instructed His people in hopes that they might return to and benefit from His Word. Though God had their best interests in mind, the people would not and did not listen. They continued to make choices that led them farther away from God's blessings. Amazingly, because of His great mercies, God did not forsake them. Instead, He was gracious and merciful.

Nehemiah 9:32-33

> ³² Now, therefore, our God, the great, the mighty, and the awesome God, who keeps covenant and steadfast love, let not all the hardship seem little to you that has come upon us, upon our kings, our princes, our priests, our prophets, our fathers, and all your people, since the time of the kings of Assyria until this day.
> ³³ Yet you have been righteous in all that has come upon us, for you have dealt faithfully and we have acted wickedly.

These Israelites (who had returned from captivity) prayed and affirmed that God is great, mighty, and awesome! They acknowledged that even when they behaved wickedly, God always behaved rightly. God had always kept His covenant agreement with Israel but the people had not. Thus the Israelites declared that in all that came upon them, God was always righteous and just.

Three Unusual Expressions

In this passage from Nehemiah 9, we saw three expressions similar to each other and similar to ones throughout this study. Each of the following expressions seems to say that God did something to the people of Israel that may appear contrary to His nature. They are:
- He gave them into the hand of their enemies (vs. 27).
- He abandoned them to the hand of their enemies (vs. 28).
- He gave them into the hand of the peoples of the lands (vs. 30).

We have already considered these expressions in their context, so we will next consider some related scriptures.

Related Scriptures

The prophet Jeremiah gave insight into why God's people were in the hand of their enemies.

> Jeremiah 2:13-14, 17-19
>
> [13] For my people have committed two evils: they have forsaken me, the fountain of living waters, and hewed out cisterns for themselves, broken cisterns that can hold no water.

Did God Do It?

> ¹⁴ Is Israel a slave? Is he a homeborn servant? Why then has he become a prey?
>
> ¹⁷ Have you not brought this upon yourself by forsaking the LORD your God, when he led you in the way?
>
> ¹⁸ And now what do you gain by going to Egypt to drink the waters of the Nile? Or what do you gain by going to Assyria to drink the waters of the Euphrates?
>
> ¹⁹ Your evil will chastise you, and your apostasy [abandonment of God] will reprove you. Know and see that it is evil and bitter for you to forsake the LORD your God; the fear [reverence] of me is not in you, declares the Lord GOD of hosts.

During the time of Jeremiah, God's people had gone into captivity because they had forsaken God. God led them in the way that would lead to blessings and success. However, they abandoned God and brought captivity upon themselves.

Ezra has another related passage.[4]

> Ezra 9:7
>
> From the days of our fathers to this day we have been in great guilt. And for our iniquities we, our kings, and our priests have been given into the hand of the kings of the lands, to the sword, to captivity, to plundering, and to utter shame, as it is today.

Ezra adds that the people, their kings, and the priests went into captivity due to their own iniquities. The same was also true in each

---

4. See also Ezekiel 39:23 "…the house of Israel went into captivity for their iniquity…."

10. Nehemiah 9 and God's Great Mercy

situation referenced by the three expressions in Nehemiah 9 that say God delivered or gave His people into the enemies' hands. The reason Israel became a slave and prey to enemies was that they had forsaken the Lord God. Jeremiah 2:17 enlightens with a question, "Have you not brought this upon yourself by forsaking the LORD your God, when he led you in the way?"

Summary: Figurative, Literal, or We Do Not Know

This chapter handles three expressions that *seem* to say God did something contrary to His nature or a person's freedom of will. They are:

- He gave them into the hand of their enemies (vs. 27).
- He abandoned them to the hand of their enemies (vs. 28).
- He gave them into the hand of the peoples of the lands (vs. 30).

At the end of the historical books of Kings and Chronicles, Israel and Judah had repeatedly forsook God. Their abandonment of God resulted in them being taken captive. As Israel and Judah fell into captivity, expressions that say God gave His people to their enemies occur frequently. Therefore, these kind of expressions are often seen in the latter half of the Old Testament.

So the question for the purpose of this study is: Are these expressions in Nehemiah 9 figurative or literal, or do we not know? For these three occurrences in Nehemiah 9, one could make the case that these unusual expressions are literal, that God literally gave the people into the hand of their enemies. One could also make the case that these expressions are figurative, that they idiomatically show the spiritual cause as the rejection of God and His Word. At this time, neither seems certain from the Scriptures. Therefore, at this point we simply do not know. So we let it sit until we have learned more.

In the latter half of the Old Testament, there are many similar expressions regarding Israel's captivity. Some such expressions may be literal and some may be figurative. The context and related passages of each occurrence need to be carefully considered and evaluated on a case-by-case basis.

To further consider these types of expressions regarding Israel's captivity, one might ask: Did God physically give the people into the hand of their enemies or do these expressions idiomatically show the spiritual cause as the rejection of God and His Word?

For the three expressions in Nehemiah 9, we do not have enough Scriptural evidence at this time to determine whether they are figurative or literal, or a mix of the two. Therefore, we are choosing not to guess and instead to say that we do not know.

Even so, let us keep in mind what we learned from this passage in Nehemiah 9. The people of Israel faced situations that resulted out of their own choices. God always respects people's freedom of will. God gave His Word to Israel. He admonished them many times with right instruction that they might return to and benefit from His Word. He warned them what would happen if they turned their back on Him and went after other gods. It was not God's primary desire that an enemy would capture His people; their capture was a consequence that they brought upon themselves. Although it may seem desirable, God would not and did not overstep anyone's freedom of will to ensure that people would accept His goodness. God always allows people to choose which source of information they believe.

So although at this time we are not certain if these expressions in Nehemiah 9 are literal or figurative, we are certain that God's involvement was righteous. That is to say, God was just in all that He did.

At times, we might not understand an unusual expression in a particular record enough to determine if statements about God's actions are literal or figurative. Sometimes we simply do not know and that's okay. We can set such a passage aside for the time being and continue in the Scriptures. When not sure about an unusual expression in the Scriptures, let us not guess. When we do not know, let us put it aside for a season. Let us continue to read and be thankful for the wonderful truths we do understand from the Scriptures.

Our Faithful and Merciful God

In these closing notes, let us review a few verses from Nehemiah 9.

> Nehemiah 9:8
> You found his heart faithful before you, and made with him the covenant to give to his offspring the land of the Canaanite, the Hittite, the Amorite, the Perizzite, the Jebusite, and the Girgashite. And you have kept your promise, for you are righteous.

God was faithful to His promise regarding the coming savior and to His covenant with Israel. God consistently and reliably performs His Word. He is true to His Word and to His nature throughout the Scriptures.

> Nehemiah 9:17
> …But you are a God ready to forgive, gracious and merciful, slow to anger and abounding in steadfast love, and did not forsake them.

According to God's great mercies, He did not forsake the people of Israel in the wilderness as they left Egypt, nor did He forsake them as they faced enemies. God's mercies were multiplied, numerous, and great.

> Nehemiah 9:32-33
> [32] Now, therefore, our God, the great, the mighty, and the awesome God, who keeps covenant and steadfast love, let not all the hardship seem little to you that has come upon us, upon our kings, our princes, our priests, our prophets, our fathers, and all your people, since the time of the kings of Assyria until this day.
> [33] Yet you have been righteous [just] in all that has come upon us, for you have dealt faithfully and we have acted wickedly.

In Nehemiah 9, we saw that whenever the people of Israel chose to forsake God, He was ready to pardon and forgive. He did not forsake them. God was mighty and awesome on behalf of His people; He is just. The Lord God delivered His people from many dark situations according to His very great mercies.

11

No Wrongdoing and What It Is not

In each of the previous chapters we have seen abounding evidence that God is good, merciful, just, equitable, compassionate, and loving in all that He does. Each record that we have looked at contained a potentially difficult expression that appears to credit God with seemingly negative actions. In some of the records, the context and related passages show that the contradictory wording was not true to fact but was an occurrence of a biblical idiom. In other records, God executed necessary judgment according to the standard of justice of that time. In each of these literal records, the context and related passages showed that God was just and merciful as He administered necessary judgment.

In most of the records that we have considered so far, the context showed that God gave information that could have led to deliverance. Regrettably, in most of the previous records, information from God was ignored and consequences followed. Noting this context is useful to identify certain unusual expressions in the Scriptures. However, this characteristic is not generally applicable to everyday life. We ought never think that every affliction in life is because somebody did something wrong. This study is not making a general statement about choices and consequences in life. Instead, this study is identifying a particular pattern of words in the Scriptures. To that end, this chapter will look at expressions that are similar to previous chapters, however with some significant differences in the context.

Background

Let us recall that God had placed Adam and Eve in a very good environment. However, Adam's sin caused several losses including the loss of the very good environment that God spoke into being. The very good environment God intended for man became corrupted. This corrupt environment hinders people's physical bodies. Moreover, because of Adam's actions, sin, death, and condemnation came into the world and spread to all people. John 10:10 adds that the devil comes to steal, kill, and to destroy; he holds the power of death.[1] The devil's ways bring death and bondage; he is an enemy of all that is just and right. The devil (or Satan, the god of this world, or whatever name he goes by) is the reason darkness, death, and afflictions are in the world.

On the other hand, many clear scriptures affirm that God is good, just, light, and full of steadfast love. God's ways bring life and deliverance to people. His goodness is abundant and available to all, especially to those who seek Him.

Naomi and Ruth

The book of Ruth begins by telling us there was a famine in the land of Judah. The very good environment in which God placed Adam

---

1. See Hebrews 2:14. In John 10:10, the devil is figuratively called the thief.

11. No Wrongdoing and What It Is Not

and Eve did not include famines.

> Ruth 1:1-5
>
> ¹ In the days when the judges ruled there was a famine in the land, and a man of Bethlehem in Judah went to sojourn in the country of Moab, he and his wife and his two sons.
>
> ² The name of the man was Elimelech and the name of his wife Naomi, and the names of his two sons were Mahlon and Chilion. They were Ephrathites from Bethlehem in Judah. They went into the country of Moab and remained there.
>
> ³ But Elimelech, the husband of Naomi, died, and she was left with her two sons.
>
> ⁴ These took Moabite wives; the name of the one was Orpah and the name of the other Ruth. They lived there about ten years,
>
> ⁵ and both Mahlon and Chilion died, so that the woman was left without her two sons and her husband.

We have not read anything in these verses that indicate that Naomi, her husband, nor her sons did anything wrong to bring about their deaths. God did not cause the famine nor was He responsible for the deaths.

> Ruth 1:6-19
>
> ⁶ Then she arose with her daughters-in-law to return from the country of Moab, for she had heard in the fields of Moab that the LORD had visited his people and

Did God Do It?

given them food.

⁷ So she set out from the place where she was with her two daughters-in-law, and they went on the way to return to the land of Judah.

⁸ But Naomi said to her two daughters-in-law, "Go, return each of you to her mother's house. May the LORD deal kindly with you, as you have dealt with the dead and with me.

⁹ The LORD grant that you may find rest, each of you in the house of her husband!" Then she kissed them, and they lifted up their voices and wept.

¹⁰ And they said to her, "No, we will return with you to your people."

¹¹ But Naomi said, "Turn back, my daughters; why will you go with me? Have I yet sons in my womb that they may become your husbands?

¹² Turn back, my daughters; go your way, for I am too old to have a husband. If I should say I have hope, even if I should have a husband this night and should bear sons,

¹³ would you therefore wait till they were grown? Would you therefore refrain from marrying? No, my daughters, for it is exceedingly bitter to me for your sake that <u>the hand of the LORD has gone out against me</u>."[2]

¹⁴ Then they lifted up their voices and wept again. And Orpah kissed her mother-in-law, but Ruth clung to her.

---

2. Underlining added to point out the unusual expressions being considered.

11. No Wrongdoing and What It Is Not

¹⁵ And she said, "See, your sister-in-law has gone back to her people and to her gods; return after your sister-in-law."
¹⁶ But Ruth said, "Do not urge me to leave you or to return from following you. For where you go I will go, and where you lodge I will lodge. Your people shall be my people, and your God my God.
¹⁷ Where you die I will die, and there will I be buried. May the LORD do so to me and more also if anything but death parts me from you."
¹⁸ And when Naomi saw that she was determined to go with her, she said no more.
¹⁹ So the two of them went on until they came to Bethlehem....

When Naomi heard that there was no longer a famine in Judah she determined to return home. But what was she to do with her two daughters-in-law who still resided with her? She selflessly told them to return to their families. Naomi encouraged them in the Lord saying, "The Lord deal kindly with you...the Lord grant that you may find rest...(v. 8-9)" Orpah returned to her people. However, Ruth clung to Naomi and said, "Your people shall be my people, and your God my God." Naomi and Ruth returned together to Naomi's hometown of Bethlehem in Judah.

Regarding Naomi's relationship with God, Naomi encouraged her daughters-in-law that her God was worthy of their trust. Naomi's

267

Did God Do It?

example inspired Ruth to turn to the One True God. Thus there is no indication that Naomi was not upright before God.

> Ruth 1:19-22
>
> [19] ...And when they came to Bethlehem, the whole town was stirred because of them. And the women said, "Is this Naomi?"
>
> [20] She said to them, "Do not call me Naomi; call me Mara, for <u>the Almighty has dealt very bitterly with me</u>. [21] I went away full, and <u>the LORD has brought me back empty</u>. Why call me Naomi, when <u>the LORD has testified against me</u> and <u>the Almighty has brought calamity upon me</u>?"
>
> [22] So Naomi returned, and Ruth the Moabite her daughter-in-law with her, who returned from the country of Moab. And they came to Bethlehem at the beginning of barley harvest.

The last time these townspeople saw Naomi, her husband and two sons lived with her. Now, Naomi walked into town without her husband and sons but instead with someone they did not know. The whole town was stirred and unsettled by Naomi and Ruth's arrival. Perhaps this bittersweet reunion brought a flood of grief and sorrow for Naomi and the townspeople. The Scriptures do not give these details.

However, what is recorded is Naomi's request that they call her "Mara." In the lands and times of the Bible, a name communicated more than it does in current times. A person's name was often

11. No Wrongdoing and What It Is Not

descriptive of their hopes, sorrows, character trait, or physical trait. The name Naomi means "pleasant" while the name Mara means "bitter."[3] Having lost her husband and her sons, Naomi asked them to call her "Mara." Then she expanded on "Mara" with several idiomatic expressions: "the Almighty has dealt very bitterly with me," "the Lord has brought me back empty," "the Lord has testified against me," and "the Almighty has brought calamity upon me." Each of these expressions seem to credit the Lord God with her sorrowful situation, but the context gives no such evidence. Instead, Naomi spoke idiomatically according to a manner of speech of her times. What she said was culturally understandable to those who lived in the lands and times of the Bible. However, removed by time and culture, as we are, her manner of speech *seems* to blame God. Nevertheless it is not for us to judge her words against the backdrop of our days and times. Instead, we must consider what was meant in the times and culture of the Old Testament.

Reading on in the book of Ruth we would find that Naomi's distant relative, Boaz, redeemed all that belonged to Naomi's husband and sons and married Ruth. The child that Boaz and Naomi had, became the grandfather of king David and is listed in the geneology of Jesus Christ.[4] Thus they were in the line to Christ. The redemption in the book of Ruth foreshadows the far greater redemption that Christ would one day accomplish.

---

3. Exodus 15:23 "When they came to Marah, they could not drink the water of Marah because it was bitter; therefore it was named Marah." See also I Chronicles 4:9; Genesis 27:36.

4. See Ruth 4:21-22 and Matthew 1:5-6: "And Salmon begat Boaz of Rahab; and Boaz begat Obed of Ruth; and Obed begat Jesse; and Jesse begat David the king...."

Did God Do It?

The "But Not Always" Provision

How do we understand Naomi's manner of speech? To rightly understand this unusual expression, we cannot impose our current thinking. We must take the time to understand what this idiom meant in ancient biblical times, which we have done and are doing in this study. In chapter two, we considered three aspects of the God-centered culture of the lands and times of the Bible that give us a basis for understanding the unusual expressions that Naomi spoke. First, people of Naomi's times and culture were not to speak the name of other gods and the devils they represented. Second, we saw that it was not until the earthly life and ministry of the Lord Jesus Christ that the devil and his nature were more fully revealed. Third, we saw that the Hebrew people did acknowledge and magnify God in the face of affliction.

According to the context and biblical culture, the unusual expressions that Ruth spoke are not literal; they are figurative. They are cultural idiomatic expressions that do not mean what they seem to say. Although Naomi's use of these cultural expressions may sound strange to our ears, this idiom was not intended to blame or belittle God. Instead Naomi magnified and acknowledged God as the Most High, Who is Lord overall.

Let us briefly digress and highlight once again that this study is not making a general statement about choices and consequences in life. Instead, this study is identifying a particular pattern of words in the Scriptures. While it is true that many examples of this idiom occur in a context where a person made choices that led to negative

11. No Wrongdoing and What It Is Not

consequences, it is not true that negative consequences in life always mean someone did something wrong. In the record of Naomi and Ruth, their afflictions were not due to something they did wrong. So also in every day life—tribulations happen and no human is to blame. Now back to understanding the cultural idiom that Naomi used.

The following is a recap of this biblical idiom:
- Active-verb expressions in the Scriptures with the pattern of "the Lord God + action + recipient" are idiomatic when the context and related scriptures show that the words are not true to fact.
- This particular biblical idiom *seems* to say God did something contrary to His nature or a person's free will but according to the context and related scriptures He did not.
- Their meaning is understood from biblical culture, context, and related scriptures.
- Culturally they were not intended to blame God nor do they mean that He did evil. They acknowledge God Who is Lord overall.

Furthermore the context and related passages of this idiom often, *but not always*, show the following:
- Who, other than God, was responsible for the action credited to God.
- The spiritual cause behind the physical.
- That someone had information or instructions from God that he or she did not believe.

Did God Do It?

The idiomatic expressions in Ruth 1 fall into the "but not always" provision. The context in Ruth does not indicate who is responsible. The context does not say that Naomi had information from God that she did not believe. There is no indication in the context or in any related scriptures that Naomi did or did not do anything that led to negative consequences. She did not do anything wrong.

God did not cause the famine, deaths, bitter dealings, losses, and calamities that afflicted Naomi. Naomi did not bring the consequences upon herself by something that she did or did not do. Instead, the Scriptures reveal that it is the devil who manipulates the environment to harm God's people and to misrepresent the goodness of the God of the Scriptures. Revelations 12:9-10 declares that the devil is the accuser of those who love God and the deceiver of the whole world. The devil is the source of emptiness, wrongful accusations, calamity, and loss. The devil's ways lead to death and destruction.

In contrast, God's ways lead to life and deliverance. God never gives information that leads to bitterness, but every good and perfect thing comes from the Lord God Almighty. What He gives is sweet and good and life-giving.

So we see that Naomi expressed herself with an idiom of her day and time. Had she been born after Christ accomplished works she may have said, "The hand of the adversary has gone out against me…Satan has dealt very bitterly with me…The devil has brought me back empty…and testified against me…The god of this world has brought calamity upon me." Saying it with these exchanges expresses what actually happened. It would have been culturally out of place for Naomi to speak of the devil and his doings. Instead, she spoke in the manner of speech of her day and employed an idiom of the lands and times of the Bible.

Job, The Lord, and Satan

The record of Job is familiar to many people. There is much that could be handled in the opening chapters of Job. This chapter will only expound on parts that stay within the focus of this study.

> Job 1:1-5
> ¹ There was a man in the land of Uz whose name was Job, and that man was blameless and upright, one who feared [reverenced] God and turned away from evil.
> ² There were born to him seven sons and three daughters.
> ³ He possessed 7,000 sheep, 3,000 camels, 500 yoke of oxen, and 500 female donkeys, and very many servants, so that this man was the greatest of all the people of the east.
> ⁴ His sons used to go and hold a feast in the house of each one on his day, and they would send and invite their three sisters to eat and drink with them.
> ⁵ And when the days of the feast had run their course, Job would send and consecrate them, and he would rise early in the morning and offer burnt offerings according to the number of them all. For Job said, "It may be that my children have sinned, and cursed God in their hearts." Thus Job did continually.

Did God Do It?

Job had many children and great wealth. The God-breathed Scriptures describe Job as blameless, upright, and as one who reverenced God and turned away from evil. We saw in the David chapter that burnt offerings were sweet smelling incense offerings for the purpose of intercession and prayer. The distinct feature of the burnt offering is that it was burnt entirely on the altar and thus offered wholly and completely to God. The function of the burnt offering was intercession, atonement, and dedication.[5] Therefore, Job's words in verse 5, "It may be that my children have sinned, and cursed God in their hearts" are not to be misconstrued to indicate that Job acted out of fear. Most parents have concerns regarding their children. With burnt offerings, Job cast his cares on God according to the manner and custom of his times. Job's continual offerings were representative of his upright character before God.

> Job 1:6-11
>
> [6] Now there was a day when the sons of God came to present themselves before the LORD, and Satan also came among them.
>
> [7] The LORD said to Satan, "From where have you come?" Satan answered the LORD and said, "From going to and fro on the earth, and from walking up and down on it."
>
> [8] And the LORD said to Satan, "Have you considered my servant Job, that there is none like him on the earth, a

---

5. David Bergey, *Jesus Christ Our Complete Offering: How the Levitical Offerings Foreshadowed Christ* (Printed in the United States of America, 2017). Chapter 9 "The Sweet Savor Offerings," p. 318, and chapters 13 and 14 on the burnt offering.

11. No Wrongdoing and What It Is Not

blameless and upright man, who fears God and turns away from evil?"

⁹ Then Satan answered the LORD and said, "Does Job fear God for no reason?

¹⁰ Have you not put a hedge around him and his house and all that he has, on every side? You have blessed the work of his hands, and his possessions have increased in the land.

¹¹ But stretch out your hand and touch all that he has, and he will curse you to your face."

God points out Job's uprightness in verse 8. Then Satan belittled Job's uprightness saying that it was because God protected Job that Job remained upright.

Job 1:12

And the LORD said to Satan, "Behold, all that he has is in your hand. Only against him do not stretch out your hand." So Satan went out from the presence of the LORD.

Satan went out from the presence of the Lord and used the authority that God said was in his hand. Other scriptures also help us to understand this authority. Genesis 1:26-28 says God gave Adam dominion over all the earth. However, Luke 4:5-6 says, "And the devil took him [Jesus] up and showed him all the kingdoms of the world in a moment of time, and said to him, 'To you I will give all this authority and their glory, for it has been delivered to me, and I give it to whom I will." In order for the devil to offer Jesus Christ the authority

Did God Do It?

of the world he must have had it. Putting Genesis 1-3 together with Luke 4, we understand that when Adam disobeyed God, he handed over his authority of the world to Satan.[6] With this background, we see that Satan, as the god of this world, was the one who destroyed Job's property and killed his children.

As an aside for our encouragement, let us recall what we have already seen in this study. By Christ's accomplished works, all who have believed concerning Christ[7] have been absolutely removed from Satan's authority of darkness (Colossians 1:13). Christ has triumphed over Satan now and will even more so in future times.[8]

Back to Job 1. According to verse 11, Satan claimed that if God touched all that Job had, Job would curse the Lord to His face. It was not the Lord Who stole and destroyed Job's property and then killed his children. We saw that Satan was the responsible party. But the question remains: Did Job curse God? Did Job give validity to Satan's accusation?

> Job 1:20-22
>
> [20] Then Job arose and tore his robe and shaved his head and fell on the ground and worshiped.
>
> [21] And he said, "Naked I came from my mother's womb, and naked shall I return. The LORD gave, and the LORD has taken away; blessed be the name of the LORD."

---

6. For more information regarding Adam's transfer of authority of the world to the devil see Walter J. Cummins, *The Acceptable Year of the Lord* (Franklin, Ohio: Scripture Consulting, 2005), Chapter 1, "The World's Need for a Savior" p. 8.

7. How to believe concerning Christ is stated in Romans 10:9-10.

8. Colossians 1:13 says, "He [God] has delivered us from the domain of darkness and transferred us to the kingdom of his beloved Son." Regarding triumph in Christ, see also Colossians 2:15 and I John 3:8.

11. No Wrongdoing and What It Is Not

²² In all this Job did not sin or charge God with wrong.

"Tore his robe" and "shaved his head" in verse 20 are both ancient customs that express mourning. These customs are an outward show of the inner anguish of the mourner.⁹ Job did not give validity to Satan's lying accusations. The context of verse 21 provides compelling evidence that the words in verse 21 were not intended to blame God. The words that could be misconstrued are sandwiched between: "[Job] fell on the ground and worshipped" and "blessed be the name of the Lord." Then it is followed by the explanation "In all this, Job did not sin or charge God with wrong." Job's actions and speech demonstrated his sorrow and his reverence for Lord God according to the manner of speech and customs of his day.

> Job 2:1-3
>
> ¹ Again there was a day when the sons of God came to present themselves before the LORD, and Satan also came among them to present himself before the LORD.
> ² And the LORD said to Satan, "From where have you come?" Satan answered the LORD and said, "From going to and fro on the earth, and from walking up and down on it."
> ³ And the LORD said to Satan, "Have you considered my servant Job, that there is none like him on the earth, a blameless and upright man, who fears God and turns away from evil? He still holds fast his integrity, although

---

9. James M. Freeman, *The New Manners and Customs of the Bible* (Bridge-Logos, Alachua, Florida, 1998), p. 72.

> you [Satan] incited me [the Lord] against him [Job] to destroy him without reason [cause]."

The Lord again declares that Job is blameless, upright, and one who reverenced God and turned away from evil. To this list of Job's upright characteristics, the divine record adds that Job held fast his integrity even in the face of all that happened. Without any reason or cause, Satan destroyed Job's family and possessions. Furthermore, Satan attempted to shift the blame off himself and onto the God of the Scriptures, but he did not succeed. God called his bluff!

The "But Not Always" Provision

Having considered the context and related scriptures, we see that Satan's accusations toward God and toward Job were unfounded and false. The expression, "you [Satan] incited me [the Lord] against him [Job] to destroy him" is not true to fact. This unusual expression is an idiom of the lands and times of the Bible that was culturally understandable then, but not clear in today's culture. This particular biblical idiom often, *but not always*, shows the following:

- Who, other than God, was responsible for the action credited to God.
- The spiritual cause behind the physical.
- That someone had information or instructions from God that he or she did not believe.

Job 1:1-2:3 *does* show that Satan and not God was responsible for the action credited to God. The context shows that Satan was the source of the death and destruction. Therefore, the spiritual cause behind the physical is Satan and his doings.

11. No Wrongdoing and What It Is Not

However, this record *does not* indicate that Job had information from God that He did not believe. In fact, there is clear and repeated scriptural evidence that Job was upright and blameless before God. Job repeatedly maintained his integrity in the face of unreasonable attempts to ruin him. The bad things that happened to Job are not related to anything Job did, or did not do. Job 1:22 adds that, "In all this Job did not sin or charge God with wrong." The expression "you [Satan] incited me [the Lord] against him [Job] to destroy him" is an example of the idiom that *seems* to say God did something that He did not do. Neither God nor Job were to blame for the bad things that happened to Job. Satan, and not God, was the source of the death and destruction toward Job.

Job lived in Old Testament times before it was available to be justified freely by God's grace through the redemption that is in Christ Jesus.[10] Regrettably, Job was subject to the conditions of the world of his times.

> Romans 8:33-34
>
> [33] Who shall bring any charge against God's elect? It is God who justifies.
>
> [34] Who is to condemn? Christ Jesus is the one who died—more than that, who was raised—who is at the right hand of God, who indeed is interceding for us.

Job lived before Christ was seated at the right hand of God to make intercession for us. However, today Christ Jesus is seated at the right hand of God ever ready to make intercession for us. In these

---

10. Romans 3:24: "And are justified by his grace as a gift, through the redemption that is in Christ Jesus."

Did God Do It?

times of the grace administration, all who believe concerning Jesus Christ are justified freely by God's grace.

Elijah and the Widow Woman

The record of I Kings occurs when Ahab was king of Judah.

> I Kings 16:30
> And Ahab the son of Omri did evil in the sight of the LORD, more than all who were before him.

Ahab promoted Baal worship in Judah and led God's people into idolatry. The idolatrous nations regarded Baal as the lord of the rain and dew and the god of fertility.

> I Kings 17:1
> Now Elijah the Tishbite, of Tishbe in Gilead, said to Ahab, "As the LORD, the God of Israel, lives, before whom I stand, there shall be neither dew nor rain these years, except by my word."

God sent His prophet, Elijah, with a message for the king: there would be neither dew nor rain these years, except by his word. God's divine judgment of no dew nor rain proved the Lord God of Israel more powerful than Baal.

Having delivered God's message, Elijah quickly departed and hid in a location God told him. According to God's instructions, Elijah lived by the brook Cherith and was fed by the ravens. When the brook dried up, God instructed Elijah to go to a place where he could hide in plain sight.

11. No Wrongdoing and What It Is Not

> I Kings 17:8-10
>
> [8] Then the word of the LORD came to him,
>
> [9] "Arise, go to Zarephath, which belongs to Sidon, and dwell there. Behold, I have commanded a widow there to feed you."
>
> [10] So he arose and went to Zarephath. And when he came to the gate of the city, behold, a widow was there gathering sticks. And he called to her and said, "Bring me a little water in a vessel, that I may drink."

Zarephath was not in Israel but was a town on the coast of Phoenicia between Tyre and Sidon. Baal was the chief god, not only of the Canaanites, but also of the Phoenicians. Thus, the city of Zarephath was located in enemy territory among Baal worshippers.

Elijah entered the city by the gate, which put him in the common area by the town well. According to the customs and culture of the lands and times of the Bible, men and women did not speak to each other in public places. However, it was culturally acceptable for a traveler to ask a woman for directions or for water. Elijah asked the widow woman to bring him a little water.

> I Kings 17:11-14
>
> [11] And as she was going to bring it, he called to her and said, "Bring me a morsel of bread in your hand."
>
> [12] And she said, "As the LORD your God lives, I have nothing baked, only a handful of flour in a jar and a little oil in a jug. And now I am gathering a couple of

> sticks that I may go in and prepare it for myself and my son, that we may eat it and die."
>
> ¹³ And Elijah said to her, "Do not fear; go and do as you have said. But first make me a little cake of it and bring it to me, and afterward make something for yourself and your son.
>
> ¹⁴ For thus says the Lord, the God of Israel, 'The jar of flour shall not be spent, and the jug of oil shall not be empty, until the day that the Lord sends rain upon the earth.'"

It was not culturally acceptable for Elijah to ask for more than directions or water. However, it was spiritually acceptable. Elijah walked with God as he conversed with the widow woman.

> I Kings 17:15-16
>
> ¹⁵ And she went and did as Elijah said. And she and he and her household ate for many days.
>
> ¹⁶ The jar of flour was not spent, neither did the jug of oil become empty, according to the word of the Lord that he spoke by Elijah.

The widow woman went and did as Elijah asked. God instructed Elijah, and Elijah instructed the woman. Thus the woman obeyed information that originated from God. As she did so, all her household had food for many days, in the midst of a famine.

11. No Wrongdoing and What It Is Not

I Kings 17:17-24

¹⁷ After this the son of the woman, the mistress of the house, became ill. And his illness was so severe that there was no breath left in him.
¹⁸ And she said to Elijah, "What have you against me, O man of God? You have come to me to bring my sin to remembrance and to cause the death of my son!"
¹⁹ And he said to her, "Give me your son." And he took him from her arms and carried him up into the upper chamber where he lodged, and laid him on his own bed.
²⁰ And he cried to the LORD, <u>"O LORD my God, have you brought calamity even upon the widow with whom I sojourn, by killing her son?"</u>
²¹ Then he stretched himself upon the child three times and cried to the LORD, "O LORD my God, let this child's life come into him again."
²² And the LORD listened to the voice of Elijah. And the life of the child came into him again, and he revived.
²³ And Elijah took the child and brought him down from the upper chamber into the house and delivered him to his mother. And Elijah said, "See, your son lives."
²⁴ And the woman said to Elijah, "Now I know that you are a man of God, and that the word of the LORD in your mouth is truth."

The widow woman and her son had only received good from Elijah and his God. Therefore, it is a startling turn of events that her son died. In the face of this tragedy, Elijah *seems* to blame God. Blaming God is so out of alignment with the many clear records of Elijah's reverence and obedience to God that these words are puzzling.

Luke 4 gives us more information about this widow woman.[11] In Luke 4, Jesus Christ is speaking to a group of people in the city of Nazareth where he had grown up.

> Luke 4:24
>
> And he said, "Truly, I say to you, no prophet is acceptable in his hometown.

Jesus Christ confronted the people of Nazareth with their rejection of him and hence their rejection of God. He followed up with a comparison.

> Luke 4:25-27
>
> [25] But in truth, I tell you, there were many widows in Israel in the days of Elijah, when the heavens were shut up three years and six months, and a great famine came over all the land,

---

11. I Kings 17:18 records what the widow woman said to Elijah when her son died. She asked if Elijah and his God had come to bring her sin to her remembrance and cause the death of her son. Why did she phrase her question as if the remembrance of sin was the cause of death? The widow woman was raised in a Baal-worshipping culture. For Baal worshippers, sin was remembered to punish them for their wrongdoings. Thus her questions in I Kings 17:18 would fit with her cultural upbringing. However, as we saw in chapter five, under the covenant of the law sin was remembered, not to punish, but to allow an opportunity to atone. The goal was restoration not punishment. The remembrance of sin in Old Testament times reminded them of the need for a savior and pointed the way forward. Under the covenant of the law, sacrifices foreshadowed the coming messiah and the deliverance Christ would bring. See David Bergey, *Jesus Christ Our Complete Offering: How the Levitical Offerings Foreshadowed Christ* (Printed in the United States of America, 2017).

11. No Wrongdoing and What It Is Not

²⁶ and Elijah was sent to none of them but only to Zarephath, in the land of Sidon, to a woman who was a widow.

²⁷ And there were many lepers in Israel in the time of the prophet Elisha, and none of them was cleansed, but only Naaman the Syrian."

Jesus Christ compared the unbelief of the people of Nazareth to the unbelief of the people of Israel in the days of Elijah and Elisha. He did so by recalling two incidents in the days of these prophets from I Kings 17 and II Kings 5. Even though there were many Israelite widows in that day, God chose the non-Israelite widow of Zarephath to feed Elijah. Similarly, in Elisha's day there were many lepers who needed healing but God healed the non-Israelite Naaman (as recorded in II Kings 5). What did the widow from Zarephath and Naaman have in common? Each of them believed information that originated from God at times when God's people, Israel, did not believe.

The final verse of I Kings 17 says, "And the woman said to Elijah, "Now I know that you are a man of God, and that the word of the Lord in your mouth is truth." Putting I Kings 17 together with Luke 4, we see that this widow woman believed that the information from Elijah originated from God. God's Word is truth and the widow woman believed God's truth.

The "But Not Always" Provision

So why did Elijah say, "O Lord my God, have you brought calamity even upon the widow with whom I sojourn, by killing her son?" (I Kings 17:20)? Elijah spoke in the manner of speech of the lands and times of the Bible. He employed an idiom that was common and understandable to the people of that day and time. This particular biblical idiom *seems* to say God did something contrary to His nature or a person's freedom of will but according to the context and related scriptures He did not.

The context of this particular biblical idiom often, *but not always,* shows that someone had information from God that he or she did not believe. The context of I Kings 17 and its related scriptures do *not* show that either Elijah or the widow woman had information from God that he or she did not believe. Elijah walked with and for God. The widow woman believed information that originated with God.

To clarify further, we might ask, was the death of the child because of something Elijah, the widow woman, or the son did or did not do? Did the calamity happen because of some secret sin? There is no scriptural evidence to support such a conclusion.

Elijah spoke the unusual words as he cried unto the Lord in prayer. The Lord did not reject Elijah's prayer. The Scriptures clearly state, "The Lord listened to the voice of Elijah. And the life of the child came into him again, and he revived." Thus, neither the widow woman, her son, nor Elijah did anything wrong. Moreover, God did not cause the death of the widow's son. The widow's son was sick and died. The devil is the source of sickness and death, not God. The devil was responsible for the death of the boy. God was responsible for bringing him back to life.

We saw that under the Mosaic Law, God's people were not to mention the name of other gods. Instead, they were to acknowledge and magnify the name of the Lord. Also, they did not fully understand

11. No Wrongdoing and What It Is Not

the devil and his nature because it was not until the earthly life and ministry of Jesus Christ that the devil and his nature were more fully revealed. Therefore, Elijah would not say, "the devil brought calamity upon the widow with whom I sojourn, by killing her son." While the devil and not God killed the widow's son, naming the devil would have been unacceptable speech in Elijah's day. Instead, Elijah cried to and acknowledged the Lord God in the face of affliction. Although God did not do it, the cultural idiom credited the Lord because He is the Most High and Most Powerful God, Who is Lord overall. We ought to also note that while it would have been unacceptable speech for Elijah to name the devil for his evil doings, it is not unacceptable speech since Christ came and revealed the evil nature of the devil. So we ought not to speak like Old Testament believers but like those who live in all that Christ has accomplished on our behalf.

Hannah, the Mother of Samuel

A record of Hannah, the mother of the prophet Samuel, provides our final example for this chapter. First, let us consider some background.

> Genesis 30:1 and 23
>
> [1] When Rachel saw that she bore Jacob no children, she envied her sister. She said to Jacob, "Give me children, or I shall die!"
>
> [23] She conceived and bore a son and said, "God has taken away my reproach [disgrace and humiliation[AMP]]."

Did God Do It?

> Luke 1:24-25
>
> ²⁴ After these days his wife Elizabeth conceived, and for five months she kept herself hidden, saying,
>
> ²⁵ "Thus the Lord has done for me in the days when he looked on me, to take away my reproach [disgrace] among people."

Rachel and Elizabeth were both barren. To not have children in that culture was so distressing that Rachel said, "Give me children, or I shall die." Each of them expressed that having a child removed the cultural reproach, disgrace, or humiliation.

Let us contrast this understanding of the extreme disgrace of not having children with some of God's intentions for the people of Israel.

> Exodus 23:25-26
>
> ²⁵ You shall serve the LORD your God, and he will bless your bread and your water, and I will take sickness away from among you.
>
> ²⁶ None shall miscarry or be barren in your land; I will fulfill the number of your days.

Evidently it was important to the Lord God that the people not miscarry or be barren.

> Deuteronomy 7:13-14
>
> ¹³ He will love you, bless you, and multiply you. He will also bless the fruit of your womb and the fruit of your ground, your grain and your wine and your oil, the increase of your herds and the young of your flock, in the land that he swore to your fathers to give you.

11. No Wrongdoing and What It Is Not

> ¹⁴ You shall be blessed above all peoples. There shall not be male or female barren among you or among your livestock.

The Scriptures again state God's will regarding the fruit of the womb. God's desire was to bless and multiply offspring to His people—both among the people and among their livestock.[12]

With this background let us consider Hannah.

> I Samuel 1:1-8
>
> ¹ There was a certain man of Ramathaim-zophim of the hill country of Ephraim whose name was Elkanah the son of Jeroham, son of Elihu, son of Tohu, son of Zuph, an Ephrathite.
>
> ² He had two wives. The name of the one was Hannah, and the name of the other, Peninnah. And Peninnah had children, but Hannah had no children.
>
> ³ Now this man used to go up year by year from his city to worship and to sacrifice to the LORD of hosts at Shiloh, where the two sons of Eli, Hophni and Phinehas, were priests of the LORD.
>
> ⁴ On the day when Elkanah sacrificed, he would give portions to Peninnah his wife and to all her sons and daughters.
>
> ⁵ But to Hannah he gave a double portion, because he loved her, though <u>the LORD had closed her womb.</u>

---

12. See also Psalm 113:9: "He gives the barren woman a home, making her the joyous mother of children. Praise the LORD!" Psalm 128:3-4 gives similar information.

Did God Do It?

> ⁶ And her rival used to provoke her grievously to irritate her, because <u>the Lord had closed her womb</u>.
>
> ⁷ So it went on year by year. As often as she went up to the house of the Lord, she used to provoke her. Therefore Hannah wept and would not eat.
>
> ⁸ And Elkanah, her husband, said to her, "Hannah, why do you weep? And why do you not eat? And why is your heart sad? Am I not more to you than ten sons?"

Elkanah had two wives but he loved Hannah more and favored her when he made sacrifices. The other wife, Peninnah, is called Hannah's rival. Instead of offering comfort in a culturally disgraceful situation, Peninnah rubbed it in at each opportunity. She sought to irritate and humiliate Hannah for being childless. However, Hannah's husband encouraged her. How did Hannah next respond to this difficult situation?

> I Samuel 1:9-18
>
> ⁹ After they had eaten and drunk in Shiloh, Hannah rose. Now Eli the priest was sitting on the seat beside the doorpost of the temple of the Lord.
>
> ¹⁰ She was deeply distressed and prayed to the Lord and wept bitterly.
>
> ¹¹ And she vowed a vow and said, "O Lord of hosts, if you will indeed look on the affliction of your servant and remember me and not forget your servant, but will give to your servant a son, then I will give him to the

11. No Wrongdoing and What It Is Not

Lord all the days of his life, and no razor shall touch his head."

¹² As she continued praying before the Lord, Eli observed her mouth.

¹³ Hannah was speaking in her heart; only her lips moved, and her voice was not heard. Therefore Eli took her to be a drunken woman.

¹⁴ And Eli said to her, "How long will you go on being drunk? Put your wine away from you."

¹⁵ But Hannah answered, "No, my lord, I am a woman troubled in spirit. I have drunk neither wine nor strong drink, but I have been pouring out my soul before the Lord.

¹⁶ Do not regard your servant as a worthless woman, for all along I have been speaking out of my great anxiety and vexation."

¹⁷ Then Eli answered, "Go in peace, and the God of Israel grant your petition that you have made to him."

¹⁸ And she said, "Let your servant find favor in your eyes." Then the woman went her way and ate, and her face was no longer sad.

Hannah responded by taking her affliction and request to the Lord God. She cast her cares on Him and made a vow that she would give her firstborn to the service of the Lord God. Hannah had good reason in their culture to be deeply distressed and troubled, but her response is what sets her apart. She prayed, continued praying, and

Did God Do It?

poured out her soul in prayer to God. These are not the actions of a woman who set God aside in the face of affliction. While the expressions in verse 5 and 6 *seem* to blame God, Hannah's actions and prayer do not. Instead, she trusted in God's power and deliverance.

> I Samuel 1:19-22
>
> [19] They rose early in the morning and worshiped before the LORD; then they went back to their house at Ramah. And Elkanah knew Hannah his wife, and the LORD remembered her.
>
> [20] And in due time Hannah conceived and bore a son, and she called his name Samuel, for she said, "I have asked for him from the LORD."
>
> [21] The man Elkanah and all his house went up to offer to the LORD the yearly sacrifice and to pay his vow.
>
> [22] But Hannah did not go up, for she said to her husband, "As soon as the child is weaned, I will bring him, so that he may appear in the presence of the LORD and dwell there forever."

Though God was credited with shutting Hannah's womb, He did not do it, nor did Hannah do anything wrong. Instead, when faced with this difficult situation, Hannah went to God in earnest prayer. Her prayer showed that she trusted in and relied on the Lord God. God answered her prayer while at the same time providing one who would become a prophet for the people of Israel. So, the context does not indicate any choices by the recipient that led to what occurred. Moreover, there are no related passages that say the Lord shut up

11. No Wrongdoing and What It Is Not

Hannah's womb. The divine narrative of I Samuel employed a cultural expression, a biblical idiom, that *seems* to say God did something contrary to His nature, but He did not. Culturally the idiom credited the Lord because He is the Most High and Most Powerful God, Who is Lord overall.

Summary—No Wrongdoing

The unusual expressions in this chapter are cultural expressions, figures of speech, a biblical idiom. This particular biblical idiom *seems* to say God did something contrary to His nature or a person's freedom of will but according to the context and related scriptures He did not.[13]

The idiomatic expressions in this chapter fall into the "but not always" provision. This is so because the context and related scriptures of these occurrences do not record an occasion when God gave His Word to a person who neglected or rejected that information. The context and related scriptures of the examples in this chapter show that Naomi, Job, Elijah, and Hannah each had a working relationship with the Lord God.

In Ruth 1, neither Naomi, her husband, their sons, nor their wives, including Ruth did anything wrong to cause the famine and deaths. Naomi encouraged her daughters-in-law in the Lord. Job was blameless and upright before God. Job reverenced God and believed information from God. On the other hand, Satan brought unfounded accusations against Job and persecuted him without cause. Elijah walked obediently with and for God. The widow woman believed

---

13. This biblical idiom's word pattern is "the Lord God + action + recipient."

information that originated from God. Hannah cast her cares on the Lord God and prayed for deliverance. In each of these records, there is no evidence in the context or related scriptures that the recipients did or did not do anything to cause the calamities that came upon them. Moreover, Satan, and not God, is the source of the calamities and deaths that happened to the upright people of these records.

We have consistently seen that God's ways are just and lead to life and deliverance. His justness and justice are consistently linked with His steadfast love, mercy, and goodness. On the other hand, the devil is an enemy of all that is just and good. Satan's injustices are consistently linked with darkness, affliction, lack of mercy, and death.

What It Is Not and Closing Notes

As we near the end of this study, let us again acknowledge something that this study is not saying. This study is about a particular pattern of words in the Bible that may be figurative or literal depending on the context. We have found that these unusual expressions often occur in a context where a person made choices that led to negative consequences. Please do not misconstrue a characteristic of this particular biblical idiom to be generally applicable to present-day life. In other words, we ought never think that every affliction in life is because somebody did something wrong. This would not be based in the Scriptures and this is not what this study is saying. Instead, let us continue to acknowledge that we live in an evil world in which the devil, as the god of this world, causes bad things to happen. However, we can take comfort knowing that Christ has triumphed over the devil—both now and in the future. As Jesus Christ said in John 16:33,

11. No Wrongdoing and What It Is Not

"Take heart; I have overcome the world."

> I Corinthians 15:57
>
> But thanks be to God, who gives us the victory through our Lord Jesus Christ.

God gives us the victory over death through our Lord Jesus Christ. There is a time coming when God and His Son, Jesus Christ will bring that victory to a final end.

> Revelation 20:10
>
> And the devil who had deceived them was thrown into the lake of fire...

> Revelation 21:4
>
> He [God] will wipe away every tear from their eyes, death shall be no more, neither shall there be mourning, nor crying, nor pain anymore, for the former things have passed away.

At a future time, the things that the god of this world orchestrates will pass away. In the future, when the former things of this evil age have passed away, there will be no more death, nor mourning, nor crying, nor pain. We can count on it!

We will close with a passage from Colossians. The following is addressed to and true of those who have believed concerning Jesus Christ.[14]

---

14. To believe concerning Jesus Christ is concisely set forth in Romans 10:9-10: "Because, if you confess with your mouth that Jesus is Lord and believe in your heart that God raised him from the dead, you will be saved. For with the heart one believes and is justified, and with the mouth one confesses and is saved."

> Colossians 3:1-4
>
> ¹ If then you have been raised with Christ, seek the things that are above, where Christ is, seated at the right hand of God.
>
> ² Set your minds on things that are above, not on things that are on earth.
>
> ³ For you have died, and your life is hidden with Christ in God.
>
> ⁴ When Christ who is your life appears, then you also will appear with him in glory.

In Colossians 3:1, "if" is used to introduce a simple condition. As such, it may be rendered "since" which fits the context of the Pauline epistles. Then it would read, "*Since you have been* raised with Christ!" Thus we see more clearly that our position in Christ is an accomplished, completed reality. When we use the access we have to God through our Lord Jesus Christ no one can pry us out of God's hands. Since we have been raised with Christ and hidden in God, we ought to focus not on the temporal things of this earth but on heavenly realities. As we do so, we look forward to that future time, when Christ will appear and we will appear with him in glory. While we wait for the glory to come, we can live in this world with an awareness of what Christ has already accomplished for us, including being our ever-present intercessor. We can wait, knowing that God and His Son are actively present to help and deliver.

12

Considerations and Summary

Throughout this study, we have seen that God is without iniquity in all that He does. God is light and His light never has any dark shadows. The Lord God is true to His nature from Genesis to Revelation; He is worthy of our reverence and trust from beginning to end.

We began this study to make sense of certain Bible passages that *seem* to connect God with negative actions. Misunderstanding certain unusual and potentially difficult expressions has caused some people to misjudge the God of the Scriptures. These unusual expressions seem to say God did something that He may, or may not, have done. Therefore, this study's objective has been to understand the context of these unusual expressions to determine, from the Scriptures, if they are literal or figurative, or if we do not know. To that end, we have considered passages with unusual expressions in the pattern of "the Lord God + action + recipient."[1] Our approach has been to respectfully consider what the Scriptures say, above all else. In doing so, we aim to let the Scriptures interpret themselves.

1. For example: the Lord did evil to this people; the Lord hardened the heart of Pharaoh; the Lord struck down all the firstborn in the land of Egypt; the Lord had closed all the wombs of the house of Abimelech; the Lord put Saul to death; the Lord sent a pestilence on Israel.

We recognize that the pattern "the Lord God + action + recipient" is commonly found and often literal. However, it may be figurative when the context shows that it is not true to fact. Thus, for each occurrence of this pattern of words, we have considered the context and related scriptures to determine if the expression is literal or figurative, or if we do not know.

Working Considerations

The intent of this section is to provide a pattern for further study of other similar expressions in the Scriptures. To that end, the following are working considerations. These considerations are not exhaustive nor are they the final word on the subject.

- *First:* Check your approach to the Scriptures in light of Proverbs 1:7; II Timothy 3:16; and II Peter 1:21.[2] Reverence for the Lord God and respect for the integrity of His Word is the starting point. As you read, consider God's point of view rather than your feelings, opinions, or current societal values; let the Word of the Lord speak.
- *Read:* Start by reading the context of the unusual expression under consideration in the Scriptures. Include both the closer and wider contexts. It may be necessary to read large sections of the Scriptures to get enough context. Read it in multiple versions. Also read related scriptures on the same subject or event.
- *Consider:* Do the Scriptures say that someone other than God did it? If so, the action credited to God is figurative; it is a biblical idiom. The context or

---

2. To review these verses see chapter one, subsection "This Study's Approach."

12. Considerations and Summary

related scriptures often, but not always, show who actually did it.

- *Note the word "heart"*: If the expression involves someone's heart, then that "someone" is responsible for the believing, thoughts, choices, and actions that come from his or her heart. If the expression includes the word "heart," the action credited to God is often figurative.

- *Allow the Scriptural evidence to speak*: If the Scriptures and all related passages do not say someone else other than God did it, then God may have done it. If someone (such as an angel) carried out instructions from God, then God is the source; He did it. If God gave explicit instructions, such as a covenant agreement with a person or people, and someone disobeyed those explicit instructions, then God may have performed necessary justice according to the standard of justice of those times.

- *No Wrongdoing:* While certain records in this study show that someone had information from God that he or she did not believe and consequences followed (for example, the Pharaoh records in Exodus), we have also seen examples when there was no wrongdoing (for example, the records in chapter eleven). Both of these fit the pattern of the biblical idiom we have considered.

Other things to keep in mind are different time periods in the Scriptures (often called administrations), God's standard of justice established for each administration, God's covenants with people, and God's purpose in Christ as declared throughout the Scriptures.

God would never work against His own standards of justice and purpose in Christ. These standards and purpose, as well as many other matters regarding God's good intentions for man, are recorded in the Scriptures. God is always faithful to fulfill the Scriptures. He always has, does, and will perform His Word. Thus God is reliable and trustworthy.

We must recognize that at times it was necessary for God to take strong measures, in order to preserve those who believed according to His purpose in Christ. The magnitude of God's mercy in the face of practices of evil should also be appreciated. In some cases, we find that God acted to protect against ungodly and evil people as well as those who were enemies of God's people. To nations that set themselves in opposition against God and His people, God was merciful, long-suffering, and just as He executed merited judgment. Certain records indicate that God executed necessary justice to the people of Israel when they broke the covenant of the law, especially regarding the worship of other gods, or the worship of the Lord God contrary to His explicit instructions. In these cases, God's swift justice demonstrated His mercy by preventing further calamity and preserving lives.

It is important to recognize that this study is not making a general statement about choices and consequences in life. We ought never think that every affliction in life is because someone did something wrong. Instead, this study is identifying a particular pattern of words in the Scriptures that may or may not be figurative.

12. Considerations and Summary

It is also important to recognize that most of the scriptures that record God's actions are literal and true to fact. God does many literal things in the Scriptures that are clear and true as written and that are also easily understood.

While God's Word is timeless, cultural understanding is not. We will not find biblical answers by holding God's actions up against attitudes, philosophies, or standards of justice of present-day cultures. What God says in the Scriptures stands above all other sources of information.

Finally, sometimes we may need to grow more in our understanding of the Scriptures to appreciate the scriptural evidence necessary to make a figurative or literal determination. Sometimes we simply do not know and that is okay. The wiser course of action may, on occasion, be to set a troublesome passage aside for the time and come back to it when we learn more. As noted many times throughout this study, we always have the assurance that God is the God of light, love, and justice; and we can rejoice in His goodness as we continue to grow in our understanding of His wonderful Word.

Summary

In our times and in the societies and cultures in which we live, God's good and just nature has been belittled, criticized, and slandered. These patterns of thinking advanced around us may derail even those who love God from sure and certain confidence that God is good. Instead of hearing that God is good, just, kind, and loving, we are surrounded with words that suggest that God is unreliable, unjust, cruel, and eager to punish. These patterns of thinking are contrary to what the Scriptures say about God's nature. Romans 2:4 addresses those who despise the goodness of God.

> Romans 2:4
>
> Or do you presume on the riches of his kindness and forbearance and patience, not knowing that God's kindness is meant to lead you to repentance?

To not recognize God's good nature hinders people from turning to God. This study has set forth scriptural evidence that God is indeed good throughout the Scriptures, even in the Old Testament. As we bring our minds to the sure and certain truth that God is good, we build a pattern of thinking that provides a solid foundation to receive God's blessings. God's goodness is associated with His light, love, kindness, mercy, and faithfulness. The Scriptures assure us that God's goodness is just and His justice is good.

Malachi 3:6 says, "For I the LORD do not change." God's nature does not waver. He is not more good in the New Testament than He is in the Old Testament. Over time, cultural ways of thinking may have shifted but God has not. God's good nature does not change. God's goodness, kindness, mercy, grace, faithfulness, light, compassion, and justness are just as valid in the Old Testament as they are in the New Testament. From Genesis through Revelations, God's goodness is just and His justice is good. We can trust and rely on God to always be Who He says He is throughout the Scriptures.

As we sum up this study, let us consider a passage in Micah regarding God's light.

12. Considerations and Summary

Micah 7:7-9

⁷ But as for me, I will look to the LORD; I will wait for the God of my salvation; my God will hear me.

⁸ Rejoice not over me, O my enemy; when I fall, I shall rise; when I sit in darkness, the LORD will be a light to me.

⁹ I will bear the indignation of the LORD because I have sinned against him, until he pleads my cause, and executes judgment for me. He will bring me out to the light; I shall look upon his vindication [righteousness [NIV, NASB, KJV]].

What an exhortation for all times: to know God will hear us, to look unto the Lord and wait for His salvation. Under the covenant of the law, people waited for a future deliverance of the coming savior, who we know to be the Lord Jesus Christ. The execution of judgment under the law brought light for deliverance, righteousness [justness] from keeping of the law, and a relationship with the Lord God. We saw in chapter one, that whenever God executes judgment it is based on His standards of justice applicable at the time and which are rooted in His good and just ways. When God executes judgment, His actions reflect His nature. God's nature is true, just, good, faithful, merciful, gracious, and long-suffering. When God executed merited judgment under the law, the Scriptures call that light and good. Throughout the history of the relationship of God and man, God always had people's best interests in mind as He worked to restore the losses to mankind due to Adam's sin. God's formal relationship by the covenant of the law with the nation of Israel provided a far greater means for God to bless than He had prior to that point. The keeping of the law pointed toward Christ and preserved the descendants of Abraham until Christ came.

Therefore, it is vital that those who live since Christ's accomplished works acknowledge that the necessary judgments under the old covenant of the law in the Old Testament are absolutely no longer applicable in our day and time. As students of God's Word we have much to learn from the Old Testament but we ought never think that the kinds of judgment seen in the Old Testament apply to those who have believed concerning Christ.[3] In this day and time of the administration of God's grace,[4] God has graciously provided a new standard of justice in Christ Jesus.

> Romans 3:21-24 and 28[WTJ]
>
> [21] Now, however, the justice of God without the law has been manifested, being witnessed to by the law and the prophets.
> [22] Yes, the justice of God *is* by the believing of Jesus Christ to all those who believe, for there is no difference.
> [23] In fact, all have sinned and come short of the glory of God,

---

3. How to believe concerning Jesus Christ is concisely set forth in Romans 10:9-10: "Because, if you confess with your mouth that Jesus is Lord and believe in your heart that God raised him from the dead, you will be saved. For with the heart one believes and is justified, and with the mouth one confesses and is saved."

4. See Ephesians 3:2[NIV]: "Surely you have heard about the administration of God's grace that was given to me for you."

> ²⁴ being justified freely by His grace through the redemption that *is* in Christ Jesus.
>
> ²⁸ Therefore, we conclude that a person is justified by believing without works of the law.

Adam's sin spread to all people so that all came short of the glory of God. However, since Christ has now accomplished God's plan of redemption and salvation for all people, all who believe concerning Christ are judged and found not guilty in Christ. By Christ's redeeming work, those who believe in him are no longer condemned or found guilty due to Adam's sin or according to the works of the law. In our times, God's justice is not by works but is by believing concerning Jesus Christ. All who believe concerning him are justified freely by God's grace. God's standard of justice in Christ demonstrates the goodness of His justice. What a wonderful day and time in which we live!

We began in I John and let us conclude there.

> I John 1:5
> This is the message we have heard from him and proclaim to you, that God is light, and in him is no darkness at all.

God is light and in Him is no darkness—none at all. The Scriptures declare that even though administrations and standards of justice have shifted over time, each new standard demonstrates God's love and kindness toward man. The goodness of God's justice has never wavered. God was good and just in the times of the Old Testament, He is good and just in present times, and He will be good and just in times yet to come! Therefore, having considered true and faithful words from God about His good, just, and merciful ways, may we be assured in the depth of our souls that the God of the Scriptures is indeed good in all that He does.

Appendix A

Justice and Judgment

Even those who love God sometimes need to grow in their appreciation of God's justice and judgment. We briefly considered God's justness in chapter one of this study.[1] This appendix will expand on these matters.

Two Hebrew Words for Justice

There are two Hebrew words for judgment and justice that this appendix will consider. They are defined in the following ways in the Scriptures:[2]

· Hebrew: *tsedeq*: justice, righteousness, or justness
· Hebrew: *mishpat*: judgment, ordinance, statute. The root form of this word means to judge or to admin-

---

1. See subsection, "Essential Background: God is Just" in chapter one of this study.
2. Resources for reading more about these Hebrew words: (1.) R. Laird Harris, Gleason L. Archer, and Bruce K. Waltke, *The Theological Wordbook of the Old Testament* (Chicago, Illinois: Moody Publishers 1980), p. 947, number 2443. (2.) Walter J. Cummins, *Scripture Consulting Select Studies* (Franklin, Ohio: Scripture Consulting, 2010), Chapter 10, "Justification" . (3.) William L. Holliday, *A Concise Hebrew and Aramaic Lexicon of the Old Testament* (Grand Rapids, Michigan: William B. Eerdmans Publishing Company, 1988), *mishpat* p. 221 and its root form *shaphat* p. 380. (4.) William Wilson, *Wilson's Old Testament Word Studies* (Grand Rapid, Michigan: Kregel Publications, 1978), *mishpat* p. 236 "just" number 4, and its root form *shaphat* p. 235 "judge" number 10.

ister justice. *Mishpat* may be used of decisions based on an established standard of justice.

This appendix uses "justice" for *tsedeq* and "judgment" for *mishpat*.

Things Associated With God's Justice

Let us consider what the Scriptures associate with God's justice and judgment.

> Psalm 36:5-7
>
> ⁵ Your steadfast love [mercy], O Lord, extends to the heavens, your faithfulness to the clouds.
> ⁶ Your righteousness [*tsedeq*] is like the mountains of God; your judgments [*mishpat*] are like the great deep; man and beast you save [deliver, preserve], O Lord.
> ⁷ How precious is your steadfast love [mercy], O God! The children of mankind take refuge in the shadow of your wings.

God's justice and judgments are sandwiched between His steadfast love, which extends to the heavens. The Lord's justice and judgments are so high and so deep as to be all encompassing. The Hebrew word for "save" means "deliver" in the sense of to preserve or to provide for the needs of.[3] The all-encompassing nature of God's justice and judgment preserves and provides for both man and beast.

---

3. See the Hebrew word, *yasha*, rendered "thou preservest" in KJV and "you save" in ESV. Francis Brown, Samuel Rolles Driver, Charles Augustus Briggs, *A Hebrew and English Lexicon of the Old Testament* (Oxford, England, UK: Clarendon Press, 1906) as offered in the e-lexicon on Parallel Plus by TheBible.org ©2017.
See also Robert G. Bratcher and William D. Reyburn, *A Handbook on Psalms* (United Bible Societies, New York, New York, USA, 1991), p. 345.

A. Justice and Judgment

Psalm 111:7-8

⁷ The works of his hands are faithful and just [*mishpat*];
all his precepts are trustworthy;
⁸ they are established forever and ever, to be performed
with faithfulness and uprightness.

The works of God's hands are faithful and just, and they are based on an established standard of justice. They are not fickle or newly imagined but are established, reliable, and trustworthy. God's just acts are performed with faithfulness and uprightness.

Psalm 37:28

For the Lord loves justice [*mishpat*, judgment]; he will
not forsake his saints. They are preserved forever, but the
children of the wicked shall be cut off.

Psalm 99:4-5

⁴ The King in his might loves justice [*mishpat*, judgment].
You have established equity; you have executed justice
[*mishpat*, judgment] and righteousness [*tsedeq*] in Jacob.
⁵ Exalt the Lord our God; worship at his footstool!
Holy is he!

Psalm 33:4-5

⁴ For the word of the Lord is upright, and all his work
is done in faithfulness.
⁵ He loves righteousness [*tsedeq*] and justice [*mishpat*,
judgment]; the earth is full of the steadfast love [goodness[KJV]] of the Lord.

The Lord God loves justice and judgment. The saints in the context of Psalm 37 are those who reverence God. The Scriptures associate God's justice and judgment with the preservation of His saints, equity, and steadfast love.

> Jeremiah 9:24
>
> But let him who boasts boast in this, that he understands and knows me, that I am the LORD who practices steadfast love, justice, and righteousness in the earth. For in these things I delight, declares the LORD."

God both loves and delights in justice and judgment. Moreover, God delights in steadfast love, which He associates with justice and judgment. The Hebrew word for steadfast love may also be rendered mercy. God's steadfast love includes mercy.

> Proverbs 2:6-9
>
> ⁶ For the LORD gives wisdom; from his mouth come knowledge and understanding;
> ⁷ he stores up sound wisdom for the upright; he is a shield to those who walk in integrity,
> ⁸ guarding the paths of justice [*mishpat*, judgement] and watching over the way of his saints.
> ⁹ Then you will understand righteousness [*tsedeq*] and justice [*mishpat*, judgment] and equity, every good path.

Proverbs 2 is about the value of God's wisdom, which He gives to the upright. To the upright, He gives wisdom, knowledge, and understanding. In this context, saints are those who are upright before God and walk in integrity. God guards the paths of justice and judgment and watches over the way of His saints. The path of justice is a good path. God's justice, judgment, and equity are a good path.

The Scriptures associate deliverance for man and beast, equity, and steadfast love with God's justice and judgment. God's just acts are established, upright, and a good path.

What God Calls Good and Desirable

Today, people hold many different points of view regarding what constitutes justice and judgment, as well as what constitutes injustice. In our times, there are many social movements that advocate for things like animal rights, judicial reform, or fair trade that define justice and fairness according to the standards of those movements. People have different criteria, values, or moral standards that give them a frame of reference from which they interpret justice and judgment. However, this study is careful not to mix in standards from outside the Scriptures. Instead, we are vitally concerned with appreciating God's point of view from the Scriptures. What God and His Word say is just, good, and desirable *is* just, good, and desirable.

The next verse from Isaiah contains a list of woes directed to the wicked. However, the exhortation regarding good and evil is generally applicable.

> Isaiah 5:19-21
>
> [19] ...Let the counsel of the Holy One of Israel draw near, and let it come, that we may know it!
> [20] Woe to those who call evil good and good evil, who put darkness for light and light for darkness, who put bitter for sweet and sweet for bitter!

> ²¹ Woe to those who are wise in their own eyes, and shrewd in their own sight!⁴

The people to whom the woes were addressed substituted darkness for light and called dark things the opposite of what God called them. They were wise in their own eyes. In contrast, we want to be wise in God's eyes and call things what God calls them. We want to call what God calls good, good; what God calls evil, evil; what God calls dark, dark; what God calls light, light; what God calls bitter, bitter; and what God calls sweet, sweet. What God calls good is good. God calls His justice and judgment good. The Scriptures are the only valid frame of reference to call something good or evil. What the God of the Scriptures says is good or evil defines what is good or evil.

> Psalm 19:7-10
>
> ⁷ The law of the LORD is perfect, reviving the soul; the testimony of the LORD is sure, making wise the simple;
>
> ⁸ the precepts of the LORD are right, rejoicing the heart; the commandment of the LORD is pure, enlightening the eyes;
>
> ⁹ the fear [reverence] of the LORD is clean, enduring forever; the rules [*mishpat*, judgments] of the LORD are true, and righteous [*tsedeq*, just] altogether.

---

4. See also the Amplified Version of Isaiah 5:18 and 20: "Woe (judgment is coming) to those who drag along wickedness with cords of falsehood..." "Woe (judgment is coming) to those who call evil good, and good evil; Who substitute darkness for light and light for darkness; Who substitute bitter for sweet and sweet for bitter!"

¹⁰ More to be desired are they than gold, even much fine gold; sweeter also than honey and drippings of the honeycomb.

These verses are a celebration of the benefits of God's Word. Contrary to what some may say, God's judgments are desirable. What God says of Himself in the Scriptures is more valuable, far weightier, and more reliably true than what any other source may say. God's judgments are true, just, desirable, and sweet.

Administering Justice

We saw that the Scriptures link God's steadfast love with His judgments and justice and calls them a good path. We noted that the Hebrew words for judgment and justice are broad terms that cover many aspects of justice in the culture of the lands and times of the Bible. This section will consider things the Scriptures associate with justice and judgment when administered or executed.

> Zechariah 7:9
>
> Thus says the LORD of hosts, Render true judgments [*mishpat*], show kindness and mercy to one another.

> Zechariah 8:16
>
> These are the things that you shall do: Speak the truth to one another; render in your gates judgments [*mishpat*] that are true and make for peace.

God instructed His people to administer true judgment and to show kindness and mercy. At another time, He exhorted His people to speak the truth and to administer judgments in their gates. In the lands and times of the Bible, the gates were where people gathered, disputes were settled, and justice was administered.[5] In these scriptures, God associated administering judgment with showing kindness and mercy as well as with making peace. We noted earlier that God's justice reflects His nature. Here the characteristics associated with administering justice reflect God's nature. God is just, kind, merciful, and abounding in steadfast love. His wisdom makes for peace; God's ways bring life and deliverance to people.

The next two verses consider the timing of justice.

> Ecclesiastes 8:11
> Because the sentence against an evil deed is not executed speedily [quickly], the heart of the children of man is fully set to do evil.

> Jeremiah 21:12
> O house of David! Thus says the LORD: Execute justice in the morning, and deliver from the hand of the oppressor him who has been robbed...

Both of these passages comment on the benefit of not delaying the administration of justice. In Ecclesiastes when an evil deed was not speedily judged and sentenced, the evildoers fully set their heart to do evil. In Jeremiah, when justice was executed early, the oppressed were delivered. From these two verses we see that quick execution of justice prevented the hearts of evil doers from being fully set to do

---

5. See James M. Freeman, *Manners and Customs of the Bible* (Logos International, Plainfield, New Jersey, 1972), "The Gate A Place of Justice," p. 110.

A. Justice and Judgment

evil and brought deliverance to the oppressed. The prompt administration of justice brought both immediate and ongoing benefit.

The next verses consider who: who was judged and who was to be benefitted.

> Psalm 103:6
>
> The Lord works righteousness [*tsedeq*] and justice [*mishpat*] for all who are oppressed.

The Lord works or administers justice to benefit all who are oppressed.

> Psalm 119:84
>
> How long must your servant endure? When will you judge those who persecute me?

Judgment was intended for those who persecuted God's servant.

> Psalm 9:16
>
> The Lord has made himself known; he has executed judgment; the wicked are snared in the work of their own hands. *Higgaion. Selah*

The wicked are to whom God has executed judgment. The wicked received the consequences of their own freewill choices. The Lord God has made Himself known by His acts of justice. Knowing and reverencing God are important throughout the Scriptures. In Old Testament times, the administration of justice was one way God made Himself known.

Did God Do It?

> Jeremiah 22:3
>
> Thus says the LORD: Do justice [*mishpat*, judgments] and righteousness [*tsedeq*], and deliver from the hand of the oppressor him who has been robbed. And do no wrong or violence to the resident alien, the fatherless, and the widow, nor shed innocent blood in this place.

The stranger, the fatherless, and the widow are often listed together in the Old Testament as ones who could not provide for themselves and for whom God made special provision. God commanded that His people do no violence to the stranger, the fatherless, and the widow. He instructed that the oppressed and innocent should see justice and deliverance by the execution of judgment against wicked persecutors.

Thus administering justice according to God's instructions had many benefits. Swift justice avoided the deepening of evil in people's hearts. Administering God's justice brought deliverance to people and saved lives. God's judgments are associated with mercy, kindness, making peace, and benefitting people in many desirable ways.

Jesus Christ Spoke Regarding Judgment

When speaking with a Pharisee about Pharisees, Jesus Christ associated judgment in an interesting way.

> Luke 11:42
>
> But woe to you Pharisees! For you tithe mint and rue and every herb, and neglect justice and the love of God. These you ought to have done, without neglecting the others.

A. Justice and Judgment

Jesus Christ reproved the Pharisees for their neglect of the more important matters of justice and the love of God. He said that judgment and the love of God ought not be left undone. Jesus Christ closely aligned judgment with the love of God.

Summary

The Scriptures declare God is just, light, merciful, and abounding in steadfast love and faithfulness. God's justice reflects His nature. We have considered several scriptures that associate God's justice with mercy, love, kindness, making peace, and deliverance to the oppressed. These characteristics of God's justice are in alignment with God's nature.

The Scriptures say God loves and delights in His justice and judgment. When He administers judgment and justice the way of the upright is preserved, the deepening of evil in people's hearts is avoided, lives are saved, and people are delivered. God's administration of justice shows that He is Lord. God introduces the light of His Word into dark situations to deliver people and to avoid further evil. We see over and over again that God acts in alignment with Who He is—that He is just, merciful, compassionate, and faithful to His Word.

The Scriptures closely associate many good things with His justice and judgment. God's justice and judgment are associated with His steadfast love, equity, truth, making peace, benefitting people, mercy, kindness, and love. The Scriptures are the only valid frame of reference to call something good or evil, light or dark, or sweet or bitter. The Scriptures declare many good, light, and sweet things about God's justice and judgment. God's good path includes His justice. His justice is good and God's goodness is just.

Appendix B

Working List—Literal

This working list provides additional examples of unusual expressions in the Scriptures that seem to say God did something that He may or may not have done. According to the best understanding at this point, the unusual expressions in this appendix are literal.

Throughout this study, we have endeavored to handle the Scriptures with integrity and by applying sound practices of allowing the Scriptures to interpret themselves. Appendix B is presented as a working list for further study. It is neither comprehensive nor the final word on the subject.

In appendices B and C, the underlined words are the unusual expression under consideration. Each expression follows the word pattern of "the Lord God + action + recipient." This pattern of words is commonly found and often literal. By considering the context and related scriptures, we have found the expressions presented in appendix B to be literal. Those found to be figurative are in the next and final appendix.

The following list of literal expressions is presented in canonical order; that is to say, in the order of the books of the Bible.

Did God Do It?

In the Time of Noah – Genesis 6:13 and 17

> Genesis 6:5, 11-13 and 17
>
> ⁵ The LORD saw that the wickedness of man was great in the earth, and that every intention of the thoughts of his heart was only evil continually.
>
> ¹¹ Now the earth was corrupt in God's sight, and the earth was filled with violence. ¹² And God saw the earth, and behold, it was corrupt, for all flesh had corrupted their way on the earth. ¹³ And God said to Noah, "I have determined to make an end of all flesh, for the earth is filled with violence through them. Behold, <u>I will destroy them</u> with the earth.
>
> ¹⁷ For behold, <u>I will bring a flood of waters upon the earth to destroy all flesh</u> in which is the breath of life under heaven. Everything that is on the earth shall die.

See the context recorded in Genesis 6:1-7:5.

See also Matthew 24:37-39; Hebrews 11:7, 39; and II Peter 2:4-9.

This record speaks regarding the inhabitants of the earth at that time. The Scriptures say those inhabitants were wicked, evil, violent, and corrupt. God's justice can be seen in that He protected the world from ungodly and wicked men and preserved Noah who was in the line to Christ.

B. Working List—Literal

Abraham – Genesis 20:18

> Genesis 20:18
>
> For <u>the LORD had closed all the wombs of the house of Abimelech</u> because of Sarah, Abraham's wife.

This record is handled in chapter six of this study entitled "Abraham." Regarding God and closing wombs, consider the Hannah section in chapter eleven and the Sarah section in appendix C. Both the Hannah and Sarah records are figurative—God did not close their wombs.

Abraham – Genesis 12:17

> Genesis 12:17
>
> But <u>the LORD afflicted Pharaoh and his house</u> with great plagues because of Sarai, Abram's wife.

This record is handled in chapter six of this study entitled "Abraham."

Sodom and Gomorrah – Genesis 19:24-25 and 29

> Genesis 19:24-25 and 29
>
> ²⁴ Then <u>the LORD rained on Sodom and Gomorrah sulfur and fire</u> from the LORD out of heaven.
> ²⁵ And <u>he overthrew those cities, and all the valley, and all the inhabitants of the cities, and what grew on the ground</u>.
>
> ²⁹ So it was that, when <u>God destroyed the cities of the valley</u>, God remembered Abraham and sent Lot out of

Did God Do It?

> the midst of the overthrow when he overthrew the cities in which Lot had lived.

See the context recorded in Genesis 18:16-19:29.

See also Genesis 13:10-13; Jeremiah 50:40; Lamentations 4:6; Luke 17:28-29; II Peter 2:4-9; and Jude 1:5-15.

God's covenant with Abraham has a bearing on understanding this record because Lot was Abraham's nephew. Consider God and Abraham's relationship in the previous two entries about Abraham. Note that God promised Abraham that He would not allow anyone to wrong or harm him and those for whom he was responsible (see Genesis 12:3 and I Chronicles 16:21-22).

It is also noteworthy that the sin of the inhabitants of the cities that were destroyed is described as very grievous, wicked, unjust, and ungodly. God protected the world from ungodly and wicked men, and fulfilled His promise to Abraham.

Pharaoh and the Passover — Exodus 12:12

> Exodus 12:12
>
> For I will pass through the land of Egypt that night, and <u>I will strike all the firstborn in the land of Egypt, both man and beast</u>; and <u>on all the gods of Egypt I will execute judgments</u>: I am the LORD.

See chapter four of this study, "Pharaoh and the Passover."

B. Working List—Literal

Aaron and the Golden Calf – Exodus 32:35

Exodus 32:1, 8, 26-28 and 35

[1] When the people saw that Moses delayed to come down from the mountain, the people gathered themselves together to Aaron and said to him, "Up, make us gods who shall go before us. As for this Moses, the man who brought us up out of the land of Egypt, we do not know what has become of him."

[8] They have turned aside quickly out of the way that I commanded them. They have made for themselves a golden calf and have worshiped it and sacrificed to it and said, 'These are your gods, O Israel, who brought you up out of the land of Egypt!

[26] Then Moses stood in the gate of the camp and said, "Who is on the LORD's side? Come to me." And all the sons of Levi gathered around him.

[27] And he said to them, "Thus says the LORD God of Israel, 'Put your sword on your side each of you, and go to and fro from gate to gate throughout the camp, and each of you kill his brother and his companion and his neighbor.'"

> ²⁸ And the sons of Levi did according to the word of Moses. And that day about three thousand men of the people fell.
>
> ³⁵ Then <u>the Lord sent a plague on the people,</u> because they made the calf, the one that Aaron made.

See the context recorded in Exodus 32:1-35.

See also Deuteronomy 9:11-29; Nehemiah 9:18; Psalm 106:19-23; Acts 7:41; I Corinthians 10:6-14.

By worshiping the calf, the people of Israel broke their covenant agreement with God and violated explicit instructions from the Lord God.

The quick execution of justice prevented the hearts of evildoers from being fully set to continue doing evil. Swift justice also brought deliverance to the oppressed. The Lord God executed swift justice against those who desired to worship a golden calf. God's swift justice brought deliverance from the furtherance of evil at that time. God's actions also preserved some to carry on the line of Christ. Thus God's swift justice brought both immediate and ongoing benefit.

Nadab and Abihu – Leviticus 10:2

> Leviticus 10:1-3
>
> ¹ Now Nadab and Abihu, the sons of Aaron, each took his censer and put fire in it and laid incense on it and offered unauthorized fire before the Lord, which he had not commanded them.
>
> ² And <u>fire came out from before the Lord and consumed them,</u> and they died before the Lord.

> ³ Then Moses said to Aaron, "This is what the Lord has said: 'Among those who are near me I will be sanctified, and before all the people I will be glorified.'" And Aaron held his peace.

See the context recorded in Leviticus 9:22-10:20.

See also Exodus 28:1 and 35-43; Exodus 30:1-9, 34-38; Leviticus 6:8-9, 12-13; 16:1-3, 12-13; and 22:9; Leviticus 8 (similar to Exodus 28); Numbers 3:4; 16:46; 26:61; and II Chronicles 26:17-20.

The covenant of the law gave explicit instructions about how to approach the presence of God in the tabernacle and who was to do so. Aaron and his sons (Eleazar, Ithamar, Nadab and Abihu) were anointed and ordained as priest to serve God in the tabernacle. God provided fire from heaven for the altar, which was to be kept burning continually. Nadab and Abihu, entered from outside the tabernacle and brought fire they had started by their own human efforts. Thus they approached God with their unauthorized fire. Their fire had not been sanctified for the things of God. The use of fire of their own making was arrogant and irreverent. Their approach was contrary to God's explicit instructions.

See David Bergey, *Jesus Christ Our Approach Offering* in general for how one was to approach God and specifically pages 138 and 188. Also see David Bergey, *Jesus Christ Our Complete Offering*, page 346.

Did God Do It?

Korah's Rebellion – Numbers 16:35

> Numbers 16:3, 9-10, and 32-35
>
> ³ They assembled themselves together against Moses and against Aaron and said to them, "You have gone too far! For all in the congregation are holy, every one of them, and the Lord is among them. Why then do you exalt yourselves above the assembly of the Lord?"
>
> ⁹ Is it too small a thing for you that the God of Israel has separated you from the congregation of Israel, to bring you near to himself, to do service in the tabernacle of the Lord and to stand before the congregation to minister to them,
>
> ¹⁰ and that he has brought you near him, and all your brothers the sons of Levi with you? And would you seek the priesthood also?
>
> ³² And the earth opened its mouth and swallowed them up, with their households and all the people who belonged to Korah and all their goods.
>
> ³³ So they and all that belonged to them went down alive into Sheol, and the earth closed over them, and they perished from the midst of the assembly.
>
> ³⁴ And all Israel who were around them fled at their cry, for they said, "Lest the earth swallow us up!"
>
> ³⁵ And <u>fire came out from the Lord and consumed the 250 men offering the incense.</u>

B. *Working List—Literal*

See the context recorded in Numbers 16:1-40.

See also Psalm 106:16-17; Numbers 3:5-10 and 38; 26:9-11; and 27:3; I Chronicles 9:19; Ephesians 2:18 and 3:12; Hebrews 2:17, 3:1; 5:5-10; 7:17; 8:1-4; 9:8; 10:19-20; and Jude 1:11.

See also David Bergey, *Jesus Christ Our Approach Offering*, page 141.

Korah and a group of wicked men (including Dathan and Abiram) treated the Lord with contempt by disregarding the laws of holiness (sanctification) that God had set up. Contrary to God's instructions, these men claimed that they, and in fact all of the children of Israel, were holy and thus could enter God's presence. Furthermore, as verse 10 says, they desired the priesthood and thus access to God.

From the perspective of the New Testament, we know that Christ became both the high priest and the final sacrificial offering to make atonement once and for all. When Korah, Dathan, Abiram and others denied the need for the priesthood they denied the need for the coming savior. They rejected God's plan of redemption and salvation.

The open access to God these men arrogantly sought was not available at the time of Numbers 16. However, by Christ's accomplished work, all who call on the name of the Lord are sanctified and given free access to the presence of God. See Romans 5:2 and Ephesians 2:18.

Baal Worship at Peor – Numbers 25:11

Numbers 25:1-11

¹ While Israel lived in Shittim, the people began to whore with the daughters of Moab.

² These invited the people to the sacrifices of their gods, and the people ate and bowed down to their gods.

³ So Israel yoked himself to Baal of Peor. And the anger of the Lord was kindled against Israel.

⁴ And <u>the Lord said to Moses, "Take all the chiefs of the people and hang them in the sun before the Lord</u>, that the fierce anger of the Lord may turn away from Israel."

⁵ And <u>Moses said to the judges of Israel, "Each of you kill those of his men who have yoked themselves to Baal of Peor."</u>

⁶ And behold, one of the people of Israel came and brought a Midianite woman to his family, in the sight of Moses and in the sight of the whole congregation of the people of Israel, while they were weeping in the entrance of the tent of meeting.

⁷ When Phinehas the son of Eleazar, son of Aaron the priest, saw it, he rose and left the congregation and took a spear in his hand

⁸ and went after the man of Israel into the chamber and pierced both of them, the man of Israel and the woman through her belly. Thus the plague on the people of Israel was stopped.

⁹ Nevertheless, those who died by the plague were twenty-four thousand.

¹⁰ And the Lord said to Moses,

¹¹ "Phinehas the son of Eleazar, son of Aaron the priest, has turned back my wrath from the people of Israel, in

that he was jealous with my jealousy among them, so that I did not consume the people of Israel in my jealousy.

Numbers 31:16
Behold, these [Midianite women], on Balaam's advice, caused the people of Israel to act treacherously against the LORD in the incident of Peor, and so the plague came among the congregation of the LORD.

See the context recorded in Numbers 25:1-18.

See also Judges 2:11-13, I Corinthians 10:8-14, Joshua 13:22; and Revelation 2:14.

Balak, king of Moab, made a league with the Midianites to oppose Israel (Numbers 22:4). Balak also enlisted a crooked prophet, Balaam to curse Israel (Numbers 22-24) but God intervened and Balaam was unable to curse Israel. Even so, together they seduced the people of Israel to worship Baal. God's people broke their covenant agreement with God. Then when at Peor, an Israelite man brought a Midianite woman to his family in the congregation of Israel. This act was a display of extreme contempt for the Lord God.

God did not cause the problem but He did provide a solution. God gave Moses instructions to have the judges kill all who had "yoked themselves to Baal of Peor." Phinehas obeyed God and carried out God's justice. Thus the plague was stopped and lives were saved. In this manner, the Lord God executed swift justice against those who desired to worship Baal and pollute the hearts of many Israelites.

Did God Do It?

> Deuteronomy 4:1 and 3-4
>
> ¹ And now, O Israel, listen...
>
> ³ Your eyes have seen what the LORD did at Baal-peor, for <u>the LORD your God destroyed from among you all the men who followed the Baal of Peor</u>.
> ⁴ But you who held fast to the LORD your God are all alive today.

God's swift justice delivered many Israelites from the spread of evil. God's actions preserved as many as possible. God protected His purpose in Christ and His plan of redemption and salvation for all.

Verse 3 says "the anger of the Lord was kindled against Israel" and verse 11 says the swift execution of justice "turned back my wrath." From a human perspective, anger often has a negative connotation because humans often misbehave when angry. To rightly understand the Scriptures, we cannot import this negative association with God's anger. The basic meaning of the Hebrew word for anger is nostril and gives the mind picture of one's nostrils flaring in anger. The anger of the Lord is related to the sin of God's people. "The anger of the Lord is not sinful, evil, or the source of capricious attitudes or deeds."[1] Instead, the use of this Hebrew word personifies God's displeasure with sin. When His people sin, it displeases God but it also causes Him grief and sorrow. God deals with sin according to the established standard of justice of the time. Even in His displeasure God is just.

---

1. R. Laird Harris, Gleason L. Archer, and Bruce K. Waltke, *The Theological Wordbook of the Old Testament* (Chicago, Illinois: Moody Publishers 1980), p. 58, number 133a.

B. *Working List—Literal*

The Sin of Achan at Ai – Joshua 7:25

> Joshua 6:2-3
>
> ² And the LORD said to Joshua, "See, I have given Jericho into your hand, with its king and mighty men of valor. ³ You shall march around the city, all the men of war going around the city once. Thus shall you do for six days.

The record of the fall of Jericho is familiar to many. What occurred in Joshua 7 must be understood in light of God's instructions regarding how to take Jericho.

> Joshua 6:16-19
>
> ¹⁶ And at the seventh time, when the priests had blown the trumpets, Joshua said to the people, "Shout, for the LORD has given you the city.
>
> ¹⁷ And the city and all that is within it shall be devoted to the LORD for destruction. Only Rahab the prostitute [innkeeper] and all who are with her in her house shall live, because she hid the messengers whom we sent.
>
> ¹⁸ But you, keep yourselves from the things devoted to destruction, lest when you have devoted them you take any of the devoted things and make the camp of Israel a thing for destruction and bring trouble upon it.
>
> ¹⁹ But all silver and gold, and every vessel of bronze and iron, are holy to the LORD; they shall go into the treasury of the LORD."

Did God Do It?

The Lord was with Joshua and the Israelites took the city of Jericho that day. As we continue, let us bear in mind God's instructions in verse 18, "keep yourselves from the things devoted to destruction, lest...you take any of the devoted things and make the camp of Israel a thing for destruction and bring trouble upon it."

> Joshua 7:1
> But the people of Israel broke faith in regard to the devoted things, for Achan the son of Carmi, son of Zabdi, son of Zerah, of the tribe of Judah, took some of the devoted things....

After Achan stole some of the devoted things. It was not initially known. So Israel went into battle against the city of Ai. Because of the Achan's sin the men of Ai defeated the Israelites and killed about 36 of them. Then Joshua fell on his face before the Lord.

> Joshua 7:10-25
> [10] The LORD said to Joshua, "Get up! Why have you fallen on your face?
> [11] Israel has sinned; they have transgressed my covenant that I commanded them; they have taken some of the devoted things; they have stolen and lied and put them among their own belongings.
> [12] Therefore the people of Israel cannot stand before their enemies. They turn their backs before their enemies, because they have become devoted for destruction. I will be with you no more, unless you destroy the devoted things from among you.

¹³ Get up! Consecrate the people and say, 'Consecrate yourselves for tomorrow; for thus says the Lord, God of Israel, "There are devoted things in your midst, O Israel. You cannot stand before your enemies until you take away the devoted things from among you."

¹⁴ In the morning therefore you shall be brought near by your tribes. And the tribe that the Lord takes by lot shall come near by clans. And the clan that the Lord takes shall come near by households. And the household that the Lord takes shall come near man by man.

¹⁵ And <u>he who is taken [by the Lord] with the devoted things shall be burned with fire, he and all that he has</u>, because he has transgressed the covenant of the Lord, and because he has done an outrageous thing in Israel.'"

¹⁶ So Joshua rose early in the morning and brought Israel near tribe by tribe, and the tribe of Judah was taken.

¹⁷ And he brought near the clans of Judah, and the clan of the Zerahites was taken. And he brought near the clan of the Zerahites man by man, and Zabdi was taken.

¹⁸ And he brought near his household man by man, and Achan the son of Carmi, son of Zabdi, son of Zerah, of the tribe of Judah, was taken.

¹⁹ Then Joshua said to Achan, "My son, give glory to the Lord God of Israel and give praise to him. And tell me now what you have done; do not hide it from me."

²⁰ And Achan answered Joshua, "Truly I have sinned against the Lord God of Israel, and this is what I did:

> ²¹ when I saw among the spoil a beautiful cloak from Shinar, and 200 shekels of silver, and a bar of gold weighing 50 shekels, then I coveted them and took them. And see, they are hidden in the earth inside my tent, with the silver underneath."
> ²² So Joshua sent messengers, and they ran to the tent; and behold, it was hidden in his tent with the silver underneath.
> ²³ And they took them out of the tent and brought them to Joshua and to all the people of Israel. And they laid them down before the LORD.
> ²⁴ And Joshua and all Israel with him took Achan the son of Zerah, and the silver and the cloak and the bar of gold, and his sons and daughters and his oxen and donkeys and sheep and his tent and all that he had. And they brought them up to the Valley of Achor.
> ²⁵ And Joshua said, "Why did you bring trouble on us?² <u>The LORD brings trouble on you</u> today." And all Israel stoned him with stones. They burned them with fire and stoned them with stones.

See the context recorded in Joshua 6:15-7:26. These verses show that the Lord executed judgement on Achan because he transgressed the covenant of the Lord and did an outrageous thing in Israel.

---

2. See also I Chronicles 2:7: "The son of Carmi: Achan, the troubler of Israel, who broke faith in the matter of the devoted thing."

B. Working List—Literal

To understand what the Scriptures say regarding "devoted things"[3] see the following:

- Leviticus 27:21-28: "Every devoted thing is most holy to the Lord."
- Numbers 18:14: "Every devoted thing in Israel shall be yours [the Lord's]."
- Deuteronomy 7:25-26: "The carved images of their gods you shall burn with fire. You shall not covet the silver or the gold that is on them or take it for yourselves, lest you be ensnared by it, for it is an abomination to the LORD your God. And you shall not bring an abominable thing into your house and become devoted to destruction like it. You shall utterly detest and abhor it, for it is devoted to destruction."
- Deuteronomy 13:11-18

Regarding judgment by stoning when God's commandments were broken, see Numbers 15:30-36.

While entering the promised land, an Israelite, Achan, took things God had previously commanded that he should not take. They were to keep away from devoted things so that they would not be snared by them and bring trouble on Israel. God determined to devote or to set these things apart to come into the treasury of the Lord. Only those who were sanctified, such as the priest, were to touch devoted

---

3. The Hebrew word for "devoted things" is used here in the sense of a "thing hostile to theocracy, and therefore to be either destroyed, or, in the case of certain objects (e.g. silver and gold, vessels of brass and iron Joshua 6:19, 24), set apart to sacred uses." See Brown, Driver, and Briggs *A Hebrew and English Lexicon of the Old Testament* (Oxford, England, UK: Clarendon Press, 1906) as offered in the e-lexicon on Parallel Plus by TheBible.org ©2017.

things. So first off, Achan was not to take the devoted things; and secondly he was not to touch them. Thus, Achan violated explicit instructions from God. God had lovingly and justly informed Israel, that if an Israelite violated the devoted things, it would be an abomination to the Lord, a transgression against the covenant of the Lord, and the cause of destruction and trouble to all Israel. Achan's sin brought these consequences upon Israel. Notably the inhabitants of the city of Ai were able to defeat the Israelites and 36 Israelites died.

Achan received the justice due to him as stated in Joshua 7:15: "And he who is taken with the devoted things shall be burned with fire, he and all that he has, because he has transgressed the covenant of the Lord, and because he has done an outrageous thing in Israel."

Let us recall that the covenant of the law was a collective covenant so that an individual's sin could affect others (see Joshua 22 in chapter five of this study). God's just actions prevented further defeat and preserved many of His people that day.

In the record about Achan in Joshua 7, there is also an unusual expression in Joshua 7:7 that is figurative (idiom). This figurative occurrence is listed in appendix C.

Joshua against Amorite Enemies – Joshua 10:8 and 11

> Joshua 10:5
> Then the five kings of the Amorites, the king of Jerusalem, the king of Hebron, the king of Jarmuth, the king of Lachish, and the king of Eglon, gathered their forces and went up with all their armies and encamped against Gibeon and made war against it.

B. Working List—Literal

When the king of Jerusalem heard that Joshua had captured Ai and was heading his way, he gathered other kings into a coalition to outnumber Israel. These kings drew Israel into battle by attacking the Gibeonites who had made peace with Israel. As expected, the Gibeonites called Israel to come to their defense.

> Joshua 10:8-12
>
> [8] And the LORD said to Joshua, "Do not fear them [the inhabitants], for <u>I have given them into your hands</u>. Not a man of them shall stand before you."
>
> [9] So Joshua came upon them suddenly, having marched up all night from Gilgal.
>
> [10] And the LORD threw them into a panic before Israel, who struck them with a great blow at Gibeon and chased them by the way of the ascent of Beth-horon and struck them as far as Azekah and Makkedah.
>
> [11] And as they fled before Israel, while they were going down the ascent of Beth-horon, <u>the Lord threw down large stones from heaven on them</u> as far as Azekah, and they died. There were more who died because of the hailstones than the sons of Israel killed with the sword.
>
> [12] At that time Joshua spoke to the LORD in the day when the LORD gave the Amorites over to the sons of Israel...

Joshua walked with God and obeyed information from Him.

Did God Do It?

> Joshua 10:42
>
> And Joshua captured all these kings and their land at one time, because the LORD God of Israel fought for Israel.

See the context recorded in Joshua 10:7-42.

God promised that as the people of Israel entered the promised land, He would defeat their enemies. In this record, He did so.

The following verses provide insight into the corrupt character of Israel's enemies.

> Deuteronomy 9:4-5
>
> [4] ...Whereas it is because of the wickedness of these nations that the LORD is driving them out before you. [5] Not because of your righteousness or the uprightness of your heart are you going in to possess their land, but because of the wickedness of these nations the LORD your God is driving them out from before you, and that he may confirm the word that the LORD swore to your fathers, to Abraham, to Isaac, and to Jacob.

> Deuteronomy 12:31
>
> You shall not worship the LORD your God in that way, for every abominable thing that the LORD hates they [the inhabitants] have done for their gods, for they even burn their sons and their daughters in the fire to their gods.

The inhabitants were wicked, doing abominable acts for the sake of their gods; they opposed the One True God and were enemies to His people.

In addition to Deuteronomy 9:4-5 and 12:31 as seen above, also consider the following about why the inhabitants were to be utterly destroyed. See Exodus 34:10-28; Leviticus 18:24-25; Numbers 33:51-56; Deuteronomy 7:1-6 and 25; 18:12; and 20:16-18; Ezra 9:11-14; I Kings 14:24. II Kings 23 tells of the reforms under King Josiah and demonstrates just how necessary it was to utterly destroy the nations as they entered the promised land.

God had committed Himself to those who committed themselves to Him. God fought for His people Israel. We have seen that the people of Israel were in the line of Christ and thus important to God's plan of redemption and salvation for all. God's instructions were always for the good of His people as they awaited the coming savior. As they entered the promised land God gave instructions that spared His people from being ensnared by the inhabitant's idolatrous practices. God was faithful to His Word and protected His people.

In the context of this Joshua 10 record, there is another unusual expression in verse 10: "the Lord threw them into a panic." These words are figurative (idiom) and are handled in appendix C.

Did God Do It?

Joshua against Enemy Kings – Joshua 11:6 and 8

> Joshua 11:5-9 and 12
>
> ⁵ And all these kings joined their forces and came and encamped together at the waters of Merom to fight against Israel.
> ⁶ And the LORD said to Joshua, "Do not be afraid of them, for tomorrow at this time <u>I will give over all of them, slain, to Israel</u>. You shall hamstring their horses and burn their chariots with fire."
> ⁷ So Joshua and all his warriors came suddenly against them by the waters of Merom and fell upon them.
> ⁸ And <u>the LORD gave them into the hand of Israel</u>, who struck them and chased them as far as Great Sidon and Misrephoth-maim, and eastward as far as the Valley of Mizpeh. And they struck them until he left none remaining.
> ⁹ And Joshua did to them just as the LORD said to him…
>
> ¹² And all the cities of those kings, and all their kings, Joshua captured, and struck them with the edge of the sword, devoting them to destruction, just as Moses the servant of the LORD had commanded.

See the context recorded in Joshua 11:1-20.

God fought for His people as they entered the promised land. This passage is similar to Joshua 10:8-12 above. The information about the corrupt character of their enemies and why to utterly destroy them in the previous entry is also applicable here.

B. Working List—Literal

In the context of this Joshua 11 record, there is another unusual expression in verse 20: "For it was the Lord's doing to harden their hearts." These words are figurative and are handled in appendix C.

The Ark of God and the Philistines – I Samuel 5:6-7 and 9

> I Samuel 5:2-9
>
> ² Then the Philistines took the ark of God and brought it into the house of Dagon and set it up beside Dagon.
> ³ And when the people of Ashdod rose early the next day, behold, Dagon had fallen face downward on the ground before the ark of the Lord. So they took Dagon and put him back in his place.
> ⁴ But when they rose early on the next morning, behold, Dagon had fallen face downward on the ground before the ark of the Lord, and the head of Dagon and both his hands were lying cut off on the threshold. Only the trunk of Dagon was left to him.
> ⁵ This is why the priests of Dagon and all who enter the house of Dagon do not tread on the threshold of Dagon in Ashdod to this day.
> ⁶ <u>The hand of the Lord was heavy against the people of Ashdod</u>, and <u>he terrified and afflicted them</u> with tumors, both Ashdod and its territory.
> ⁷ And when the men of Ashdod saw how things were, they said, "The ark of the God of Israel must not remain with us, for <u>his hand is hard against us and against Dagon our god</u>."

Did God Do It?

> [8] So they sent and gathered together all the lords of the Philistines and said, "What shall we do with the ark of the God of Israel?" They answered, "Let the ark of the God of Israel be brought around to Gath." So they brought the ark of the God of Israel there.
> [9] But after they had brought it around, <u>the hand of the Lord was against the city</u>, causing a very great panic, and <u>he afflicted the men of the city</u>, both young and old, so that tumors broke out on them.

See the context recorded in I Samuel 4:1-5:12. See also the related account of I Samuel 4:3 in appendix C.

The Ark of God represented God's presence; it was to be treated with great honor and respect. It was one of the holy, or sanctified, things of God, set apart for God's purposes; it was to be treated according to God's explicit instructions. Some of those instructions are found in the following scriptures: Exodus 25:10-22; Numbers 1:50-54; 4:1-20; and 18:25-26, and 31-32.

Dagon was one of the chief gods of the Philistines and was associated with Baal. The Philistines were some of the wicked inhabitants who did abominable acts for the sake of their gods. They were enemies of God and of His people. The Philistines received the consequences of their irreverent actions. The Lord God demonstrated that He is the Most Powerful and Most High God.

The Ark of God and Men of Beth-shemesh — I Samuel 6:19

> I Samuel 6:19
>
> And <u>he [the Lord] struck some of the men of Beth-shemesh</u>, because they looked upon the ark of the LORD. <u>He struck seventy men of them</u>, and the people mourned because <u>the LORD had struck the people</u> with a great blow.

See the context recorded in I Samuel 5:1-7:14.

This is a continuation of the events discussed in the previous entry of I Samuel 5. The points made in the previous entry also apply here.

The Ark of God and Uzzah — II Samuel 6:7

> II Samuel 6:6-7
>
> ⁶ And when they came to the threshing floor of Nacon, Uzzah put out his hand to the ark of God and took hold of it, for the oxen stumbled.
>
> ⁷ And the anger of the LORD, was kindled against Uzzah, and <u>God struck him down</u> there because of his error, and he died there beside the ark of God.

See the context recorded in II Samuel 6:1-11.

See also Exodus 19:11-13; Exodus 25:10-16 and 21-22; Exodus 30:26-29; Numbers 1:50-51; 3:5-10 and 38; 4:1, 4-5, 15, and 20; and I Chronicles 13:3 and 9-11.

The Ark of God represented God's presence; God said He would commune with His people there.

Exodus 25:21-22

²¹ And you shall put the mercy seat on the top of the ark, and in the ark you shall put the testimony that I shall give you.
²² There I will meet with you, and from above the mercy seat, from between the two cherubim that are on the ark of the testimony, I will speak with you about all that I will give you in commandment for the people of Israel.

The ark of God was one of the holy things of God in the tabernacle, which were to be treated according to God's explicit instructions.

Numbers 1:50-51

⁵⁰ But appoint the Levites over the tabernacle of the testimony, and over all its furnishings, and over all that belongs to it. They are to carry the tabernacle and all its furnishings, and they shall take care of it and shall camp around the tabernacle.
⁵¹ When the tabernacle is to set out, the Levites shall take it down, and when the tabernacle is to be pitched, the Levites shall set it up. And if any outsider comes near, he shall be put to death.

Numbers 4:15

And when Aaron and his sons have finished covering the sanctuary and all the furnishings of the sanctuary, as the camp sets out, after that the sons of Kohath shall come to carry these, but they must not touch the holy things,

> lest they die. These are the things of the tent of meeting that the sons of Kohath are to carry.

God designated certain Levites for the care and transportation of the furnishings, which included the ark of God. Additionally, the Levites were to transport the Ark of God by using poles inserted into rings at the four corners of the ark; the poles were not to be removed (Exodus 25:10-16). In this way, no one had any need to touch the ark, and it could be successfully transported without harm to anyone. As recorded in II Samuel 6, the Ark of God was transported upon a new cart and not according to God's explicit instructions, which would have been by Levites using the transport poles.

Uzzah put out his hand to the ark of God and took hold of it because the oxen stumbled. Would not God be able to stabilize the ark Himself? Was it not presumptuous of Uzzah to think to help God?

Uzzah was not a Levite. The covenant of the law said that if a non-Levite came near he would be put to death. Even the Levites were not to touch the holy things lest they die. While transporting the Ark of God, Uzzah touched it and died accordingly.

David — II Samuel 24:15 and I Chronicles 21:14

> II Samuel 24:15
> So <u>the LORD sent a pestilence on Israel</u> from the morning until the appointed time. And there died of the people from Dan to Beersheba 70,000 men.

Did God Do It?

> I Chronicles 21:14
>
> So <u>the Lord sent a pestilence on Israel, and 70,000 men of Israel fell.</u>

See chapter eight of this study about David.

Uzziah, King of Judah – II Chronicles 26:20

> II Chronicles 26:3-5
>
> ³ Uzziah was sixteen years old when he began to reign, and he reigned fifty-two years in Jerusalem. His mother's name was Jecoliah of Jerusalem.
> ⁴ And he did what was right in the eyes of the Lord, according to all that his father Amaziah had done.
> ⁵ He set himself to seek God in the days of Zechariah, who instructed him in the fear of God, and as long as he sought the Lord, God made him prosper.

Uzziah started his reign doing what was right in the sight of the Lord. Uzziah made a decision to set himself to seek God.

> II Chronicles 26:16-20
>
> ¹⁶ But when he [Uzziah, King of Judah] was strong, he grew proud, to his destruction [his heart was so proud that he acted corruptly^{NASB}]. For he was unfaithful to the Lord his God and entered the temple of the Lord to burn incense on the altar of incense.
> ¹⁷ But Azariah the priest went in after him, with eighty priests of the Lord who were men of valor,
> ¹⁸ and they withstood King Uzziah and said to him, "It

is not for you, Uzziah, to burn incense to the LORD, but for the priests, the sons of Aaron, who are consecrated to burn incense. Go out of the sanctuary, for you have done wrong, and it will bring you no honor from the LORD God."

[19] Then Uzziah was angry. Now he had a censer in his hand to burn incense, and when he became angry with the priests, leprosy broke out on his forehead in the presence of the priests in the house of the LORD, by the altar of incense.

[20] And Azariah the chief priest and all the priests looked at him, and behold, he was leprous in his forehead! And they rushed him out quickly, and he himself hurried to go out, because <u>the LORD had struck him</u>.

See the context recorded in II Chronicles 26:1-21.

See also Exodus 28:43; 30:1-9, 26-37; Leviticus 10:3; 11:44-45; and 16:11-13.

The covenant of the law gave explicit instructions about how to approach the presence of God in the tabernacle and who was to do so. All who entered God's presence were to be sanctified and approach God according to God's explicit instructions. Only Aaron and his sons were authorized to offer incense on the altar.

Uzziah started out with his heart right toward God and was instructed in the things of God. However, once God had prospered him, he grew proud and acted corruptly. With full knowledge of his error, he arrogantly approached the altar of incense.

Did God Do It?

To better understand how and who was to approach the altar, see *Jesus Christ Our Approach Offering* by David Bergey, page 188.

Herod – Acts 12:23

> Acts 12:1-3
> ¹ About that time Herod the king laid violent hands on some who belonged to the church.
> ² He killed James the brother of John with the sword,
> ³ and when he saw that it pleased the Jews, he proceeded to arrest Peter also. This was during the days of Unleavened Bread.

Herod set about to harm some of those in the church. First he killed James, and then he arrested Peter.

> Acts 12:19-24
> ¹⁹ And after Herod searched for him and did not find him, he examined the sentries and ordered that they should be put to death. Then he went down from Judea to Caesarea and spent time there.
> ²⁰ Now Herod was angry with the people of Tyre and Sidon, and they came to him with one accord, and having persuaded Blastus, the king's chamberlain, they asked for peace, because their country depended on the king's country for food.
> ²¹ On an appointed day Herod put on his royal robes, took his seat upon the throne, and delivered an oration to them.
> ²² And the people were shouting, "The voice of a god,

and not of a man!"

²³ Immediately <u>an angel of the Lord struck him down</u>, because he did not give God the glory, and he was eaten by worms and breathed his last.

²⁴ But the word of God increased and multiplied.

See the context recorded in Acts 11:19-12:25.

Herod persecuted God's people. Then, on an appointed day, Herod sat on the royal throne or judgment seat and addressed the assembly. The historian Josephus recorded in *Jewish Antiquities* 19.344 that Herod's royal robes were made of silver that sparkled in the sun and provoked the crowd's acclamation that he was a god. Herod did not deny their response and accepted the people's voice that he was a god. He accepted glory due only to God Who is Lord overall. Verse 23 says an angel, or messenger, of the Lord struck Herod down because he did not give the glory to God.

Observations

By reading the context and related passages of the unusual expressions in this appendix, we have determined the expressions presented here are literal. Please again note that this appendix is a working list; it is neither comprehensive nor the final word on the subject. If we learn more, we will reevaluate.

Now what have we learned by collecting these records, reading them over and over, and looking for patterns? We have identified some common elements in these kinds of records. One or more of the following factors may occur in the context or related passages of expressions that appear literal.

- Actions by a person or people contrary to explicit instructions from God, including explicit instructions regarding:
  - Keeping the covenant of the law
  - Idolatrous worship of other gods
  - Irreverent worship of the Lord God
- The recipient(s) of the consequences were often ungodly, wicked people and/or enemies of God's people
- In all that God did, He was faithful to His Word.
  - God was faithful to His standards of justice.
  - God was faithful to His eternal purposes in Christ.
  - God was faithful to His nature, including mercy to enemies.

To close, let us proclaim, to God be the Glory!

Jude 1:25

To the only God, our Savior, through Jesus Christ our Lord, be glory, majesty, dominion, and authority, before all time and now and forever. Amen.

Appendix C

Working List—Figurative

This working list provides additional examples of unusual expressions in the Scriptures that seem to say God did something that He may or may not have done. According to the best understanding at this point, the unusual expressions in this appendix are figurative.

Throughout this study, we have endeavored to handle the Scriptures with integrity and by applying sound practices of allowing the Scriptures to interpret themselves. Appendix C is presented as a working list for further study. It is neither comprehensive nor the final word on the subject.

The unusual expressions in appendix C are a biblical idiom that may be represented as "the Lord God + action + recipient." This pattern of words is commonly found and often literal. However, expressions with the pattern "the Lord God + action + recipient" may be figurative when the context and related passages shows that it is not true to fact. Thus the following is a working list of other unusual expressions found to be figurative.

Review from Chapter Two of this Study

We have seen that the following characteristics often accompany the particular biblical idiom under consideration in this study.

- This particular biblical idiom seems to say God did something contrary to His nature or a person's freedom of will, but according to the context and related scriptures, He did not.
- When the unusual expression has the word "heart" and seems to say God made someone's heart do or believe something, the expression is usually figurative and not literal.
- The idiom's meaning is understood from biblical culture, context, and related scriptures.
- Culturally this idiom was not intended to blame God nor was it intended to say He did evil. While the devil is the source of evil, in the culture of the lands and times of the Bible, the devil was not named. Instead, God Who is Lord overall was named. The Lord God was magnified in the face of affliction.

Furthermore the context and related scriptures of this idiom often, but not always, show the following:

- Who, other than God, was responsible for the action credited to God.
- That someone had information or instructions from God that he or she did not believe.
- The spiritual cause behind the physical.

This appendix is provided to assist those who read this book and would like to consider more similar expressions in the Scriptures.

How this Appendix Is Organized

In this appendix, the underlined words are the unusual expression under consideration. The examples of those expressions are organized in the following way:

- Idiom (Basic)
- Idiomatic expressions with the word "heart"
- Idiom without wrongdoing

Within each section the lists are presented in canonical order; that is to say, in the order of the books of the Bible.

Idiom (Basic)

Moses – Exodus 5:22

> Exodus 5:6-9 and 22-23
>
> ⁶ The same day Pharaoh commanded the taskmasters of the people and their foremen,
>
> ⁷ "You shall no longer give the people straw to make bricks, as in the past; let them go and gather straw for themselves.
>
> ⁸ But the number of bricks that they made in the past you shall impose on them, you shall by no means reduce it, for they are idle. Therefore they cry, 'Let us go and offer sacrifice to our God.'

Did God Do It?

> ⁹ Let heavier work be laid on the men that they may labor at it and pay no regard to lying words."
>
> ²² Then Moses turned to the LORD and said, <u>"O Lord, why have you done evil to this people?</u> Why did you ever send me?
>
> ²³ For since I came to Pharaoh to speak in your name, he has done evil to this people, and you have not delivered your people at all."

See the context recorded in Exodus 3:10-6:13.

This record is handled in chapter two of this study entitled, "Moses and an Unusual Expression."

Joshua and the City of Ai – Joshua 7:7

> Joshua 7:1 and 7
>
> ¹ But the people of Israel broke faith in regard to the devoted things, for Achan the son of Carmi, son of Zabdi, son of Zerah, of the tribe of Judah, took some of the devoted things. And the anger of the LORD burned against the people of Israel.
>
> ⁷ And Joshua said, "Alas, O LORD God, why have you brought this people over the Jordan at all, <u>to give us into the hands of the Amorites, to destroy us</u>? Would that we had been content to dwell beyond the Jordan!

See the context recorded in Joshua 6-7.

As background, consider what God had promised Joshua as he led God's people into the promised land.

C. Working List—Figurative

> Joshua 1:3, 5, and 7
>
> ³ Every place that the sole of your foot will tread upon I have given to you, just as I promised to Moses.
>
> ⁵ No man shall be able to stand before you all the days of your life. Just as I was with Moses, so I will be with you. I will not leave you or forsake you.
>
> ⁷ Only be strong and very courageous, being careful to do according to all the law that Moses my servant commanded you. Do not turn from it to the right hand or to the left, that you may have good success wherever you go.

God's plan for Israel as they entered the promised land was for success. God promised that He would not allow anyone to withstand His people. Deuteronomy 3:22 recaps this truth saying to Israel, "You shall not fear them, for it is the Lord your God who fights for you." Moreover, God instructed Joshua and Joshua instructed the Israelites on how to avoid trouble.

> Joshua 6:18-19
>
> ¹⁸ But you, keep yourselves from the things devoted to destruction, lest when you have devoted them you take any of the devoted things and make the camp of Israel a thing for destruction and bring trouble upon it.
>
> ¹⁹ But all silver and gold, and every vessel of bronze and iron, are holy to the Lord; they shall go into the treasury of the Lord."

Again, Deuteronomy recaps.

Did God Do It?

> Deuteronomy 7:1 and 25-26
>
> ¹ When the LORD your God brings you into the land that you are entering to take possession of it, and clears away many nations before you....
>
> ²⁵ The carved images of their gods you shall burn with fire. You shall not covet the silver or the gold that is on them or take it for yourselves, lest you be ensnared by it, for it is an abomination to the LORD your God.
>
> ²⁶ And you shall not bring an abominable thing into your house and become devoted to destruction like it....

With this background let us return to Joshua 7. After Israel was defeated at Ai, Joshua expressed his great distress and deep grief in the manner and custom of his day; he tore his clothes and fell on his face before the ark of the Lord. The elders too put dust on their heads to express their great distress and deep grief. Joshua continued to express his distress when he cried to the Lord in Joshua 7:7 saying, "Alas, O LORD God, why have you brought this people over the Jordan at all, to give us into the hands of the Amorites, to destroy us?" This unusual manner of speech is a biblical idiom in the manner and custom of the lands and times of the Bible. Let us read on and come back to this unusual expression.

After expressing their distress and grief, the Lord God informed Joshua that Israel had transgressed their covenant agreement with God as well as how to handle the breach. We will pick the record up in verse 20, once God identified Achan as the wrongdoer.

C. Working List—Figurative

Joshua 7:20-26

20 And Achan answered Joshua, "Truly I have sinned against the LORD God of Israel, and this is what I did: 21 when I saw among the spoil a beautiful cloak from Shinar, and 200 shekels of silver, and a bar of gold weighing 50 shekels, then I coveted them and took them. And see, they are hidden in the earth inside my tent, with the silver underneath."

22 So Joshua sent messengers, and they ran to the tent; and behold, it was hidden in his tent with the silver underneath.

23 And they took them out of the tent and brought them to Joshua and to all the people of Israel. And they laid them down before the LORD.

24 And Joshua and all Israel with him took Achan the son of Zerah, and the silver and the cloak and the bar of gold, and his sons and daughters and his oxen and donkeys and sheep and his tent and all that he had. And they brought them up to the Valley of Achor.

25 And Joshua said, "Why did you bring trouble on us? The LORD brings trouble on you today." And all Israel stoned him with stones. They burned them with fire and stoned them with stones.

Joshua 7:21 tells us that Achan had coveted and taken the silver and gold that had been set apart to go into the treasury of the Lord. God's heart behind not allowing them to have the spoils of silver and gold was love—to keep trouble away from His people and to prevent anyone from becoming ensnared and destroyed. God had informed them that by bringing an abominable thing into one's house, the wrongdoer would bring destruction on himself. Achan's disobedience caused many Israelites to be killed in the battle against the city of Ai as well as the destruction of himself and all who belonged to him. God's just actions saved the rest of Israel that day from also being destroyed.

Let us return to the unusual expression spoken by Joshua: "Alas, O Lord God, why have you brought this people over the Jordan at all, to give us into the hands of the Amorites, to destroy us?" Is this what happened? No, Achan, not God, brought trouble on Israel. Achan brought the pre-warned consequences upon himself and all who belonged to him. Joshua spoke in the manner of speech of his day and employed a common Hebrew idiom. From the context and related scriptures, we see that the unusual words are not true to fact but instead are figurative. It is a biblical idiom. To our ears what Joshua said seems to blame God. However, according to the culture of the lands and times of the Bible, such expressions were not intended to blame God. God did not cause harm to Israel. Figuratively Joshua cried to the Lord in his distress and grief and magnified the Lord in the face of affliction. Both the manner of expressing grief and distress as well as Joshua's manner of speech are examples of manners and customs of the Scriptures that we need to recognize in order to rightly understand what God is communicating.

C. Working List—Figurative

Elders of Israel – I Samuel 4:3

I Samuel 4:1-4

¹ And the word of Samuel came to all Israel. Now Israel went out to battle against the Philistines. They encamped at Ebenezer, and the Philistines encamped at Aphek. ² The Philistines drew up in line against Israel, and when the battle spread, Israel was defeated before the Philistines, who killed about four thousand men on the field of battle. ³ And when the people came to the camp, the elders of Israel said, "<u>Why has the LORD defeated us</u> today before the Philistines? Let us bring the ark of the covenant of the LORD here from Shiloh, that it may come among us and save us from the power of our enemies." ⁴ So the people sent to Shiloh and brought from there the ark of the covenant of the LORD of hosts, who is enthroned on the cherubim. And the two sons of Eli, Hophni and Phinehas, were there with the ark of the covenant of God.

See the context recorded in I Samuel chapters 2-4.

Concerning the significance of the ark of the covenant (also called the ark of God) consider the following.

Exodus 25:21-22

²¹ And you shall put the mercy seat on the top of the ark, and in the ark you shall put the testimony that I shall give you.

> ²² There I will meet with you, and from above the mercy seat, from between the two cherubim that are on the ark of the testimony, I will speak with you about all that I will give you in commandment for the people of Israel.

The ark of the covenant represented the presence of God to the people of Israel. Numbers 10:33-36 adds that the ark of the covenant was to go before Israel into battle and scatter their enemies before them.

Consider the spiritual environment leading up to the incident in I Samuel 4.

> I Samuel 3:1 and 13
>
> ¹ Now the boy Samuel was ministering to the LORD in the presence of Eli. And the word of the LORD was rare in those days; there was no frequent vision.
>
> ¹³ ...Because his [Eli's] sons were blaspheming God, and he did not restrain them.

God's Word was rare and infrequent in those days and Eli's son's were blaspheming God without restraint.

With this background, we see that the ark of the covenant represented the presence of God. The Israelites were to carry the ark of God into battle with them. This act ought to have been out of genuine reverence for the Lord God. However, I Samuel 4:4 says that the ark of the covenant was accompanied by Eli's sons who blasphemed God. This association does not show reverence for the Lord God. There is no indication in this record that the ark of the covenant was transported to the battlefield because of reverence for the Lord God.

C. Working List—Figurative

Instead the context hints that they may have brought the ark of the covenant as some sort of good luck relic. Without the appropriate accompanying acknowledgment and reverence for the Lord God, the ark of the covenant did not scatter their enemies. The Philistines defeated them once again and captured the ark. What happened to the ark of the covenant in the hands of the Philistines is handled in appendix B "The Ark of God and the Philistines-I Samuel 5:6 and 9."

The elders spoke in the manner of speech of the people of Old Testament times and idiomatically credited God for actions He did not do. The idiom focuses on God Who is Lord overall but was not intended to blame Him. The context shows that it was the irreverent attitude of the people that removed God's protection. They brought consequences upon themselves.

Saul and the Harmful Spirit – I Samuel 16:14-16 and 23

> I Samuel 16:14-16 and 23
>
> ¹⁴ Now the Spirit of the Lord departed from Saul, and <u>a harmful spirit from the Lord tormented him</u>.
>
> ¹⁵ And Saul's servants said to him, "Behold now, <u>a harmful spirit from God is tormenting you</u>.
>
> ¹⁶ Let our lord now command your servants who are before you to seek out a man who is skillful in playing the lyre, and when <u>the harmful spirit from God is upon you</u>, he will play it, and you will be well."
>
> ²³ And whenever <u>the harmful spirit from God was upon Saul</u>, David took the lyre and played it with his hand. So

Saul was refreshed and was well, and the harmful spirit departed from him.

See the context recorded in I Samuel 10-31, which begins with Samuel anointing Saul with spirit and ends with Saul killing himself.

Chapter seven of this study showed from the Scriptures that Saul chose to rebel against God and to transgress against God and His Word. When he did so, he lost the spirit from God. The subsequent spirit that Saul had was from another source.

In I Samuel 16:15-16, the servants said that the evil spirit was from God. While it is true that the servants said it, it is not true of God. The servants' expression was not true to fact.

Consider the following related scripture on the subject of the nature of God's spirit: Nehemiah 9:20, Psalm 143:10, and Luke 11:11-13. Each of these scriptures declares that the spirit from God is good. Then add that many records throughout the Scriptures show that the operation of God's spirit produces much good (for example, consider I Corinthians 12-14). Thirdly, Jesus Christ always did the will of the Father (John 5:30 and 6:38). Jesus Christ gave his disciples (Matthew 10:1) power over unclean and evil spirits as well as delivering people from unclean spirits himself (Luke 7:21). See also Mark 1:21-29; 9:25; and Acts 19:10-17.

Therefore, by the context and related scriptures, we see that God does not give spirits that are characterized by evil. Instead, the Scriptures reveal that spirits of an evil nature are from the devil and not from God. In the Scriptures, spirit beings from the devil are

C. Working List—Figurative

called: devils, demons, unclean spirits, or evil spirits depending on the version.

The Hebrew people of the lands and times of the Bible used these unusual expressions for the reasons covered in chapter two. In brief, in their culture they did not mention the name of other gods. It was not until the life and ministry of the Lord Jesus Christ that the devil and his evil nature were revealed. Therefore, in the speech and idioms of the God-centered culture of the Hebrews of the Old Testament, the devil was not named for his evil deeds. However, they did name God Who gave His Word and is Lord overall. God did not give an evil spirit to Saul—for God only gives a good spirit. The unusual expressions in this record are all figurative.

The End of Saul's Life – I Chronicles 10:14

> I Chronicles 10:13-14
>
> ¹³ So Saul died for his breach of faith. He broke faith with the LORD in that he did not keep the command of the LORD, and also consulted a medium, seeking guidance.
>
> ¹⁴ He did not seek guidance from the LORD. Therefore <u>the LORD put him [Saul] to death</u> and turned the kingdom over to David the son of Jesse.

This record is handled in chapter seven of this study entitled, "Saul."

Idiomatic Expressions with the Word "Heart"

Chapters one and three of this study set forth what the Scriptures say regarding freedom of will and who is responsible for the heart. We summarized our findings as follows. It is essential to keep these in mind in order to understand occurrences of this idiom with the word "heart."

- According to God's original design, people have freedom of will to choose between available sources of information.
- God never oversteps an individual's free will, but always respects people's freedom of will to choose from available sources of information.
- In the Scriptures, thoughts, choices, understanding, and believing are said to occur in the heart.
- Each person is responsible for his or her own heart and the believing, thoughts, choices, and actions that come from the heart.

The records in this subsection include the word "heart." Additionally, in certain context the word "spirit" is used figuratively to refer to person's inner being and what issues from it. Therefore, "spirit" may be used in a similar manner as the word "heart" in the Scriptures, *if* the context supports such a conclusion.

Pharaoh – Exodus 4:21; 7:3; 9:12; 10:1, 20, 27; 11:10

> Exodus 4:21
>
> And the LORD said to Moses, "When you go back to Egypt, see that you do before Pharaoh all the miracles

C. Working List—Figurative

that I have put in your power. But <u>I will harden his heart</u>, so that he will not let the people go.

Exodus 7:3

But <u>I will harden Pharaoh's heart</u>, and though I multiply my signs and wonders in the land of Egypt.

Exodus 9:12

But <u>the Lord hardened the heart of Pharaoh</u>, and he did not listen to them, as the Lord had spoken to Moses.

Exodus 10:1, 20, and 27

[1] Then the Lord said to Moses, "Go in to Pharaoh, for <u>I have hardened his heart and the heart of his servants</u>, that I may show these signs of mine among them,

[20] But <u>the Lord hardened Pharaoh's heart</u>, and he did not let the people of Israel go.

[27] But <u>the Lord hardened Pharaoh's heart</u>, and he would not let them go.

Exodus 11:10

Moses and Aaron did all these wonders before Pharaoh, and <u>the Lord hardened Pharaoh's heart</u>, and he did not let the people of Israel go out of his land.

To consider these occurrences of the idiom, see chapter three of this study "Pharaoh and the Heart."

King Sihon – Deuteronomy 2:30

> Deuteronomy 2:30
> But Sihon the king of Heshbon would not let us [people of Israel] pass by him, for <u>the Lord your God hardened his spirit</u> and <u>made his heart obstinate</u>, that he might give him into your hand, as he is this day.

See the context recorded in Deuteronomy 2:1-37. The people of Israel asked to pass through the land of the Amorites. King Sihon stubbornly refused to give safe passage to them. The same event is also recorded in Numbers 21:21-24.

In Deuteronomy 2:30, "spirit" is used figuratively to refer to person's inner being and what issues from. As such it conveys a similar meaning as "heart." The words "hardened his spirit" and "made his heart obstinate" are two different ways of saying the same thing. Together these expressions say that Sihon willfully and obstinately hardened his heart.

Israel against the Amorite Enemies – Joshua 10:10

> Joshua 10:10
> And <u>the Lord threw them into a panic</u> before Israel, who struck them with a great blow at Gibeon and chased them by the way of the ascent of Beth-horon and struck them as far as Azekah and Makkedah.

See the context recorded in Joshua 10:1-42.

The Hebrew word "threw them into a panic" means "to confuse, discomfit or vex."[1] From the Scriptures, we know that each individual is responsible for his or her own heart, as well as the believing, thoughts, choices, and actions that come from the heart. Whatever God did, He did not overstep anyone's freedom of will. If God had literally thrown Israel's enemies into a panic, then He would have overstepped their freedom of will and would have controlled their response to information received. Instead, God provided information and they responded. The underlined expression "the Lord threw them into a panic" is figurative. On the other hand, in this same verse "[the Lord] struck them with a great blow" is literal and is handled in appendix B.

Joshua against Enemy Kings – Joshua 11:20

> Joshua 11:20
>
> For <u>it was the LORD's doing to harden their hearts</u> that they should come against Israel in battle, in order that they should be devoted to destruction and should receive no mercy but be destroyed, just as the LORD commanded Moses.

See the context recorded in Joshua 10:1-11:23. While reading, please note Joshua 10:42 and 11:15, which agree with the verse above and tell us that it was at God's command and with His assistance that Israel won the battle. Reviewing the two literal records found in appendix B will assist the readers understanding of this

---

1. Brown, Driver, and Briggs, *A Hebrew and English Lexicon of the Old Testament* as seen online at Parallel Plus by TheBible.org.

record. Please review: "Joshua against Amorite Enemies-Joshua 10:8 and 10-12" and "Joshua against Enemy Kings-Joshua 11:6 and 8." In the previous appendix, we noted that God instructed the people of Israel to utterly destroy the inhabitants of the promised land, so they would not be ensnared by their idolatrous practices.

We must also recall that God had committed Himself to those who committed themselves to Him. God and Israel had a covenant relationship whereby He was their God and they were His people.

As recorded in Joshua 11:1, the kings heard of God's might on behalf of Israel. Instead of acknowledging that God is the Most Powerful Lord overall, several kings chose to band together to fight against God's people. These kings had information regarding God's might, but instead of acknowledging God in the situation, they hardened their hearts. Joshua 11:20 figuratively states that it was the Lord's doing that the enemies of His people hardened their hearts. However, God never makes anyone's heart do something against his or her own freedom of will. Whatever God did, He did not overstep the enemies' freedom of will.

David – II Samuel 24:1

> II Samuel 24:1
> Again the anger of the LORD was kindled against Israel, and he [the Lord] incited David against them, saying, "Go, number Israel and Judah."

See chapter eight of this study entitled "David."

In chapter eight, we saw that Satan, and not God incited David to make such a decision in his heart.

C. Working List—Figurative

Darius, King of Assyria – Ezra 6:22 and 7:27

Ezra 6:20-22

¹⁹ On the fourteenth day of the first month, the returned exiles kept the Passover.
²⁰ For the priests and the Levites had purified themselves together; all of them were clean. So they slaughtered the Passover lamb for all the returned exiles, for their fellow priests, and for themselves.
²¹ It was eaten by the people of Israel who had returned from exile, and also by every one who had joined them and separated himself from the uncleanness of the peoples of the land to worship the LORD, the God of Israel.
²² And they kept the Feast of Unleavened Bread seven days with joy, for the <u>LORD had made them joyful and had turned the heart of the king of Assyria to them</u>, so that he aided them in the work of the house of God, the God of Israel.

Ezra 7:9-11 and 27-28

⁹ For on the first day of the first month he began to go up from Babylonia, and on the first day of the fifth month he came to Jerusalem, for the good hand of his God was on him.
¹⁰ For Ezra had set his heart to study the Law of the LORD, and to do it and to teach his statutes and rules in Israel.

> ¹¹ This is a copy of the letter that King Artaxerxes gave to Ezra the priest, the scribe, a man learned in matters of the commandments of the LORD and his statutes for Israel:
>
> ²⁷ Blessed be <u>the LORD, the God of our fathers, who put such a thing as this into the heart of the king</u>, to beautify the house of the LORD that is in Jerusalem,
> ²⁸ And who extended to me his steadfast love before the king and his counselors, and before all the king's mighty officers. I took courage, for the hand of the LORD my God was on me, and I gathered leading men from Israel to go up with me.

See the context recorded in Ezra 4:24-7:28.

In Ezra 6:2-5, a scroll was found; it was a decree, previously issued by King Cyrus, to rebuild the house of God and pay for the project from the royal treasury. The current king, Darius, reissued the decree and further decreed that the project's adversaries stop hindering its progress. Once the house of God was successfully completed, it was dedicated and the returned exiles of Israel observed the Passover. In Ezra 7, the scribe Ezra went up to Jerusalem. The next king (possibly Artaxerxes) acknowledged that Ezra was learned in matters of the commandments of the Lord. The king referred to the Lord as the God of heaven and chose to provide resources to beautify the house of the Lord.

Ezra 6:22 verse has two idiomatic word groups—one regarding the returned exiles and one regarding the king: "for the Lord had made them joyful" and "had turned the heart of the king of Assyria to them." Ezra 7:27 has one idiomatic expression: "the Lord, the God of our fathers, who put such a thing as this into the heart of the king."

Information regarding the blessings of keeping the Passover and the many ways God had blessed His people over the decades was available for the recipients in these expressions to know. Chapter 7 says, Ezra studied the law of the Lord and taught it to the people of Israel (though this may have occurred after the expressions in Ezra 6:22). After Ezra taught God's statutes and ordinances in Israel, the king sent a letter to Ezra. In his letter to Ezra, the king refers to Ezra's God as the God of heaven four times (Ezra 7:12, 21, 23 twice). This title implies that the king saw Ezra's God as the Most High God.

To understand the expression in Ezra 7:27, we must first recall that each individual is responsible for his or her own heart and the thoughts, believing, choices, and actions that come from the heart. Secondly, we have seen that God may influence a person's heart by making information from Him available in whatever way He chooses. With that solid understanding, we see that the king was responsible for what was in his heart. However God chose to work in the king's heart, He did not overstep the king's freedom of will to do so.

Thirdly, let us recall a similar expression in Acts 16, which we saw in chapters three and nine of this study.

> Acts 16:13-14
> [13] And on the Sabbath day we [Paul, Silas, and Timothy] went outside the gate to the riverside, where we sup-

> posed there was a place of prayer, and we sat down and spoke to the women who had come together.
> ¹⁴ One who heard us was a woman named Lydia, from the city of Thyatira, a seller of purple goods, who was a worshiper of God. The Lord opened her heart to pay attention to what was said by Paul.

Lydia heard and gave attention to God's Word that Paul spoke. Lydia responded favorably to information that originated from God. When Lydia heard and paid attention to God's Word, she decided to open her heart to the Lord. In Ezra, the king believed information that originated from God even though the Scriptures do not give the details of how he came to have that information. Just as Lydia opened her own heart to God's Word spoken by Paul, so the king opened his own heart to the things of God. If God literally did as these expressions say, it would be contrary to God's nature. However, God did not, for He never oversteps anyone's freedom of will.

God was indeed at work in the situation for the good of His people. The returned exiles of Israel kept the Passover with joy according to each person's own freewill response. The king also acted according to his own free will. He aided the people of Israel in the work of the house of God and helped to beautify the house of God.

Zerubbabel, Governor of Judah – Haggai 1:14

> Haggai 1:12-14
> ¹² Then Zerubbabel the son of Shealtiel, and Joshua the son of Jehozadak, the high priest, with all the remnant of the people, obeyed the voice of the LORD their God,

C. Working List—Figurative

and the words of Haggai the prophet, as the LORD their God had sent him. And the people feared [reverenced] the LORD.

¹³ Then Haggai, the messenger of the LORD, spoke to the people with the LORD's message, "I am with you, declares the LORD."

¹⁴ And <u>the LORD stirred up the spirit of Zerubbabel the son of Shealtiel, governor of Judah, and the spirit of Joshua the son of Jehozadak, the high priest, and the spirit of all the remnant of the people</u>. And they came and worked on the house of the LORD of hosts, their God.

See the context recorded in Haggai 1:1-15. Haggai was a prophet during the rebuilding of the Temple in Jerusalem, as recorded in Ezra and Nehemiah.

In this record, "spirit" is figuratively put for a person's inner being. Thus in Haggai 1:14, "spirit" is employed in a similar way as "heart." The Scriptures tell us that believing, thoughts, decisions, and actions come from the heart. We also know that God may influence a person's heart, or stir up a person's spirit, by making information from Him available in whatever way He chooses. We must also recognize that a prophet speaks for God to the people.

These people received the Word of the Lord spoken by Haggai, the prophet. They obeyed information from God and reverenced the Lord God. According to each person's own freedom of will, their "spirit" was stirred up because of the Word of the Lord they had put into their own "spirit," that is to say into their own hearts. Therefore, they worked on the house of the Lord of hosts, their God.

Lydia – Acts 16:14

> Acts 16:14
> One who heard us was a woman named Lydia, from the city of Thyatira, a seller of purple goods, who was a worshiper of God. <u>The Lord opened her heart </u>to pay attention to what was said by Paul.

See chapter three of this study entitled "Pharaoh and the Heart," near the end of the chapter.

Unjust People – Romans 1:24, 26, and 28

> Romans 1:20-28
> [20] For his invisible attributes, namely, his eternal power and divine nature, have been clearly perceived, ever since the creation of the world, in the things that have been made. So they are without excuse.
> [21] For although they [unjust people] knew God, they did not honor him as God or give thanks to him, but they became futile in their thinking, and their foolish hearts were darkened.
> [22] Claiming to be wise, they became fools,
> [23] and exchanged the glory of the immortal God for images resembling mortal man and birds and animals and creeping things.
> [24] Therefore <u>God gave them up in the lusts of their hearts</u>

C. Working List—Figurative

to impurity, to the dishonoring of their bodies among themselves,
²⁵ because they exchanged the truth about God for a lie and worshiped and served the creature rather than the Creator, who is blessed forever! Amen.
²⁶ For this reason God gave them up to dishonorable passions. For their women exchanged natural relations for those that are contrary to nature;
²⁷ and the men likewise gave up natural relations with women and were consumed with passion for one another, men committing shameless acts with men and receiving in themselves the due penalty [recompense] for their error [delusion].
²⁸ And since they did not see fit to acknowledge God, God gave them up to a debased mind to do what ought not to be done.

See the context recorded in Romans 1:18-3:20.

According to this passage, the unjust people knew God's eternal power and divine nature by means of His workmanship so that they were without excuse in their choices and actions. They chose to not honor or give thanks to the Lord God even though they had observed and experienced His power and nature. Instead, they put vain and foolish thoughts into their hearts to the end that they believed lies about God and worshipped something God had made, instead of the Creator Himself.

Let us recall that God designed people with freedom of will, which He always honors. That is to say God never caused or causes anyone to do or say something contrary to his or her own freedom of will. Thus when the unjust people allowed lust and uncleanness into their minds and lives, God did not overstep their freewill choice to put uncleaness into their minds. The unjust people's actions were dishonorable, contrary to nature, and shameless. Since they did not think it worthwhile to acknowledge God and instead made unprofitable choices, their minds became debased and unfit. These people were responsible for what they put in their minds and the resulting actions from the heart. Thus they brought just consequences upon themselves. God is idiomatically credited with what these people brought upon themselves. God did not make them think or act in the manner they did. God demonstrated His power and nature so that they could acknowledge Him and be delivered. However, they rejected God's good intentions for their lives.

Titus – II Corinthians 8:16

> II Corinthians 8:13-17
>
> [13] For *I mean* not that other men be eased, and ye burdened:
>
> [14] But by an equality, *that* now at this time your abundance *may be a supply* for their want, that their abundance also may be *a supply* for your want: that there may be equality:
>
> [15] As it is written, He that *had gathered* much had nothing over; and he that *had gathered* little had no lack.

C. Working List—Figurative

¹⁶ But thanks be to <u>God, who put into the heart of Titus the same earnest care I have for you</u>.

¹⁷ For he not only accepted our appeal, but being himself very earnest he is going to you of his own accord.

See the context recorded in II Corinthians chapters 8-9.

Chapters 8 and 9 of II Corinthians discuss the topic of giving and receiving in the church. These chapters exhort the Corinthians to give cheerfully and to help others in the Church who had needs. Verse 16 says God "put the same earnest care into the heart of Titus for you." Verse 17 goes on to say that Titus accepted the exhortation to care for the Corinthian believers and acted voluntarily of his own accord. This verse agrees with many other scriptures that say that each person is responsible for the content and maintenance of his or her own heart. Moreover, in II Corinthians 8:23, the apostle Paul says of Titus, "he is my partner and fellowhelper concerning you [the Corinthian believers]." In Titus 1:4, Paul further says that Titus believed what "was to be commonly believed among those in the Church."[2] Thus we see that Titus believed God's Word.

So, by putting together the context of these words and related passages regarding who is responsible for the heart and information about Titus, we see that saying that God put earnest care for the believers into Titus' heart cannot be literal but is figurative. It is an idiom that focuses on God Who gave His Word and credits God for people's response to His Word. God works in people's hearts

---

2. See *A Journey through Acts and Epistles* translated and edited by Walter J. Cummins, (Franklin, Ohio: Scripture Consulting, 2006 first edition), see footnote for "faith" on p.529.

by making information from Him available by whatever means He chooses. In this record, Titus had God's Word and decided to demonstrate earnest care for the Corinthian believers, according to his own freedom of will.

Some in Future Times – II Thessalonians 2:11

> II Thessalonians 2:11
> Therefore <u>God sends them a strong delusion</u>, so that they may believe what is false.

See the context recorded in II Thessalonians 2. See chapter nine of this study entitled "II Thessalonians 2 and God's Enduring Mercy."

Idiom without Wrongdoing

This study has considered a pattern of an idiom found in the Scriptures. The context of many of the occurrences of this biblical idiom show that someone had information from God that he or she could believe or not. Such occurrences often show that someone did not believe information from God and consequences followed. However, some occurrences of this biblical idiom give no scriptural evidence that the recipients disobeyed God or did anything wrong.

This pattern of the idiom without wrongdoing idiomatically credited God, even though He did not do it. These cultural expressions grew out of the beliefs of the people of Old Testament times as covered in chapter two of this study and summarized here:

- Those who lived in Old Testament times were not to mention the name of other gods.

C. Working List—Figurative

- Generally, those who lived in Old Testament times did not know nor mention the devil because it was not until the earthly life and ministry of Jesus Christ that the devil and his nature were more fully revealed.
- Those who lived in Old Testament times did mention God Who is the Most High and Most Powerful Lord overall.

The vocabulary and idioms of those who lived in Old Testament times reflected their God-centered culture. These idiomatic expressions without wrongdoing fit the basic definition of this pattern of a biblical idiom, because the words seem to say that God acted toward someone in a manner contrary to His nature or a person's freedom of will, when the context or related passages indicate that He did not. However, they differ from the previous records in this study because there is no scriptural evidence that the recipients in the following records disobeyed God or did anything wrong.

Sarah – Genesis 16:2

Genesis 16:2
And Sarai said to Abram, "Behold now, <u>the LORD has prevented me from bearing children</u>. Go in to my servant; it may be that I shall obtain children by her." And Abram listened to the voice of Sarai.

See the context recorded in Genesis 12:1-17:27. See also Genesis 13:16; Galatians 3:16; and Matthew 1:1-2.

Though God was idiomatically credited with restraining Sarah from bearing children, He did not do it. Nor did Sarah do anything wrong. The longing for children by women of Bible times is well expressed in Genesis 30:1 saying, "When Rachel saw that she bore Jacob no children, she envied her sister. She said to Jacob, 'Give me children, or I shall die!'" Luke 1:24-25 adds the following about the importance of bearing children in biblical culture, "After these days his wife Elizabeth conceived, and for five months she kept herself hidden, saying, 'Thus the Lord has done for me in the days when he looked on me, to take away my reproach among people.'" In that culture it was considered a disgrace not to have children. Not bearing children was a source of great anguish and affliction for Sarah. In her distress, she spoke in the manner of speech of the people of that time and credited God.

Earlier in this study, we saw that Christ would come through Abraham's descendants. Genesis 17 says this birth would be by Sarah. For the Lord to restrain Sarah from bearing children in a literal way would have been at cross purposes with His plans recorded in His Word. For background, see chapters five and six of this study.

Joseph's Brothers – Genesis 42:28

> Genesis 42:23-28
>
> [25] They did not know that Joseph understood them, for there was an interpreter between them.
>
> [26] Then he turned away from them and wept. And he returned to them and spoke to them. And he took Simeon from them and bound him before their eyes.
>
> [25] And Joseph gave orders to fill their bags with grain, and to replace every man's money in his sack, and to

C. Working List—Figurative

give them provisions for the journey. This was done for them.

²⁶ Then they loaded their donkeys with their grain and departed.

²⁷ And as one of them [Joseph's brothers] opened his sack to give his donkey fodder at the lodging place, he saw his money in the mouth of his sack.

²⁸ He said to his brothers, "My money has been put back; here it is in the mouth of my sack!" At this their hearts failed them, and they turned trembling to one another, saying, "<u>What is this that God has done to us?</u>"

See the context recorded in Genesis 41:39-42:38. For broader context include Genesis 37:1-36 and Genesis 39:1-41:38. For related scriptures, see Acts 7:8-15.

As background, Genesis 37 tells us that Joseph's brothers hated Joseph and were jealous of him. They did so because their father favored Joseph and because of the dreams Joseph had about ruling over his brothers.[3] Therefore, the brothers conspired to kill Joseph but as the events unfolded they ended up selling him to a passing caravan. The caravan traders sold Joseph to an Egyptian who was an officer of Pharaoh. Through all these things, the Lord was with Joseph and Joseph walked with God. Years passed and one day Pharaoh had a dream, which no one could interpret except Joseph. The interpretation of the dream that God showed to Joseph was that there

---

3. Genesis 37: 4-5, 11 But when his brothers saw that their father loved him more than all his brothers, they hated him...and when he told it [Joseph's dream] to his brothers they hated him even more... and his brothers were jealous of him....

Did God Do It?

would be seven years of plentiful crops followed by seven years of famine. To manage these difficult times, Pharaoh made Joseph second in command in all of Egypt. As the famine affected people far and wide, Joseph's brothers came to buy grain. Since Joseph was dressed as an Egyptian, the brothers did not recognize him. After buying provisions, Joseph had his servants return his brothers' money into their sacks. Later, when they found it, they were afraid of the possible consequences.

Although Joseph's brothers were not always upright in their ways, in the case of payment for this corn, they acted in an upright manner. Since the record says that Joseph put money in his brothers' sacks, God did not do it in a literal sense. The responsible parties were Joseph, who gave the command, and his servants, who carried it out. According to their cultural manner of speaking the brothers credited God although the context clarifies that God did not do it.

Moses – Numbers 11:11

> Numbers 11:1-6 and 10-15
>
> ¹ And the people complained in the hearing of the Lord about their misfortunes, and when the Lord heard it, his anger was kindled, and the fire of the Lord burned among them and consumed some outlying parts of the camp.
>
> ² Then the people cried out to Moses, and Moses prayed to the Lord, and the fire died down.
>
> ³ So the name of that place was called Taberah, because the fire of the Lord burned among them.

C. Working List—Figurative

⁴ Now the rabble that was among them had a strong craving. And the people of Israel also wept again and said, "Oh that we had meat to eat!
⁵ We remember the fish we ate in Egypt that cost nothing, the cucumbers, the melons, the leeks, the onions, and the garlic.
⁶ But now our strength is dried up, and there is nothing at all but this manna to look at."

¹⁰ Moses heard the people weeping throughout their clans, everyone at the door of his tent. And the anger of the Lord blazed hotly, and Moses was displeased.
¹¹ Moses said to the Lord, "<u>Why have you dealt ill with your servant? And why have I not found favor in your sight, that you lay the burden of all this people on me?</u>
¹² Did I conceive all this people? Did I give them birth, that you should say to me, 'Carry them in your bosom, as a nurse carries a nursing child,' to the land that you swore to give their fathers?
¹³ Where am I to get meat to give to all this people? For they weep before me and say, 'Give us meat, that we may eat.'
¹⁴ I am not able to carry all this people alone; the burden is too heavy for me.
¹⁵ If you will treat me like this, kill me at once, if I find favor in your sight, that I may not see my wretchedness."

See the context recorded in Numbers 11:1-35.

Did God Do It?

This event occurs when the people of Israel departed from Egypt and journeyed across Sinai. Along the way, God provided manna as the perfect food for His people to eat. Yet, Numbers 11 begins by saying, "and the people complained in the hearing of the Lord." Verse 4 adds that "the rabble that was among them had a strong craving. And the people of Israel also wept again and said, "Oh that we had meat to eat!" Who were this rabble? According to Exodus 12:38 when the people of Israel left Egypt "a mixed multitude also went up with them."[4] In Numbers 11, this mixed group of non-Israelites had a strong craving for food other than the perfect manna God had provided. Their complaints seemed to incite some of the Israelites (who knew God's great mercy and provision) to also complain and rebel against God.

Verse 10 speaks of the anger and displeasure of the Lord. Let us review what we saw in chapter eight about the anger of the Lord. The Lord's anger is related to the sin of His people. The use of the Hebrew word for anger personifies God's displeasure with sin. When God's people sin, it displeases God but it also causes Him grief and sorrow. God deals with sin according to the established standard of justice of the time. "The anger of the Lord is not sinful, evil, or the source of capricious attitudes or deeds."[5] Humans may misbehave when angry but God does not. Even in His anger, God is just.

---

4. See Exodus 12:30-38 and Leviticus 24:10-11. See also *New American Standard Study Bible* footnote on Numbers 11:4.

5. R. Laird Harris, Gleason L. Archer, and Bruce K. Waltke, *The Theological Wordbook of the Old Testament* (Chicago, Illinois: Moody Publishers 1980) p. 58, number 133a.

C. Working List—Figurative

Moses was afflicted (troubled, burdened) by the continual complaints. Numbers 11:11 records some things that Moses said. It is true that Moses said these things but the negative intent we may read into these statements are not true of God. God had laid the burden of all this people on Moses but it was not intended for ill. It was in the best interest of God's people that Moses would lead them. However, the people of Israel did not always appreciate God's many blessings.

In Numbers 11, the people of Israel wept and complained. In response, Moses expressed his burdens to God employing a Hebrew idiom. The idiom was not intended to blame God; instead, these idiomatic expressions magnified God in the face of affliction. According to the context, it was the burden of the care of the Israelites and their complaints that afflicted Moses and not God.

Ruth – Ruth 1:13 and 20-21

Ruth 1:5-9, 13, and 20-21

⁵ And both Mahlon and Chilion died, so that the woman was left without her two sons and her husband.
⁶ Then she arose with her daughters-in-law to return from the country of Moab, for she had heard in the fields of Moab that the Lord had visited his people and given them food.
⁷ So she set out from the place where she was with her two daughters-in-law, and they went on the way to return to the land of Judah.
⁸ But Naomi said to her two daughters-in-law, "Go,

Did God Do It?

> return each of you to her mother's house. May the LORD deal kindly with you, as you have dealt with the dead and with me.
>
> ⁹ The LORD grant that you may find rest...
>
> ¹³ would you therefore wait till they were grown? Would you therefore refrain from marrying? No, my daughters, for it is exceedingly bitter to me for your sake that <u>the hand of the LORD has gone out against me</u>."
>
> ²⁰ She said to them, "Do not call me Naomi; call me Mara, for <u>the Almighty has dealt very bitterly with me</u>. ²¹ I went away full, and <u>the LORD has brought me back empty</u>. Why call me Naomi, when <u>the LORD has testified against me</u> and <u>the Almighty has brought calamity upon me</u>?"

See the context recorded in Ruth 1:1-4:22, especially the redemption God provided for Ruth as recorded in Ruth 4.

This record is handled in chapter eleven of this study entitled, "No Wrongdoing and What It Is Not."

There is no scriptural evidence that God caused Naomi's afflictions, nor does the context say that she made a choice that would have led to her affliction. God did not cause her afflictions. Naomi did not bring these consequences upon herself. However, Naomi did idiomatically credit God using a cultural expression of her day. God was credited because He is the Most High and Most Powerful God, Who is Lord overall. Other reasons why this cultural expression developed in the lands and times of the Bible are handled in chapter two and eleven of this study.

Hannah – I Samuel 1:5-6

> I Samuel 1:5-6 and 10-12
>
> ⁵ But to Hannah he gave a double portion, because he loved her, though <u>the LORD had closed her womb</u>.
> ⁶ And her rival [the other wife, Peninnah] used to provoke her grievously to irritate her, because <u>the LORD had closed her womb</u>.
>
> ¹⁰ She was deeply distressed and prayed to the LORD and wept bitterly.
> ¹¹ And she vowed a vow and said, "O LORD of hosts, if you will indeed look on the affliction of your servant and remember me and not forget your servant, but will give to your servant a son, then I will give him to the LORD all the days of his life, and no razor shall touch his head."
> ¹² As she continued praying before the LORD, Eli observed her mouth.

See the context recorded in I Samuel 1:1-2:11.

This record is handled in chapter eleven of this study entitled, "No Wrongdoing and What It Is Not."

Though God was credited with shutting Hannah's womb, He did not do it, nor did Hannah do anything wrong. Although He did not do it, God was credited because He is the Most High and Most Powerful

Did God Do It?

God, Who is Lord overall and because the people of Old Testament times did not name the devil for the tribulation he orchestrated.

See also the following promises God made regarding offspring and childbearing: Exodus 23:26; Leviticus 26:9; Deuteronomy 7:14 and 28:2-4; and Psalm 113:9 and 128:3-4.

Elijah and the Son of the Widow Woman – I Kings 17:20

> I Kings 17:14-22
>
> ¹⁴ For thus says the LORD, the God of Israel, 'The jar of flour shall not be spent, and the jug of oil shall not be empty, until the day that the LORD sends rain upon the earth.'"
>
> ¹⁵ And she went and did as Elijah said. And she and he and her household ate for many days.
>
> ¹⁶ The jar of flour was not spent, neither did the jug of oil become empty, according to the word of the LORD that he spoke by Elijah.
>
> ¹⁷ After this the son of the woman, the mistress of the house, became ill. And his illness was so severe that there was no breath left in him.
>
> ¹⁸ And she said to Elijah, "What have you against me, O man of God? You have come to me to bring my sin to remembrance and to cause the death of my son!"
>
> ¹⁹ And he said to her, "Give me your son." And he took him from her arms and carried him up into the upper chamber where he lodged, and laid him on his own bed.
>
> ²⁰ And he cried to the LORD, "O <u>LORD my God, have</u>

C. Working List—Figurative

<u>you brought calamity even upon the widow with whom I sojourn, by killing her son?"</u>

²¹ Then he stretched himself upon the child three times and cried to the LORD, "O LORD my God, let this child's life come into him again."

²² And the LORD listened to the voice of Elijah. And the life of the child came into him again, and he revived.

See the context recorded in I Kings 17:1-24.

This record is handled in chapter eleven of this study entitled, "No Wrongdoing and What It Is Not."

Elijah cried unto the Lord and used an idiomatic expression common in his day and time. Elijah idiomatically credited God because He is the Most High and Most Powerful God, Who is Lord overall. Neither the woman, nor Elijah, nor God were responsible for the negative situation.

To read more about Elijah's life and walk with God, see I Kings 17:1- II Kings 2:13. See also James 5:17-18.

Job – Job 2:3

Job 2:3

And the LORD said to Satan, "Have you considered my servant Job, that there is none like him on the earth, a blameless and upright man, who fears God and turns away from evil? He still holds fast his integrity, although <u>you [Satan] incited me [the Lord] against him [Job] to destroy him</u> without reason."

See the context recorded in Job 1:1-2:7.

This record is handled in chapter eleven of this study entitled, "No Wrongdoing and What It Is Not."

Satan tried to move God to destroy Job, but God refused to harm Job. Neither God nor Job was responsible for the deaths and destruction. Job was blameless and upright; he did not do anything to warrant such tribulation from Satan. Satan destroyed Job without cause. Because of God's protection, Satan could not take Job's life.

To Close

This study has looked at some unclear and oft-misunderstood verses. As we have done so, we have held in mind that God is light and in Him is absolutely no darkness at all.

In closing, let us again note that the position this study takes is that the idiom, that seems to say God did something He did not do, is a figure of meaning or thought and not a figure of grammar. That is to say this idiom is not understood by a shift in grammar (such as active put for passive) but is understood from the context and related scriptures as well as the culture of Old Testament times.

The working lists in appendices B and C give you additional examples of this idiom and the pattern it follows. These appendices are provided so that you can more effectively recognize when certain unusual expressions about God's actions are literal or figurative, or if we do not know.

As these working lists go to press, we recognize that they are not comprehensive nor are they all that could be said on the subject. That is to say, this study is not the final word on the subject. Instead, this study is intended to provide a framework for continued study in the Scriptures.

> Proverbs 1:7
>
> The fear [reverence] of the LORD is the beginning of knowledge...

May the pattern of study presented here give you tools to begin to understand more difficult sections of Scriptures so that your confidence in our good God remains steadfast. May this study help you know in the depth of your soul that God is reliably good from Genesis to Revelation.

You may reach the author at jcoad@Godislight.com.

Did God Do It?

Scripture Index

This is an alphabetical listing of Scripture quoted in this study. It does not include quotes within the body of a single paragraph.

Reference	Page	Reference	Page
Acts 4:25-26	140	Deuteronomy 30:10-16 and 19	26
Acts 5:3	63	Deuteronomy 32:4 NASB	31
Acts 12:1-3	348	Deuteronomy 32:16-17	61
Acts 12:19-24	348	Ecclesiastes 8:11	314
Acts 13:9-10	37	Ephesians 1:7-9	153
Acts 14:15-17	140	Ephesians 3:2 NIV	151
Acts 16:10	92	Ephesians 3:11	153
Acts 16:10 and 13-14	227	Ephesians 3:11	177
Acts 16:13-14	371	Exodus 1:11-14	42
Acts 16:13-15	92	Exodus 1:13-14	115
Acts 16:14	374	Exodus 2:24-25	43
Acts 26:16-18	21	Exodus 3:6-11	43
Colossians 1:12-13	22	Exodus 3:19-20	45
Colossians 3:1-4	296	Exodus 4:21	364
Deuteronomy 2:30	366	Exodus 5:1-5	45
Deuteronomy 4:1 and 3-4	330	Exodus 5:6-9	47
Deuteronomy 6:24 and 25	135	Exodus 5:6-9 and 22-23	353
Deuteronomy 7:1 and 25-26	356	Exodus 5:10-16	47
Deuteronomy 7:13-14	288	Exodus 5:17-21	48
Deuteronomy 9:4-5	338	Exodus 5:22	11
Deuteronomy 11:16	88	Exodus 5:22	42
Deuteronomy 12:31	338	Exodus 5:22-23	49
Deuteronomy 15:7	87	Exodus 6:1	75
Deuteronomy 17:14-15	181	Exodus 6:4-7	75
Deuteronomy 17:18-20	181	Exodus 7:2-6	78
Deuteronomy 26:6-7	50	Exodus 7:3	365
Deuteronomy 30:10	89	Exodus 7:8-14	79

Exodus 7:17-23	80	Genesis 12:9-10	164
Exodus 7:22	74	Genesis 12:11-13	165
Exodus 8:1-2	82	Genesis 12:14-16	165
Exodus 8:8	82	Genesis 12:17	158
Exodus 8:13-15	82	Genesis 12:17	321
Exodus 8:32	74	Genesis 12:17-20	167
Exodus 9:1-7	83	Genesis 14:18-19	67
Exodus 9:12	11	Genesis 15:4-6	128
Exodus 9:12	74	Genesis 15:7-8	131
Exodus 9:12	365	Genesis 15:13-14	76
Exodus 9:18-22	84	Genesis 15:17-18	131
Exodus 9:27-30	85	Genesis 16:2	379
Exodus 9:34-35	86	Genesis 17:1	67
Exodus 10:1-4 and 20	100	Genesis 17:3-7	132
Exodus 10:1, 20, and 27	365	Genesis 17:15-16 and 19	132
Exodus 11:1	102	Genesis 17:15-16 and 19	159
Exodus 11:10	365	Genesis 19:24-25 and 29	321
Exodus 12:1-3, 6-11	102	Genesis 20:1-2	170
Exodus 12:12	12	Genesis 20:3-11	170
Exodus 12:12	98	Genesis 20:6	166
Exodus 12:12	322	Genesis 20:12-16	172
Exodus 12:12-13	103	Genesis 20:17-18	173
Exodus 12:23	98	Genesis 20:18	158
Exodus 12:23-31	104	Genesis 20:18	321
Exodus 13:15	111	Genesis 30:1 and 23	287
Exodus 19:5-8	134	Genesis 42:23-28	380
Exodus 20:1-5	59	Haggai 1:12-14	372
Exodus 23:13	60	Hebrews 2:14-15^{NASB}	154
Exodus 23:25-26	288	Hebrews 2:14^{WTJ}	24
Exodus 25:21-22	344	I Chronicles 10:1-6	185
Exodus 25:21-22	359	I Chronicles 10:4	180
Exodus 32:1, 8, 26-28 and 35	323	I Chronicles 10:13-14	186
Exodus 34:6	19	I Chronicles 10:13-14	363
Ezekiel 18:32	219	I Chronicles 10:14	11
Ezra 6:20-22	369	I Chronicles 10:14	180
Ezra 7:9-11 and 27-28	369	I Chronicles 16:15-23	162
Ezra 9:7	258	I Chronicles 17:21-22	139
Galatians 3:6-8	129	I Chronicles 21:1	203
Galatians 3:16-17	130	I Chronicles 21:2	208
Galatians 3:19, 22-25^{WTJ}	136	I Chronicles 21:3-7	208
Genesis 1:2-4 and 31	17	I Chronicles 21:8-10	210
Genesis 2:7^{KJV}	122	I Chronicles 21:11-15	211
Genesis 2:15-17	25	I Chronicles 21:14	12
Genesis 3:15	125	I Chronicles 21:14	346
Genesis 6:5, 11-13 and 17	320	I Chronicles 21:14-15	203
Genesis 12:1-4 and 7	127	I Chronicles 21:15-22	213
Genesis 12:1-5	160	I Chronicles 21:23-28	215

Scripture Index

I Corinthians 5:7	114
I Corinthians 6:14-15	239
I Corinthians 15:57	295
II Chronicles 26:3-5	346
II Chronicles 26:16-20	346
II Corinthians 2:10-11	64
II Corinthians 4:3-6	23
II Corinthians 8:13-17	376
II Corinthians 9:7	90
II Corinthians 10:5	118
II Peter 1:20-21	14
II Peter 1:20-21	225
II Samuel 6:6-7	343
II Samuel 24:1	203
II Samuel 24:1	207
II Samuel 24:1	368
II Samuel 24:15	203
II Samuel 24:15	345
II Thessalonians 2:1-3	231
II Thessalonians 2:1-3	240
II Thessalonians 2:3-6	241
II Thessalonians 2:7-9	242
II Thessalonians 2:9-12	243
II Thessalonians 2:11	229
II Thessalonians 2:11	378
II Timothy 2:15^{NASB}	15
II Timothy 3:16	14
I John 1:5	3
I John 1:5	17
I John 1:5	305
I John 3:8	63
I Kings 16:30	280
I Kings 17:1	280
I Kings 17:8-10	281
I Kings 17:11-14	281
I Kings 17:14-22	388
I Kings 17:15-16	282
I Kings 17:17-24	283
I Peter 1:18-19^{WTJ}	114
I Peter 5:8-9	20
I Peter 5:8-9	64
Isaiah 2:11-12	233
Isaiah 5:19-20	118
Isaiah 5:19-21	35
Isaiah 5:19-21	311
Isaiah 13:9 and 11	233
I Samuel 1:1-8	289
I Samuel 1:5-6 and 10-12	387
I Samuel 1:9-18	290
I Samuel 1:19-22	292
I Samuel 3:1 and 13	360
I Samuel 4:1-4	359
I Samuel 5:2-9	341
I Samuel 6:19	343
I Samuel 8:4-5 and 22	182
I Samuel 8:5-7	146
I Samuel 10:1	183
I Samuel 10:6 and 9-10	183
I Samuel 15:1-3 and 9-11	187
I Samuel 15:11	195
I Samuel 15:19-21	188
I Samuel 15:22-26	189
I Samuel 16:14	190
I Samuel 16:14-16 and 23	361
I Samuel 28:3-7	191
I Samuel 28:8-10	192
I Samuel 28:11-14	193
I Samuel 28:15-17	194
I Samuel 31:1-6	184
I Samuel 31:4	180
I Thessalonians 1:5-10	229
I Thessalonians 2:17-18	63
I Thessalonians 4:14	239
I Thessalonians 4:14-18	236
I Thessalonians 5:2-5	233
I Thessalonians 5:8-9	234
James 1:17	18
Jeremiah 2:13-14, 17-19	257
Jeremiah 9:24	34
Jeremiah 9:24	310
Jeremiah 21:12	314
Jeremiah 22:3	316
Jeremiah 31:31-34	148
Job 1:1-5	273
Job 1:6-11	274
Job 1:12	275
Job 1:20-22	276
Job 2:1-3	277
Job 2:3	389
Joel 2:31-32	247
John 8:12-14	28
John 8:42-47	29
John 8:44	62
John 8:44^{NASB}	30

Did God Do It?

John 10:10	24	Numbers 33:4	111
John 10:10	62	Proverbs 1:7	14
Joshua 1:3, 5, and 7	355	Proverbs 1:7	391
Joshua 6:2-3	331	Proverbs 1:29-30	90
Joshua 6:16-19	331	Proverbs 2:6-9	310
Joshua 6:18-19	142	Proverbs 2:7-9	32
Joshua 6:18-19	355	Proverbs 4:23	89
Joshua 7:1	142	Proverbs 23:12	88
Joshua 7:1	332	Psalm 9:16	315
Joshua 7:1 and 7	354	Psalm 12:6	13
Joshua 7:10-25	332	Psalm 19:7-10	312
Joshua 7:20-26	357	Psalm 19:9-10	32
Joshua 10:5	336	Psalm 33:4-5	309
Joshua 10:8-12	337	Psalm 33:4-6	34
Joshua 10:10	366	Psalm 36:5-7	308
Joshua 10:42	338	Psalm 37:28	309
Joshua 11:5-9 and 12	340	Psalm 40:14-16	68
Joshua 11:20	367	Psalm 44:4^{NIV}	180
Joshua 22:15-16	144	Psalm 47:2	66
Joshua 22:18-20	144	Psalm 57:2-3^{KJV}	67
Joshua 23:7	60	Psalm 78:41-48	107
Jude 1:25	350	Psalm 78:49-52	108
Leviticus 10:1-3	324	Psalm 83:18	66
Luke 1:24-25	288	Psalm 86:5	247
Luke 4:24	284	Psalm 86:5 and 15	19
Luke 4:25-27	284	Psalm 91:9-11	110
Luke 6:45	88	Psalm 98:8-9	36
Luke 11:42	316	Psalm 99:4-5	309
Matthew 1:1	202	Psalm 103:6	315
Micah 7:7-9	303	Psalm 103:19-21	109
Nehemiah 9:7-8	250	Psalm 111:7-8	309
Nehemiah 9:8	261	Psalm 116:15^{NIV}	212
Nehemiah 9:9-15	250	Psalm 119:39	35
Nehemiah 9:16-19	252	Psalm 119:84	315
Nehemiah 9:17	262	Psalm 119:112	89
Nehemiah 9:20-25	253	Psalm 145:7 and 9	19
Nehemiah 9:26-28	254	Revelation 12:9	20
Nehemiah 9:29-31	255	Revelation 16:7	36
Nehemiah 9:32-33	256	Revelation 20:10	295
Nehemiah 9:32-33	262	Revelation 21:4	295
Numbers 1:50-51	344	Romans 1:20-28	374
Numbers 4:15	344	Romans 2:4	302
Numbers 11:1-6 and 10-15	382	Romans 3:21-22	33
Numbers 16:3, 9-10, and 32-35	326	Romans 3:21-23^{WTJ}	222
Numbers 20:15-16	50	Romans 3:21-24 and 28^{WTJ}	304
Numbers 25:1-11	327	Romans 3:21-24^{WTJ}	150
Numbers 31:16	329	Romans 3:24-25^{WTJ}	222

Scripture Index

Romans 5:9-10	235
Romans 5:12-16	124
Romans 5:17-21	125
Romans 5:19	26
Romans 8:1-2	149
Romans 8:3-4	150
Romans 8:33-34	279
Romans 10:9-10	151
Romans 10:10	90
Romans 16:27	7
Ruth 1:1-5	265
Ruth 1:5-9, 13, and 20-21	385
Ruth 1:6-19	265
Ruth 1:19-22	268
Zechariah 7:9	313
Zechariah 7:9 and 11-12	87
Zechariah 8:16	313
Zephaniah 1:14-15	232

www.ingramcontent.com/pod-product-compliance
Lightning Source LLC
Chambersburg PA
CBHW071656170426
43195CB00039B/2211